RETHINKING
THE AMERICAN
RACE PROBLEM

RETHINKING THE AMERICAN RACE PROBLEM

ROY L. BROOKS

UNIVERSITY OF CALIFORNIA PRESS
BERKELEY   LOS ANGELES   OXFORD

University of California Press

Berkeley and Los Angeles, California

University of California Press, Ltd.

Oxford, England

© 1990 by

The Regents of the University of California

Library of Congress Cataloging-in-Publication Data

Brooks, Roy L. (Roy Lavon), 1950–
    Rethinking the American race problem / Roy L. Brooks.
      p.   cm.
    Includes bibliographical references (p.   ) and index.
    ISBN 0–520–06886–6 (alk. paper)
    1. United States—Race relations. 2. Afro-Americans—
Social conditions—1975– 3. Social classes—United States.
4. Afro-Americans—Civil rights. I. Title.
E185.615.B73   1990
305.8'96'073—dc20   90–11227
                                                  CIP

Printed in the United States of America

1 2 3 4 5 6 7 8 9

To my wife, Penny,
and to my children,
Whitney and Courtney

Contents

Acknowledgments

I owe a debt of gratitude to the people who helped to produce this book. The idea of writing a book on the American race problem came from Geoffrey Hazard of Yale Law School. He and Boris Bittker, also a friend and former teacher at Yale, read and commented on an early draft. Wayne Shannon and Joel Kupperman are longtime friends and mentors at the University of Connecticut who commented extensively on the manuscript. They, Richard Delgado of the University of Colorado Law School, and Gerald Torres, my colleague at the University of Minnesota Law School, provided helpful suggestions and encouragement along the way. My special thanks also go to Martin Kilson of Harvard University for his perceptive comments on the book.

Valuable research and suggestions were furnished by B. James Pantone, Lincoln Smith, Linda Frakes, Sharon Kalemkiarian, Mary Reid, Tami Bass, Roberta Sistos, Polly Haisha, Gary Fields, and Marcia Stone. My editors at the University of California Press—Naomi Schneider, Marilyn Schwartz, and Mary Renaud— were simply superb.

Although they did not have a direct hand in the production of this book, George Cole, Vincent Carrafiello, and Arnold Taylor have influenced my thoughts about the American race problem over the years. Edmund Ursin, Virginia Nolan, and Virginia Shue have been my most valuable friends and supporters since I began teaching law more than a decade ago.

Preface

Nearly a half century ago, Gunnar Myrdal of the University of Stockholm assembled a team of sociologists, historians, economists, political scientists, philosophers, and lawyers to undertake what still remains the most ambitious study ever conducted of the status of African Americans in the United States. Myrdal's study unfolded an "American dilemma," detailing what is commonly known as the American race problem.[1] It is the problem of a people's painful vulnerability in a society that promises comfort and equality. And it is a problem that poses a simple question: how can African Americans be accorded genuine equal opportunity in American society? This book attempts to answer that question.

The American race problem today is quite different from the situation Myrdal described in his study. Whereas political inequality was once seen as the key element of the problem, social and economic disparities have become the central questions today. Also, in the past generation, three general socioeconomic classes have emerged with greater clarity and force in African American society—a middle class, a working class, and a poverty-stricken class, which includes an underclass subculture. The status of African Americans, therefore, can no longer be defined solely in racial terms. Considerations of race and class now criss-cross into an often puzzling portrait.

Deep class stratification within African American society is without a doubt the most significant development in the "American dilemma" since the civil rights movement of the 1960s.

Many social commentators have taken this development to mean that questions of race and color—matters that trigger civil rights laws—no longer play an important role. For them, what seem to be racial problems are now primarily or exclusively caused by class status, with the racial factor, or civil rights, having been sufficiently addressed by the passage of hundreds of civil rights laws at the federal, state, and local levels. Influenced by these commentators, the public has in the past decade given more attention to such phenomena within African American society as welfare dependency (Charles Murray), female-headed families (Daniel Moynihan), and unemployment resulting from structural changes in the economy (William Julius Wilson) than it has given to civil rights.[2] These perspectives on America's race problem not only downplay the importance of civil rights—or, more precisely, the importance of the interpretation and application of civil rights laws and policies—but also reduce the scope of the problem to a single segment of African American society— the underclass.

Commentators who may believe that other segments of African American society also experience socioeconomic inequality have still not sufficiently factored in civil rights. Some—Thomas Sowell, for example—actually discount civil rights laws and policies, instead citing an alleged deficiency of human capital among African Americans as a primary cause of socioeconomic inequality.[3] This theory, however, fails to explain the rise of a genuine African American middle class since the 1960s and, moreover, is too dismissive of the role that factors external to the market—mainly government—have played in the establishment, protection, and even loss of position and wealth. Other commentators, such as Glenn Loury, who argue that African Americans must look beyond civil rights fail to understand that many socioeconomic problems, from unemployment to housing discrimination, require government intervention because of their scope or nature.[4] And others—among them Farley and Allen, perhaps the best of the recent nonlegal commentators on the American race situation— who conclude that African Americans, in the employment context at least, are adequately protected by "a variety of government agencies . . . and an array of supportive federal court decisions" are positively wrong, as Part I of this book demonstrates.[5] Other students of race in America, such as Derrick Bell, who know better and have therefore sought to reintroduce civil rights into the current discussion have not established a systemic nexus between the interpretation and application of civil rights laws and policies and specific socioeconomic problems unique to African Americans.[6] Nor have they endeavored to analyze civil rights or the race problem from within the context of the class division that now shapes African American society or to offer comprehensive solutions.

The failure to develop a systematic critique from the perspective of both race and class stands as an across-the-board criticism of these and other recent commentators, including Gerald Jaynes and Robin Williams, Kristin Bumiller, and the polemicist and African American nationalist Harold Cruse.[7] No one addresses the relationship between race and class—racial subordination and class subordination—systematically, either in terms of understanding the problem or in terms of proposals for resolving it. And only Bell and, to a lesser extent, Bumiller come even remotely close to addressing the legal aspect of the interaction between race and class. This book attempts to fill the void left by these nonetheless gifted scholars.

The book delivers two primary messages—one is directed specifically to civil rights legal scholars, or legalists; the other is directed to the public at large, including civil rights scholars, both legal and nonlegal. To legalists, the book asserts that one can no longer talk meaningfully about the problems of African Americans and the resolution of those problems without merging the question of race (which triggers civil rights laws and policies) with that of class structure—it is not an either-or proposition. The issue of race versus class, in other words, is a red herring, a nonissue, in today's African American society. The book constructs an intellectual framework (the "subordination question") that allows the legalist to take both race, or civil rights, and class into account in arriving at an understanding of the problem (Part I) and, in addition, presents a prescription for solving the problem that likewise is sensitive to both considerations (Part II). Although this discussion, which necessarily moves through several doctrinal nuances in civil rights law, is geared primarily to the legalist, it warrants consideration both by nonlegal scholars who endeavor to write or think about racial matters and by thoughtful citizens who are attempting to understand racial concerns.

The book's message to its more general audience is that a new form of self-help offers the best hope for improving socio-economic conditions among African Americans, whether these conditions result from racial subordination or class subordination. African Americans must stop putting their lives on hold, for yet another generation, waiting for the government to come in as promised to rescue them from bad jobs, bad housing, bad schools. It is not that government cannot fulfill its civil rights promise; it is simply that government *will not* fulfill this promise. That, in truth, is our civil rights legacy, to which the entire nation must open its eyes. African American self-help will not by itself resolve the American race problem—nor should African Americans have to go it alone—because resources beyond the means or control of any one group of citizens are needed to redress employment discrimination, housing segregation, poor public schooling, and other institutionalized problems. Only government can and should supply such resources. But a well-focused, intensive program of self-help can surely ameliorate the living conditions of many African Americans, even without the government's assistance.

Introduction:
Rethinking Our
Civil Rights Legacy

In 1989 the Supreme Court issued a rush of rulings that danger-
ously chipped away at the civil rights protections African Americans had gained not only under the liberal Warren Court in the
1960s but also under the conservative Burger Court in the 1970s
and early 1980s. Anchored by the three Reagan appointees (Justices Sandra Day O'Connor, Antonin Scalia, and Anthony Kennedy), the Rehnquist Supreme Court, among other things, made
voluntary affirmative action programs more difficult to establish
and much easier to undo once established, increased the burden
of proving employment discrimination, and reduced the reach of
a hundred-year-old antidiscrimination law.[1] These rulings set pre-
cedents that so restrict the employment opportunities of African
Americans and that so diminish their ability to fight racial discrimination and segregation in employment and elsewhere—pre-
cedents, in other words, so decidedly unsupportive of their civil
rights interests—that three of the justices felt impelled to wonder aloud whether those justices voting with the majority believe
that America still faces a race problem.[2]

My view of the Court's civil rights rulings (and of civil rights
laws and policy in general) is far different from the views held
by either conservatives or liberals. To both old-line conservatives
and neoconservatives, the Court's rulings are to be celebrated as
one of former president Ronald Reagan's most enduring legacies.
To both full-time and fair-weather liberals, the Court's rulings are
to be recorded as an unhappy fortuity of political timing. To me,
they simply underscore an important message conveyed in this

book—namely, the absolute necessity for a serious program of African American self-help.

Those looking to be beguiled by easy answers to a question as complex as the American race problem might be tempted to prejudge my call for self-help as yet another song that blames the victim and exonerates the government from any responsibility for the existence or resolution of the problem. But nothing could be further from the truth. For I strongly believe, and argue in this book, that the government has helped to perpetuate the race problem in the United States since the end of the Jim Crow era (circa 1968) and that governmental resources are an indispensable ingredient in any complete solution. Furthermore, I maintain that African Americans must continue to knock on the door; they must continue to demand legal and economic assistance from the government. But I also argue that African Americans cannot rely on the government to come through, to do what government must do to help overcome the obstacles racial minorities face in the United States. That, indeed, is our civil rights legacy. And thus the necessity for self-help.

These propositions—particularly the idea that America's race problem may never be fully resolved—challenge the reader to ponder unpleasant or even unthinkable thoughts. They call into question many comfortable traditions (both conservative and liberal) regarding our civil rights legacy. But if the bonds of powerlessness are ever to be lifted or at least loosened from around African Americans, thoughtful citizens must consider the possibility that after more than three and one-half centuries of "effort," the government simply refuses to do what it needs to do and is capable of doing. If the lives of millions of African Americans are ever to improve appreciably, citizens of all races must consider the possibility that our civil rights laws and policies—even those crafted by liberal judges and members of Congress[3]—help to fuel the race problem. If African Americans are ever to jettison their de facto second-class socioeconomic status, which places them behind even new waves of immigrants who arrive here poor and powerless, serious thought must be given to the possibility that all the government's clatter about civil rights and equal rights and racial equality is nothing more than a bill of goods—a running promise of forty acres and a mule—sold to our anxiously hopeful and unsuspecting kith and kin and that what the government ultimately means by "civil rights" is that African Americans must fend for themselves.[4] We must, in short, rethink our civil rights legacy.

The process of rethinking our civil rights tradition begins by reexamining the nature of America's race problem. Historically, racial inequality or disparity was the sine qua non of the issue. African Americans under both slavery and Jim Crow lived in a state of abject, absolute inequity. In all spheres of life, they had less than whites: less income, wealth, occupational prestige, housing, education, political influence. The disparity in living conditions between the races was so discernible, so obvious that it could be established by a casual stroll through neighborhoods and workplaces.[5]

Although inequality is still the critical ingredient of the race problem today, both the magnitude and the nature of racial inequality (and hence the problem itself) have changed. Primarily as a result of the 1965 Voting Rights Act and its amendments, African Americans have almost as much political equality as their minority status and willingness to vote will allow.[6] Employment, housing, and education are now the areas in which residual racial disparity most jeopardizes African Americans' chances for worldly success and happiness.

The nature of racial inequality has changed far more substantially than have the categories of inequality. No longer can the problem be articulated solely in terms of broad statistical disparities between African Americans and white Americans in employment (including income and occupational prestige), housing, and education. During the slavery and Jim Crow eras, the great majority of African Americans were concentrated in the poverty and working classes; since the 1960s, however, a sizable number have climbed into the middle class.[7] Racial inequality must now be viewed against the grid of class inequality.

My concept of the race problem in the United States recognizes the constraints and inherent inequities of class stratification in our society. It does so by assuming, for the sake of argument, the legitimacy of class subordination, under which poor and working-class people possess less socioeconomic power or resources (and hence "equality") than members of the upper classes, of whatever color.[8] Thus, I define the American race problem as disparity in the distribution of societal hardships or burdens between Americans of different races who belong to the same socioeconomic class—the absence of racial parity in socio-economic opportunities within class lines such that the racial disparity in question is clearly traceable to the color line rather than the class line. For example, when middle-class African Americans are more vulnerable than middle-class whites to employment discrimination, when working-class African American children are asked to shoulder more of the burdens associated with school integration than are their white counterparts, or when disproportionately more poor African Americans than poor whites experience a type of poverty (namely, an underclass subculture) that removes them farther from mainstream society than the usual brand of American poverty does, then America has a race problem. Clearly, this problem involves not only African Americans and whites; other racial minorities also experience socioeconomic disparity in relation to the dominant group. The aim of this book, however, is to center our attention on African Americans.

The historical version of the American race problem focuses on socioeconomic disparity between the races without regard to class structure; and what might be called the American class problem focuses on *inter-class* socioeconomic disparity not necessarily involving the races. In contrast, a modern version of America's race problem must focus on *intra-class* socioeconomic disparity along racial lines, or, in other words, "intra-class racial disparity."

In this modern version, existing civil rights laws and policies can be seen as primary contributors to obstacles encountered at the higher end of the class ladder in African American society; factors other than civil rights appear equally if not more determinative at the lower end. Concentrating first on the African American upper classes, I argue in Part I of this book that the nation's fundamental civil rights policy—"formal equal opportunity," or, more precisely, its twin operational tenets, racial omission and racial integration—is parent to numerous legal prescriptions, practices, and more limited policies that touch the socioeconomic conditions under which middle-class and working-class African Americans live. These legal devices, which should be the instruments of promoting racial inclusion and equality, in fact have subordinated (given little or no priority to) specific civil rights interests of middle-class and working-class African Americans and, as a consequence, reduced the opportunities available through law to effectively remedy the uneven distribution of societal hardships between the races within these classes. As they are currently interpreted and applied, then, civil rights laws and policies accommodate, prolong, and intensify intra-class racial disparity.

Two points should be noted about this argument. First, it defines "civil rights interest" to mean an equality interest, an interest in equal socioeconomic opportunity. It is a claim against the government for access to a protection or privilege augmenting socioeconomic status or comfort in American society that is roughly equal to the access enjoyed by other racial groups. A civil rights interest is, by definition, "legitimate" because it speaks to a protection or privilege that is available to Americans in general or to those belonging to the claimant's socioeconomic class. Second, the argument is anchored in the belief that if employment, housing, and educational opportunities were truly open and nondiscriminatory, we should reasonably expect that over a period of time there would be no significant disparity in the distribution of social problems (such as racial discrimination or extreme poverty) between Americans of different races within the same socioeconomic class.[9] As many scholars have noted, race in American society is "more an attributed quality than a real one."[10]

At the low end of the socioeconomic ladder in African American society, civil rights policy also appears to be a potent agent in creating and sustaining intra-class racial disparity, although it is perhaps less powerful than the effect of structural changes in the American economy during the past generation or so (as analyzed by William Julius Wilson and others).[11] The tenet of racial integration itself, for example, helps to explain the rise of an underclass subculture within the African American poverty class.

Although there is clearly a negative nexus between the American race problem and civil rights policy, a relationship whose strength may vary from one end of the class ladder to the other, the problem can be resolved neither with civil rights reforms alone nor with government intervention alone. I argue in Part II that the government must provide economic as well as legal resources as part of a solution. The race problem in the United

States is not coextensive with civil rights; it is larger than civil rights—perhaps it always was. Legal reforms can effectively address racial subordination and intra-class racial disparity within the middle and working classes; but economic measures—job training, the creation of jobs, child care, and so on—are the only governmental resources that can counteract racial subordination (or, alternatively, structural changes in the economy) and intra-class racial disparity within the poverty class.

Recognizing the necessity of an economic response at the level of the poverty class may seem to provide an analytical counter to my claim of a nexus between civil rights policy and the race problem within this class. But there is no contradiction here: the latter argument addresses the question of cause, whereas the would-be counterargument addresses the question of solution. The problem, the cause, and the solution are different entities.

No amount of government intervention, with either economic or legal resources, will solve America's race problem unless it is combined with a strong private initiative on the part of African Americans—namely, self-help. African Americans must package an intensive, long-term program to prepare primarily the working class and poverty class, especially members of the underclass, to take advantage of government-created opportunities in employment, housing, and education. Once these vital socioeconomic resources become more accessible, African Americans must be mentally and behaviorally ready to compete aggressively for such resources. This book outlines a program of self-help that can respond to these needs.

Being prepared to compete aggressively for new opportunities is not the only or even the primary reason for creating a self-help program for African Americans. The most important reason is our civil rights legacy—the high probability that the government will not come through on its end of the deal and that, consequently, African Americans must fend for themselves. Effective legal reforms and strong economic measures are not likely to emanate from the government in the foreseeable future, if ever.

Indeed, opinion polls reveal that most Americans believe the government should not give special treatment to African Americans.[12] Such opinions may be based as much on perceived self-interest as on individual racism. A white working-class male, feeling the pinch of class standing, may not be in a charitable mood—understandably, perhaps, because it might appear to the white individual that his burden and the burden carried by an African American are equal in weight. But the burdens and their consequent pain are not in parity; most African Americans in fact experience the double pain of both racial and class inequality.

Even if one could suppose that the government, especially the Supreme Court, might act on behalf of African Americans in the absence of substantial support from its white constituents, it would still be unwise for African Americans to wait for a governmental rescue. Resolving America's race problem is undoubtedly not the government's highest priority. This may be the real lesson of racial subordination, discussed in Part I. The government may truly want to help its African American citizens, but it may feel constrained or may simply prefer to use our limited collective resources of time, money, energy, and moral fervor to tackle cancer, AIDS, the budget deficit, ozone depletion, national defense, or torture in Argentina first—all legitimate though not equally compelling ways for the government to conduct its business.

It may also be that the government does not ever intend to fully resolve the American race problem. After all, the problem has existed in one form or another at least since the institution of American slavery in 1638 (by New England custom) and 1641 (by Massachusetts law).[13] Perhaps this means that the government, which certainly has the resources to make substantial changes in the lives of African Americans, is simply willing to let things stand.

"The government," of course, is not a single-minded monolith. Nor can we dismiss the salutary efforts of some administrations, congresses, political parties, and courts. Yet, even in the government's finest moments, it never goes far enough. Implementation of constitutional rights is delayed; exceptions are made to anti-discrimination law (Congress has even exempted itself from Title VII of the 1964 Civil Rights Act); and, more generally, legal prescriptions and other necessary resources are consciously denied to African Americans. If it is possible to infer intent from a course of conduct, one can reasonably conclude that the government may have opted to allow the race problem to exist in some form in perpetuity.

Other evidence, less empirical than the longevity of racial issues, also supports this conclusion. It is clear that the socioeconomic inequality built into class stratification is painful for many of those in the lower classes. It is equally clear that the government will not engage in class leveling to remove this pain. Is it possible that the government likewise believes the race problem is one that society can live with, regardless of the pain it causes African Americans? Perhaps the government believes nothing more can be done about this issue without hurting more people than are helped, that African Americans must live with residual racial discrimination because society has reached the point of diminishing returns on civil rights or on other attempts to solve the problem. Perhaps it would be helpful if the government would simply level with us.[14]

It is clearly wrong, however, to regard racial subordination as a constant feature of our society, tantamount in that respect to class subordination. The two forms of subordination are quite distinguishable. For most Americans traveling in the lowest deck of society (the poverty class), class subordination is but a temporary event; the poverty class is fluid, not static.[15] But color is a permanent condition. African Americans cannot escape the race into which they were born. Thus, to the extent that the government's approach is partly motivated by an unspoken belief that some degree of racial subordination is tolerable, African Americans will have been banished to a life of second-class status by tacit consent among government officials.

Challenging our civil rights legacy is prelude to and an integral part of a broader inquiry into America's race problem. Raising questions about this issue necessitates a certain amount of self-criticism by African Americans as well as criticism of the government. Neither form of criticism is intended to be an ideological search-and-destroy mission, but rather an honest attempt to get at the truth, to discover how African Americans can experience the American dream, the essence of which is the opportunity to create a better life for oneself.

Difficult even under the best circumstances, self-criticism is an especially onerous exercise for African Americans, who live in a society that remains full of racist feelings and actions. Self-criticism must, however, go forward; as Dr. Martin Luther King, Jr., argued:

One of the sure signs of maturity is the ability to rise to the point of self-criticism. Whenever we are objects of criticism from white men, even though the criticisms are maliciously directed and mixed with half-truths, we must pick out the elements of truth and make them the basis of creative reconstruction. We must not let the fact that we are victims of injustice lull us into abrogating responsibility for our own lives.[16]

I invite the reader to join me in a search for truth and creative reconstruction. To begin, I offer an introduction to the major elements of my analysis, outlined in brief here.

Understanding the Problem

Combining elements of race and class, I attempt to establish two propositions in Part I of this book. First, certain societal hardships within socioeconomic classes are manifested along racial lines, creating racial inequalities that form today's race problem. Second, our fundamental civil rights policy, formal equal opportunity (examined in Chapter 1), denies priority to specific African American civil rights interests class by class and, as a consequence, such racial subordination accommodates, intensifies, and nurtures intra-class racial disparity, or the American race problem. At a deeper level, both of these propositions find expression in the "subordination question," a two-pronged question that asks whether formal equal opportunity (through its tenets, racial omission and racial integration) subordinates the civil rights interests of African Americans and, if so, whether such racial subordination contributes to intra-class racial disparity. Part I answers both questions in the affirmative.

In short, my response to the subordination question comes down to a simple lesson: *By giving little or no priority to the interests of African Americans in equal opportunity, civil rights laws and policies, as developed and interpreted over the past several decades, ineluctably contribute to the American race problem.*

The African American Middle Class

Compared to their white counterparts, middle-class African Americans suffer more employment discrimination ("complex racial discrimination") and segregation (racially stratified work environments), other employment hardships, housing discrimination and segregation, and low college enrollment. Chapter 2 focuses only on employment disparities; housing and education are considered later, in connection with the working class.

Formal equal opportunity's tenet of racial omission subordinates the civil rights interest of middle-class African Americans in equal employment opportunity in several ways. A primary problem is the priestly status given to the "strict scrutiny" test, a judicial construct used in constitutional litigation to vindicate this tenet. The strict scrutiny test, faithfully applied, gives low priority to the equal employment opportunity interest of middle-class African Americans by enjoining or discouraging public-sector employers from using race-conscious employment policies or practices that give qualified African Americans access to jobs from which they have been excluded in the past by societal discrimination. As a consequence of such racial subordination, there are fewer good opportunities in the legal arena to redress the socioeconomic disparity that is manifested along racial lines within the American middle class and that involves complex racial discrimination, segregation, and other job-related hardships, from loneliness and disaffection to stress and hypertension.

Similarly, judicial construction of statutory antidiscrimination law—mainly Title VII of the 1964 Civil Rights Act,[17]—shifts to the plaintiff the burden of persuasion concerning a defendant's justification for a discriminatory practice and places a relatively high standard of causation on the plaintiff. Some courts have even shown a reluctance to apply Title VII to high-level jobs. These and other features discussed later subordinate the interest of middle-class African Americans in equal employment opportunity by substantially decreasing the odds of winning cases under Title VII. Consequently, legal remedies for complex racial discrimination and racial segregation in the nation's top jobs are significantly limited.

The African American Working Class

Like middle-class African Americans, working-class African Americans experience intra-class racial disparity in employment, housing, and higher education. But unlike the more affluent members of their race, members of the working class also encounter obstacles in primary education and additional hardships on the job. Although the employment problems they face, including the lack of time, money, and flexibility to pursue Title VII litigation, are extremely important, I have chosen to focus the argument in Chapter 3 on intra-class racial disparities in housing and education, both primary (here meaning kindergarten through high school) and higher education.

Legal doctrines, procedures, and policies designed to implement or vindicate the racial omission tenet subordinate certain housing and educational interests of working-class African Americans and consequently accommodate or sustain intra-class racial disparity in these areas. Chapter 3 specifically discusses the role of the "intent" test, the strict scrutiny test, the Fair Housing Act, and the Supreme Court's decision in the *Bakke* case.

The intent test, for example—another judicial creation that reigns supreme in the realm of constitutional litigation—makes the task of proving racial discrimination in housing and racial segregation in public schools extremely difficult and often impossible. Members of the African American working class find themselves unable to use litigation, an essential governmental resource, to effectively protect their interests in equal housing and educational opportunity. The housing discrimination and segregation traceable to race within the working class thus continue unabated. In primary education, problems such as the absence of cultural diversity and the dearth of educational resources (from books to desks to computers) in racially isolated inner-city public schools remain acute.

Faithful application of the strict scrutiny test invalidates any remedial use of racial occupancy controls, or "benign housing quotas," that could counteract complex housing discrimination and prevent housing resegregation through the "tipping" phenomenon. This gives low priority to the African American working class's civil rights interest in open housing. The style of racial subordination supported by the strict scrutiny test can only contribute to the housing problems of working-class African Americans and prolong the struggle against discrimination and housing segregation—segregation that is especially pernicious not only because it usually entails poor municipal services and low-quality housing but also because it etches in the minds of both African Americans and whites an indelible image of yesteryear's racial hierarchy.

The African American working class's civil rights interest in fair housing is further frustrated by the poor structure and administration of the Fair Housing Act of 1968 and by the protracted litigation and the low amounts of monetary relief under both Section 1982 and (until recently) the Fair Housing Act.[18] In failing to support the interest of working-class African Americans in equal housing opportunity, these acts of Congress have allowed housing discrimination and segregation to continue for at least a generation.

Likewise, the Supreme Court's momentous decision in *Regents of the University of California v. Bakke*—which some have incorrectly regarded as a constitutional precedent—has given college and university admissions officers reason to abandon admissions quotas for African Americans or to place undue weight on traditional academic indicators.[19] These admissions practices, which fail to give priority to the interest of African Americans in equal opportunity in higher education, have the effect of decreasing the enrollment of African Americans in colleges and graduate schools.

The tenet of racial integration is also tied to practices that subordinate the interest of working-class African Americans in equal primary education. School officials often implement this tenet in ways that result in "second-generation discrimination" and "resegregation" within integrated schools: academic tracking patterns, biased disciplinary practices, disproportionate placements in classes for the mentally retarded, and school integration techniques that place heavy burdens on African American schoolchildren. Such racial subordination destroys not only the quality of education these children receive but also their self-esteem.

The African American Poverty Class

Intra-class racial disparity in the poverty class is reflected in the disproportionate number of poor African Americans who live in long-term poverty, who experience long-term unemployment, who remain geographically isolated within the inner city, and who, because of these socioeconomic conditions, exhibit a proclivity toward behaviors, values, and attitudes that are dysfunctional and self-defeating in American society. These ingredients constitute a subculture within the African American poverty class—that is, an underclass. Structural transformation of our smokestack economy to a service-oriented economy requiring a higher level of skills may be, as Wilson claims, the major reason for the creation of the African American underclass.[20] But slavery and Jim Crow also set in motion socioeconomic conditions—unemployment, poverty, residential isolation—that have helped to form this group.

The tenet of racial integration aggravates these conditions by subordinating the primary civil rights interest of the African American poor, which is to have an equal opportunity to achieve a decent standard of living. Integration policies have this effect by providing a first-time opportunity for middle-class and working-class African Americans to leave previously segregated communities. Although this is beneficial for those who leave and for the nation as a whole, such an exodus of stable families and talented individuals is a disaster for those who are left behind in poverty-stricken areas. It depletes from African American communities the human and economic resources—talented community leadership, role models, social stability, and dollars—that are necessary for millions of poor African Americans to attain control over their lives and a reasonable level of existence.[21] Racial integration pays little attention to this special civil rights interest of the African American poverty class. Its effect hurts rather than helps this class, leaving many of its members behind in the underclass as "unavoidable costs" of racial progress, while more stable and affluent African American households march forward with the rest of society (though at a slower pace than whites). By failing to recognize or emphasize the civil rights interest of the poverty class in achieving an adequate standard of living, racial integration helps to open a cultural and economic abyss in communities already suffering from the lingering effects of slavery and Jim Crow, creating an underworld of dysfunction and self-destruction into which millions of African Americans have fallen.

Resolving the Problem

More speculative than Part I, Part II offers a prescription for a rational response to the racial issues our society faces. Whatever its operational merits or flaws, this prescription primarily seeks to provide a theory, a logical matrix for resolving the American race problem, a vision for what needs to be done. These proposals depart both from traditional conservative ideology that rejects a governmental response and from traditional liberal ideology that relies too heavily on a governmental rescue. I believe that any realistic solution must necessarily involve both self-help on the part of African Americans *and* governmental remedies (legal and economic) and that these ingredients must be employed in a complementary rather than a contradictory manner.

I argue in Chapter 5 that, to be effective, a program of self-help must provide support for African American institutions (such as predominantly African American public schools) and for households (families and individuals). Programs offering support to institutions (for example, corporate executives who are on loan to inner-city schools or who convince their companies to finance a computer lab or a new collection of books for the library) are not new and hence are not the focus of this book. The concept of household support, however, is less familiar and *is* my focus. I envision a program of household support in which middle-class African Americans work one-on-one, long-term, with poorer families and individuals to impart and to coach the behaviors, values, and attitudes of mainstream society, as well as the survival techniques that African Americans have found essential in a racist society. The goal of such an intensive program is to position African Americans to take full advantage of government-created opportunities, or to at least improve the socioeconomic conditions (both race- and class-based) under which they live.

For its part, government must accordingly create a special support system for African Americans, which in some cases might

also be applicable to whites, that opens real or *measurable* opportunities. As discussed in Chapter 6, this effort would require federal courts and Congress to modify the manner in which formal
equal opportunity has conventionally been applied relative to
middle-class and working-class African Americans (legal remedies) and would require the president and Congress to create an
employment opportunities program for poor African Americans
(economic remedies). The level of private and public support
would decrease as socioeconomic status increases.

Although certain of the proposed legal remedies have in fact
been adopted in recent amendments to the 1968 Fair Housing
Act (discussed in Chapter 6), our civil rights legacy makes it
highly unlikely that anything approaching the full array of the
proposed legal and economic remedies will be implemented in
the foreseeable future. In spite of this forbidding reality, I argue
that civil rights advocates have no choice but to continue the
struggle for such goals. We cannot give up the fight.

I argue, furthermore, that we will maximize our slim chances
for success in the legal arena if we are able to cast our legal proposals in terms of promoting or reimplementing formal equal opportunity, society's fundamental civil rights policy, rather than as
a frontal attack on that policy or as a means of converting equality
of opportunity into equality of results in which genuine differences in ability are overlooked. Legal remedies, then, must be as
consistent as possible with the operational tenets of formal equal
opportunity—racial omission and racial integration—and they
must in the end promote their societal goal, racial inclusion.

Similarly, to stand a realistic chance of capturing needed political and public support, the economic remedies must be congru-
ent with the cultural and political values of our liberal democratic
society. These remedies must be in the tune with the existing
direction of our society. They must not attempt to effect a fundamental social transformation, such as class leveling, and they
must recognize the limited role that government plays in our society: government supplies the opportunities, not the achievements; the individual supplies the effort.

One hopes, of course, that these legal and economic remedies,
so constrained by the system, will in fact register as measurable,
even if small, victories for African Americans. A high tightrope,

but one I attempt to walk in Chapter 6. I do not walk this tight-rope without a safety net below, however. For I believe that, given the uncertainty of government assistance—the certainty of our civil rights legacy—African Americans must proceed on their own, and they must do so now rather than later, without viewing government assistance as a precondition for self-help. African Americans can do a great deal to help resolve the American race problem (although it will never be completely solved in the absence of governmental remedies). Furthermore, African Americans can do a great deal by themselves to ameliorate some of the socioeconomic problems in their lives caused by class subordination as well as racial subordination, and these efforts can help to achieve greater social and economic stability. That is added incentive for African Americans to proceed with an intensive self-help program, to refuse to wait until the government moves forward. For all these reasons, I consider African American self-help to be the most important of the proposals outlined here.

But if meaningful government assistance is uncertain, so is self-help. The advent of social and economic stratification within African American society is a reality that may militate against intra-racial, inter-class cooperation. As Part I illustrates in some detail, many of the day-to-day experiences and specific civil rights interests of middle-class, working-class, and poor African Americans are different, in some instances vastly different. African Americans may not see eye-to-eye on many issues, including the issue of self-help.

Other divisions in African American society may also threaten self-help. Among these are geographic differences, gender conflicts, and internal discord (including color prejudice and ideology) that extends back to the days of slavery and to the fierce debate between Booker T. Washington (plantation-born, trained for manual labor, and a conservative accommodator) and W. E. B. DuBois (New England-born, Harvard-educated, and an undaunted protester), a debate that raged early in this century concerning the strategy for dealing with another form of racial subordination, Jim Crow's separate-but-equal policy.[22] Add to these chasms the fact that African Americans, like all oppressed people, have always responded in different ways to racial oppression—some have offered resistance; others have been more docile, even to the point of acquiescence—and the possibility of intra-racial, cross-class cooperation at a level sufficient to create, execute, and sustain a strong program of self-help may seem remote at best.

I view socioeconomic division as the crucial variable in any program of African American self-help today. It is a new variable that remains to be tested. All the other divisions and conflicts have been in place throughout hundreds of years of racial oppression, and we know that most (though not all) African Americans were nevertheless sufficiently motivated by the commonality of race to work together in successful campaigns against slavery and Jim Crow. For example, Martin Luther King himself reported the "large number" of uneducated African Americans in Montgomery, Alabama, who not only "accepted [segregation] without protest" and seemed "resigned to segregation per se" but "also accepted the abuses and indignities which came with it."[23] Despite this, enough members of Montgomery's African American community, including many of the formerly passive citizens, were brought together under King's leadership to successfully conduct the famous bus boycott of 1955–1956. Furthermore, even African Americans who were relatively well-off under slavery and Jim Crow often sacrificed their time and in some cases their lives to help others of their race achieve a better life—from Harriet Tubman, Frederick Douglass, and W. E. B. DuBois to Malcolm X, Martin Luther King, and other modern civil rights activists.

Focusing, then, on the socioeconomic variable, I argue that most African Americans today can be motivated to work together in a program of self-help both because of altruism and, most important, because they can be shown how the program serves their own material interests. Admittedly, appeal to self-interest is not the noblest of arguments; but it is usually effective. I concentrate on the self-interest of the African American middle class, a group that would appear to have the least to gain and the most to lose by participating in a self-help program. I argue that middle-class African Americans can improve their own quality of life by taking part in a program of self-help designed to improve the quality of life of others. In part, this argument underscores my belief that in a society that remains extremely color-conscious and fraught with negative stereotyping, African Americans are still so significantly connected by color that racial kinship may in fact continue to motivate intra-racial cooperation in spite of socio-economic division or, for that matter, any other differences within African American society. *Race is still a more significant factor for African Americans than is class.*

The particulars of my prescription for resolving the American race problem—both in terms of self-help (household support) and government assistance—can be analyzed along class lines.

The African American Middle Class

The African American middle class encounters disproportionately more societal hardships in employment, housing, and higher education than does the white middle class; thus self-help and government assistance for this relatively prosperous segment of African American society must focus on these specific socioeconomic problems and the underlying racial subordination. The problems in housing and higher education are similar to those encountered by the working class and are discussed in that connection.

Focusing on employment problems, I suggest that self-help among middle-class African Americans should center on the development of self-support and networking systems. These measures can do little to redress job discrimination and segregation, but they can provide some relief for other job-related problems such as loneliness, disaffection, stress, and hypertension.

Only the government can solve the problems of employment discrimination and a racially stratified work force. Accordingly, on the public side, the federal courts must reallocate the burden of persuasion regarding a defendant's justification for a discriminatory employment decision and change the substantive standard of causation in individual cases of intentional discrimination under Title VII; must adopt a different litigation model as well as a different evidentiary standard governing a defendant's case-in-chief in "mixed-motive" litigation; and must end their reluctance to apply antidiscrimination law to high-level positions. The federal courts must also modify or abandon the strict scrutiny test in racial preference law to permit greater use of voluntary affirmative action programs in the public sector.

The African American Working Class

The African American working class needs help in redressing intra-class racial disparity and underlying racial subordination in employment, housing, and both primary and higher education. Employment burdens held in common with the middle class may be alleviated through prescriptive measures designed for that class. Other employment hardships, such as the lack of time, resources, and flexibility to pursue complex and protracted employment discrimination litigation, require a different approach. Unlike members of the middle class, working-class African Americans are caught in the pinch of both class subordination and racial subordination: as a result of insufficient income, on the one hand, they are unable to control many events in their lives or to enjoy a margin of error in their personal dealings; as a result of color, on the other hand, they face discrimination, de jure and de facto segregation, and other forms of intra-class racial disparity. For this reason, both forms of subordination are proper subjects for self-help.

Self-help in this case could focus on relatively small changes in lifestyle for working-class African Americans. To further stabilize their lives or to advance to the middle class, working-class African Americans could benefit from strengthening skills such as household budgeting, long-term family goal setting, smart consumer spending, and racial survival techniques. In addition to these household support measures, members of the middle class must provide support to African American institutions within the inner cities, not with money from their own pockets but with private funds from professional and business organizations and with a personal commitment of time, know-how, direction, and other intangibles. Predominantly African American public schools should be the major recipients of such institutional support. African American professional organizations and corporate executives working through their corporations can provide badly needed educational resources to segregated (or "voluntarily" separated) public schools—high-quality instruction, sophisticated academic programs, state-of-the-art equipment, and so on—as well as assistance in lobbying local school boards and city halls to secure badly needed public funds.

Middle-class African Americans are in the best position to provide household and institutional support, especially the former.
This statement is not intended to demean or discount the valuable mentoring efforts or other assistance that scores of white
Americans have extended to African Americans throughout the
years. Nor do I wish to suggest that white individuals and organizations have no role to play; white Americans can and must
continue to offer assistance to African American households and
institutions in whatever way feasible. My point is simply that
members of the African American middle class are likely to be
the most effective and the most desirable guides for working-class
and poor African American households. Having been through
much of the terrain before, members of the middle class possess
certain unique skills and knowledge, from how to deal with a racist boss or co-worker to how to tap into the African American
ethos for strength and perseverance. Many also have a certain
status within the African American community, which can be useful in reaching others. In addition, they are able to serve as role
models for younger African Americans, who can envision themselves duplicating the successful career paths they see. For these
and other reasons, I argue that middle-class African Americans
should, as a matter of policy, lead the private campaign to solve
the American race problem.[24]

The government must help the African American working class
by freeing the avenues of upward social and economic mobility
from invidious racial discrimination. Overhauls of Title VII and
of the 1968 Fair Housing Act (beyond the 1988 amendments) are
essential to compensate for the inability of the working class to
engage in protracted civil rights litigation. The "effects" test must
be adopted as an alternative standard of proof in school desegregation law. Having a more realistic opportunity to establish the
liability of school boards, African American parents would increase their chances of winning school desegregation lawsuits,
which are the keys to unlocking a treasure chest of educational
remedies—more resources for academic programs, racial mixing
at both student and staff levels, African American awareness programs, and so on. To counteract *Bakke's* towering negative influence on college admissions, admissions officers must return to
the use of admissions quotas for African Americans or at least

must consider the applicant's "whole person" rather than merely a traditional academic record. And the strict scrutiny test—"strict in theory and fatal in fact" when applied to racial occupancy controls and admissions quotas—should be modified or abolished.

The African American Poverty Class

Although some poor African Americans, particularly the working poor, may be able to benefit from the measures proposed for the working class, self-help and government assistance for a majority of poor African Americans (and especially for the underclass) require the most intensive effort. Once again, the assistance of the middle class would be indispensable in developing effective self-help programs. Middle-class African Americans must attempt to redirect the dysfunctional and self-defeating mores afflicting those who form the underclass subculture. They must do so by teaching not only mainstream American behaviors, values, and attitudes (including the work ethic) but also survival techniques for African Americans coping with a racist society. As in the case of the working class, these skills can be taught only on a long-term, one-on-one, "adopt a family" basis. Thus, household rather than institutional support is the primary form of self-help at the poverty level.

The government should spearhead the creation of a broad-based employment opportunities program for all poor African Americans. This program could be patterned after what Sheila Kamerman and Alfred Kahn call the "European experience" and what William Julius Wilson calls his "hidden agenda": namely, "a strategy that includes income transfers, child care services, and employment policies as central elements."[25] My proposals concerning employment opportunities modify this strategy by adding elements that fit the unique American experience. For example, although job training would be guaranteed, jobs would not. Income transfers would be provided only during the transitional job-training period. Emphasis would be placed on private-sector employment, with tax incentives to help create jobs. Employers would be involved in job training and perhaps in transportation to workplaces. Child care services could involve local schools, churches, employers, parents, or government assistance.

The complexity and range of racial issues in the United States may at times seem overwhelming. I do not pretend to offer all the answers or even to address all the pressing concerns—for example, this book does not discuss the need for a national drug policy that would affect the lives of many underclass African Americans. But I do hope to stimulate some fresh thinking and to add some substance to the shadows surrounding the American race problem.

Part One

Understanding the American Race Problem

Chapter One

Formal Equal Opportunity

Formal equal opportunity is the nation's fundamental public policy on civil rights. Like its predecessor, the separate-but-equal policy under Jim Crow,[1] formal equal opportunity seeks to regulate in rather broad terms the treatment that government and, to a lesser extent, private individuals accord to society's racial groups in relation to one another. Formal equal opportunity, in other words, determines the direction and tone of interracial relations in our society today.

Clearly, the past holds the key to understanding formal equal opportunity. The meaning and significance of this civil rights policy are rooted in the community attitudes and beliefs that fueled Jim Crow's separate-but-equal policy, for formal equal opportunity is intended to run counter to Jim Crow and all that it represents.[2]

Those historical attitudes and beliefs, which helped to shape the development of formal equal opportunity later on, are unmistakable. African Americans were regarded as an alien breed, lower than the entire community of whites. They were stereotyped as bestial, unteachable, uncouth, odious, and inferior to whites in every essential respect. In 1896 the Supreme Court in *Plessy v. Ferguson* determined that these community attitudes and beliefs had gelled into a strong community expectation concerning interracial relations: that the races were to be held separate but equal—meaning, of course, unequal.[3] The separate-but-equal policy, in which at least one prominent African American, Booker T. Washington, acquiesced, was thereby born; and a parade of laws designed to enforce it soon followed.[4] These laws, which condoned ubiquitous discrimination against African Americans and mandated "colored" and white public accommodations, schools, libraries, restrooms, drinking fountains, and so forth endured until formal equal opportunity became public policy in the 1950s and 1960s.[5]

Formal equal opportunity is a first-time blend of African American and white community expectations regarding interracial relations having the force of law. At its most basic level, formal equal opportunity can be defined as a civil rights policy in which African Americans and whites are held to be of equal legal status. The races are deemed to differ in no legally material way and are therefore entitled to equal legal treatment. Racism and its humiliating effects—segregation and discrimination—are no longer the official policies of or condoned by the government.[6]

Formal equal opportunity has certainly not reversed all the negative attitudes that whites held toward African Americans during the Jim Crow era. Racism and stereotyping continue to thrive in our society. The survival of these racial attitudes does not, however, call into question the legitimacy of formal equal opportunity as our current public policy. So many social institutions and conventions have been built around formal equal opportunity that community expectations favoring this policy are clearly stronger and more consistent with our liberal democratic society than those favoring separate-but-equal treatment.

In *The Structure of Scientific Revolutions,* Thomas Kuhn demonstrates that new paradigms often have a long and uncertain gestation period.[7] In the case of formal equal opportunity, the first serious indication that it might replace separate-but-equal as the nation's civil rights policy came during World War II. President Franklin D. Roosevelt issued Executive Order 8802 on June 25, 1941, which (in what has become standard legal jargon for creating formal equal opportunity rules of law) "prohibited discrimination on the basis of race, creed, [or] color" in certain areas of federal employment, vocational training programs administered by federal agencies, and the national defense industry. Executive Order 8802 also created a federal agency, called the Fair Employment Practices Committee, that was authorized to receive and investigate charges of employment discrimination, redress proven grievances, and make recommendations to carry out the purposes of the executive order.[8]

Further indications of the advent of formal equal opportunity appeared in the military itself during the Second World War. Before the war, African Americans in the armed services had been confined to segregated units and assigned to noncombat, low-status jobs, usually in labor details. African American soldiers during World War I, for example, were often trained in the United States using broomsticks as weapons; they fought gallantly in Europe, but as part of the French, not the American, armed forces. The experiences of these soldiers, in other words, reflected the overall experience of African Americans under Jim Crow. By the end of World War II, however, the army had desegregated most of its officer candidate schools, although Army Air Corps training was still segregated; the navy had its first African American commissioned officer, although African American sailors generally were permitted to serve on ships only as mess stewards; and the Marine Corps, which had been exclusively white since the late eighteenth century, enlisted African Americans but assigned them to segregated units.[9]

Although racial progress in the military during World War II was minor, matters were greatly improved by the time of the Korean War, when African Americans fought in desegregated units in all branches of the service. This turn of events was the direct result of Executive Order 9981, signed by President Harry Truman on July 26, 1948, which required "equality of treatment and opportunity for all persons in the armed services without regard to race, color, religion, or national origin." A companion order, Executive Order 9980, signed on the same day, brought formal equal opportunity to most areas within the federal government's civilian departments.[10]

In bringing about these early promulgations of formal equal opportunity, however, the confluence of several domestic and international conditions was more important than the altruism of lawmakers. Demographic changes in the industrialized North were crucial. Between 1940 and 1944, 470,000 African Americans moved from the rural regions of the South to the urban areas of the North looking for better jobs and better racial relations. For the first time, most African Americans lived in cities rather than in the rural South. This massive migration placed desegregative pressures on employment markets in the cities and, most important, provided a welcome supply of labor for hungry civilian industries supporting the war effort.[11]

The war itself was an important motivation for the executive orders issued by Roosevelt and Truman. Fighting for democracy abroad made it increasingly difficult to defend racial oppression at home. African Americans, who felt the contradiction intensely, applied increasing pressure on government officials through demonstrations, marches, and other forms of protests. Union leader A. Philip Randolph's threatened march on Washington in 1940, which helped to persuade Roosevelt to issue Executive Order 8802, is an example of the new activism that took hold of African Americans. The success of this activism also served to convince the followers of Booker T. Washington, who died in 1915, that it was time to jettison their support for separate-but-equal and to embrace the more assertive civil rights policy, formal equal opportunity, advocated by such leaders as W. E. B. DuBois and Randolph.[12]

Finally, the rise of Keynesian economics and the decline of laissez-faire economics in the United States during the 1930s made government intervention schemes, such as formal equal opportunity, seem proper. Indeed, the failure of laissez-faire government to prevent or to extricate the nation from severe economic depression made government regulation of institutional behavior seem not only legitimate but also necessary.[13]

Formal equal opportunity during the war years was but a community impulse struggling to become a public policy, however. Separate-but-equal was still the dominant community value—it was still "law"—although it had been significantly vitiated.

One May 17, 1954, formal equal opportunity came of age when the Supreme Court handed down its momentous decision in the cases consolidated under *Brown v. Board of Education*.[14] Against the backdrop of all the pressures that had caused Roosevelt and Truman to establish pockets of formal equal opportunity in selected areas of American life, and with the momentum of a line of its own cases chipping away at separate-but-equal,[15] the Supreme Court in *Brown I* took a decisive turn for the better in the government's approach to race relations. *Brown I* was the first act of government to make the ideal of racial equality—the push for racial inclusiveness—a constitutional imperative and, hence, unequivocally the official civil rights policy of the United States. In *Brown I*, a unanimous Supreme Court promulgated, as the Court itself would later say, "the fundamental [policy] that racial discrimination in public education is unconstitutional" and declared that "[a]ll provisions of federal, state, or local law requiring or permitting such discrimination must yield to this [policy]."[16]

Although *Brown I* dealt solely with the issue of public education, the fact that for the first time the Supreme Court had construed the Constitution, the nation's legal infrastructure, to require nonracial access to such an essential societal resource would inevitably project a towering shadow over virtually every aspect of interracial relations in this country. Indeed, *Brown I* has been credited with engendering "a social upheaval the extent and consequences of which cannot even now be measured with certainty" and with changing the *legal* status of African Americans from mere supplicants "seeking, pleading, begging to be treated as full-fledged members of the human race" to persons entitled to equal treatment under the law.[17]

In the years following *Brown I*, courts and legislatures identified and accentuated two major operational tenets derived from formal equal opportunity. These tenets have guided the way legal institutions and the community at large have applied this policy since *Brown I*. Today, formal equal opportunity is often defined in terms of these operational tenets.

The first is racial omission, what some might call color blindness or a race-neutral approach. Racial omission may be seen, in some respects, as a restatement of the fundamental meaning of formal equal opportunity, discussed earlier in this chapter—equal legal status and treatment. Racial omission is the belief that racial differences should be ignored and omitted from legal consideration. Rules of law and practices regulating access to education, employment, housing, and other social resources must be formulated without regard to race or racial dynamics. Members of all racial groups are entitled to be treated the same in all essential respects by the government. Accordingly, white Americans may not receive any opportunities not also available to racial minorities, and vice versa.

Racial integration is the sibling tenet of racial omission. Racial integration is racial mixing. It is simply any governmental policy that mandates or encourages a physical merger or juxtaposition of various racial groups. If the government favors racial integration, it necessarily must disfavor racial separation. Both policies cannot be promoted simultaneously.

Racial integration should be contrasted with desegregation. Desegregation is the removal of legal restraints on one's actions or designations placed on one's status that were intended to stigmatize. The removal of these government-imposed conditions permits a group or its members to choose to go their separate or integrated ways. In this sense, it can be said that racial integration presupposes desegregation.

There is also a sense in which racial omission presupposes desegregation. No government could logically or successfully operate a public policy that mandates the omission of race from legal considerations without first (or at least simultaneously) removing legal designations designed to exclude and stigmatize. The failure to do so would at worst create governmental dysfunction and at best engender cognitive dissonance among the public.

The ultimate purpose of formal equal opportunity is to change our society from one marked by racial exclusivity to one characterized by racial inclusion. This fundamental civil rights policy seeks to bring African Americans into the mainstream of American society, to make them first-class citizens. Racial omission and racial integration are simply specific strategies or vehicles for engendering real opportunities for racial inclusion.[18]

The Civil Rights Act of 1964, the Voting Rights Act of 1965, and the Fair Housing Act of 1968 are the most significant federal rules of law implementing these two strategies.[19] More sweeping than any other piece of civil rights legislation in American history, the 1964 Civil Rights Act has eleven titles, each of which prohibits discrimination "on the basis of race or color" in a major sector of American life: voting (Title I), public accommodations (Title II), public education (Title IV), and employment (Title VII), among others. The 1965 Voting Rights Act vastly improves the voting protections offered by Title I of the 1964 Civil Rights Act (which mainly establishes standards applicable to voter registration) by banning all forms of racial discrimination in voting, from literacy tests to complex schemes of vote dilution, and by enforcing these rights with powerful remedies. Finally, the 1968 Fair Hosing Act makes it illegal for certain property owners, real estate agencies, and lenders to discriminate "on the basis of race or color" in the sale or rental of housing.

But after all the civil rights laws and passions promoting formal equal opportunity since *Brown I*, it is nevertheless true that millions of African Americans are still living a life that in many ways reflects second-class citizenship, a life that in many respects is Jim Crow in all but name. Class by class, African Americans continue to shoulder more than their fair share of societal hardships such as racial discrimination, poor public schooling, and poverty. Why?

My answer to that question targets formal equal opportunity itself. I argue that there is a relationship between formal equal opportunity and intra-class racial disparity, the American race problem. Specifically, I argue that there is something dreadfully wrong about the way our fundamental civil rights policy has been *applied* since *Brown I*.

Some legal instrumentalists, particularly legal realists, would argue that formalism is what is wrong with formal equal opportunity, that this policy has not been grounded in the social reality it seeks to regulate. For example, the late Judge Skelly Wright, one of the most influential modern legal realists, faulted those who would apply our civil rights law and policy in a way that is too concerned with abstractionism, deductive logic, and internal consistency.[20] Wright would advise judicial decision makers implementing formal equal opportunity to proceed from the Holmesian maxim concerning the content and growth of law—"The life of the law has not been logic; it has been experience"—rather than from the Langdellian syllogism:

> All P are M [principle of law from formal equal opportunity]
> No S are M [crucial facts of problem]
> Ergo, No S are P [authoritative decision][21]

Although decision makers, both judicial and nonjudicial, have not always been attentive to socioeconomic reality when implementing formal equal opportunity, many of these decision makers, especially judges, do attempt to ground their decisions in

that reality. And many of these individuals are generally supportive of civil rights. For example, the Supreme Court in *Bakke* sin-
cerely tried to devise a remedy that could deal with the real-life
obstacles that African American students continued to face in college admissions.[22]

The real problem with the application of formal equal opportunity has less to do with formalism than with the degree of deference given to African Americans' view of reality. It is the lack of
priority given to African American civil rights interests in the implementation of formal equal opportunity that is most at fault.
Formal equal opportunity (through its operational tenets of racial
omission and racial integration) gives low priority, little weight to
African American rights interests at critical times, despite the fact
that civil rights would seem to be the one arena in American society in which these interests, damaged for so long by earlier policies, should receive top priority.

With the increased class stratification in African American
society since the 1960s, various African American civil rights interests occasionally conflict. This, of course, can make it more
difficult to emphasize or promote a particular interest. Yet in
most instances, these civil rights interests are not contraposed,
and the conundrum of which interest to promote does not usually
present itself.

At this point, some may argue that formal equal opportunity
never sought to ensure equality of results, only equality of treatment by government.[23] My initial response to this argument is to
recognize that formal equal opportunity has had a greater impact
on African Americans at the normative level than at the ground
level. In many respects, African Americans and whites are accorded equal treatment by government more in theory than in
the reality of daily life. African Americans have certainly received
a legalistic, formalistic type of equality. But that is a poor proxy
for the real thing—an equal chance to improve or protect one's
chances for worldly success and personal happiness.

This leads to a more substantial response to the argument. I
fault formal equal opportunity (or, more precisely, its implementation through racial omission and racial integration) for its inability to deliver equal opportunity for the races, not equal results.
Coming out of the Jim Crow era, the government essentially had

two choices concerning how to redress the racial disparity set in motion by centuries of unequal status and treatment. The first and more direct was simply to upgrade the living conditions of African Americans by, for example, providing housing or jobs in proportion to the racial group's percentage of the population. Although some deemed this tactic, equality of results, immoral because it undermined the principle of desert (for instance, qualified workers could be denied jobs because their employment would upset an employer's racially balanced work force), recent scholarship has demonstrated how some forms of equality of results might be morally defensible.[24]

Formal equal opportunity did not, in any event, represent this approach to the problem. Rather, it meant choosing a second, indirect strategy that focused on racial starting positions, attempting to provide African Americans with the opportunities necessary to gain parity with whites by such actions as proscribing employment discrimination and making available the means to enforce that prohibition—not a bad plan if properly implemented.

I contend, however, that formal equal opportunity is operationally flawed, even though it is conceptually sound; that although it was designed to level the playing field for African Americans and whites, too often it has done this only within the rarefied pages of the law books, not within the mundane living conditions of American society. To claim that the playing field should be level—that African Americans should have roughly the same opportunities as whites, in reality, to augment or preserve their socioeconomic position in society—is quite different from claiming that the results or the achievements of the competition should be equal. I make the former, not the latter, claim.

Chapter Two

The African American
Middle Class

Defining Characteristics

Although it is rarely defined, the term *middle class* is widely
used in American society. It is a term that purports to measure
worldly success. Because Americans like to view themselves as
successful people, there is little wonder, then, that most consider
themselves members of the middle class. Yet, as one commentator indicates, this "all-inclusive category . . . [is] so broad that it
not only blurs real distinctions in income, lifestyle, and well-being
but often clouds public discussion as well."[1] Quite simply, the
term *middle class* needs to be carefully (and perhaps narrowly)
defined before it can be gainfully employed in public discourse.

It may be impossible, however, to arrive at a definition acceptable to everyone, as illustrated by the work of a few prominent
scholars. Sociologist Bart Landry, for example, defines middle-
class status in terms of occupation. In his book *The New Black
Middle Class*, he equates middle-class status with white-collar
occupations, by which he means sales and clerical workers as
well as professionals and business managers.[2]

Some of the specific occupations Landry classifies as middle-
class may be debatable—in particular, I would categorize sales
and clerical positions as working-class occupations. Nevertheless,
Landry's occupational approach is useful, because an individual's
occupation clearly conveys certain information about his or her
socioeconomic status. Primarily, it indicates the stability of one's
stream of income. For example, an autoworker, who endures pe-
riodic layoffs and the threat of strikes or cutbacks during contract

34

negotiations, has a less stable earnings stream than does a computer analyst, who enjoys a high degree of job security and mobility, even though both workers might earn about the same amount. Occupation also tells us something about educational background: a doctor's level of education is vastly different from that of a professional wrestler, even though both may earn $200,000 annually.

But an occupational approach has its limitations. Occupational status can be a misleading indicator of income level. A Legal Aid attorney might earn only $18,000 a year, a salary ordinarily inadequate to allow one to "buy into" the middle-class dream: comfort and security, a nice home, a late-model car, household appliances such as a microwave oven or VCR, an annual vacation, savings and investments—in general, a stable, even thriving existence.[3] Yet a plumber earning $60,000 a year could easily afford such a lifestyle.

Because income level dictates the type of lifestyle one can afford, many scholars argue that individual or family income is the most important determinant of socioeconomic status and the primary measure of class standing. Sociologist Robert Hill and economists Andrew Brimmer and Andrew Hacker are among leading scholars who use income levels to define the African American middle class. For both Hill and Hacker, this class, like the white middle class, consists of families or individuals with annual incomes between $20,000 and $50,000. Brimmer defines the middle-class income range as $25,000 to $50,000.[4]

There are problems in using an income approach. All income categories and percentages based on census data that predate the March 1989 population survey (including the categories and percentages employed by Hill, Brimmer, and Hacker) have limited current value. This limitation has less to do with the passage of time—which involves only two or three years at most—than with new methods of analysis used by the Bureau of the Census. Since 1988, the target year for the March 1989 population survey, the government has used expanded income categories and a different technique for processing the raw data. For example, instead of a $10,000–$20,000 income category, the government now uses $10,000–$15,000 and $15,000–$20,000 categories. In addition, "$100,000 and over" has replaced "$50,000 and over" as the top income category.[5]

A more fundamental problem with an income approach is that it provides little information about occupational status, earnings stability and potential, or educational background. A young business lawyer who earns $40,000 a year, a janitor who moonlights as a taxicab driver and has a combined annual income of $40,000, a high school teacher who earns $40,000 after twenty years on the job, and a family in which the husband works in a factory and the wife cleans offices to earn a combined annual income of $40,000 all have the same "middle-class" income—but their occupations, their degree of job security and mobility, their future earnings potential, and their educational backgrounds are vastly different.

Nevertheless, each of these individuals and families has the ability to live a relatively stable, comfortable lifestyle. Income is the essential determinant, though it may be based on widely varying occupations and education. This book, then, takes an income approach in defining the general socioeconomic classes in African American society—the upper class, the middle class, the working class, and the poverty class. But I am less concerned with the numbers themselves than with what the numbers mean or suggest. When I use a term such as *African American middle class*, I refer in the main to an identifiable set of socioeconomic characteristics that certain households (individuals or families) normally hold in common.

Using annual household income as the chief defining characteristic of socioeconomic strata, I categorize households with incomes ranging from $75,000 to $100,000 or more as *upper-class*, those within the $25,000–$75,000 income range as *middle-class*, those within the $10,000–$25,000 range as *working-class*, and those with incomes of $10,000 or less as among the *poverty class*. Because there are so few African Americans in the upper class (fewer than 3 percent), I combine upper- and middle-class households for purposes of analysis, using the term *middle class* to generally include both groups.

Based on these considerations, 33.8 percent of African Americans belong to the middle class, compared to 56.7 percent of white Americans. The African American middle class is thus a sizable segment of African American society, but much smaller than the white middle class, which is the largest segment of white society. (See the accompanying table detailing the various

Household Income, 1988

	Percentage of African American Population	Percentage of White Population
Upper class		
Over $100,000	1.0	3.4
$75,000–$100,000	1.6	4.5
Middle class		
$50,000–$75,000	7.3	14.2
$35,000–$50,000	11.4	18.1
$25,000–$35,000	12.5	16.5
Working class		
$15,000–$25,000	19.4	18.6
$10,000–$15,000	13.1	9.8
Poverty class		
Under $10,000	33.8	14.8
Median income	$16,407	$28,781
Population	10,561,000	79,734,000

SOURCE: Based on statistics from U.S. Bureau of the Census, *Current Population Reports: Money Income and Poverty Status in the United States:* 1988, Series P-60, no. 166, advance data from the March 1989 Current Population Survey (Washington, D.C.: U.S. Government Printing Office, 1989), pp. 23–24, table 2.

NOTE: The poverty line in 1988 was set at an annual household income of $10,997 for a family of four. Id. at p. 127.

income groups and the chart indicating relative sizes of these socioeconomic strata.)

African American households within the middle-class income range have certain socioeconomic characteristics:

- Forty-three percent of the households consist of families headed by both parents. Among this group, the men are employed in three categories in approximately equal percentages: semi-skilled or unskilled blue-collar or service workers (for example, assembly-line workers, laborers, food handlers), professionals (doctors, lawyers, teachers), and business persons (managers, company sales representatives, small-business owners). The women in this group also fall into three occupational categories in roughly equal percentages: retail sales or clerical

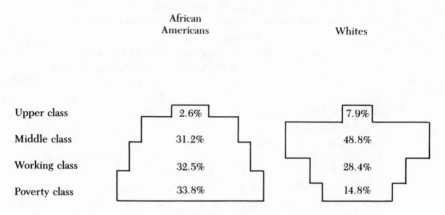

	African Americans	Whites
Upper class	2.6%	7.9%
Middle class	31.2%	48.8%
Working class	32.5%	28.4%
Poverty class	33.8%	14.8%

Socioeconomic classes

SOURCE: Based on statistics from U.S. Bureau of the Census, *Current Population Reports: Money Income and Poverty Status in the United States:* 1988, Series P-60, no. 166, advance data from the March 1989 Current Population Survey (Washington, D.C.: U.S. Government Printing Office, 1989), pp. 23–24, table 2.

workers (postal workers, officer workers, telephone operators), professionals, and homemakers (married women who are not in the paid labor force).

- Fourteen percent of the households are female-headed. About 20 percent of these women are professionals, another 20 percent are retail sales or clerical workers, and an additional 20 percent are retired. The remaining 40 percent are employed as semi-skilled or unskilled blue-collar or service workers.

- The remaining households consist of single women, single men, and male-headed families, in which the breadwinners are typically business managers or professionals.[6]

Although members of the African American middle class enjoy a comfortable and stable lifestyle relative to other African Americans, color remains a significant barrier to attaining sustained happiness and worldly success. Nowhere is this assessment more evident than in the employment arena. Here, middle-class African Americans face a combination of problems that jeopardize their level of income and status and that threaten to push them into the working class, or worse. And it is also here that middle-class African Americans face racial subordination through the judicial application of formal equal opportunity.

The Subordination Question

The subordination question analyzes the role of formal equal opportunity in engendering racial subordination and also examines how such subordination has contributed to the problem of intra-class racial disparity. It may be best to begin by discussing the nature of this intra-class disparity—that is, by describing the American race problem as it is experienced by middle-class African Americans.

Intra-Class Racial Disparity

Middle-class African Americans shoulder disproportionately more societal burdens than do middle-class whites in at least three vital areas: employment, housing, and education. Although they are not the focus of this chapter, the obstacles faced in housing and education cannot be taken lightly. Members of the African American elite encounter as much housing segregation as poor African Americans do, though the two groups remain geographically separated from each other.[7] And even though middle-class African American high school students, because of their parents' education and occupational status, are more likely to aspire to highly selective colleges and graduate schools than are working-class or poverty-stricken students, all African American high school students face a common problem—namely, low enrollment in higher education, caused in part by the use of standardized admission tests. On average, African American students whose fathers are college-educated score *lower* on standardized entrance exams (such as the SAT for college admission and the LSAT for law school admission) than white students whose fathers had only an elementary school education.[8]

Nevertheless, employment hardships probably present the most serious threat to the African American middle class overall, for they seem to affect virtually all members of this class in one way or another, and they certainly hit where it hurts most—family income. Because of the importance and complexity of these employment problems, this chapter concentrates only on that area. (Housing and educational problems are taken up in Chapter 3.) To further simplify the discussion, I also generally focus my analysis on the problems faced by corporate managers and professionals, two of the larger occupational groups in this income range. These problems are similar to many of those encountered by other middle-class African Americans.

So much fuss has been made about affirmative action hiring that little attention has been given to what happens to African American employees (whether or not they are beneficiaries of affirmative action) *after* they are hired. A closer look reveals no dearth of racial disparities hounding the African American corporate manager or professional. Loneliness, disaffection, stress and hypertension (related to "John Henryism"), "complex racial discrimination" (sophisticated or unconscious racial discrimination, frequently accompanied by nonracial factors), and de facto segregation in high-level jobs are the principal problems. Of these, employment discrimination and segregation reflect the most serious intra-class disparities.

African Americans are seriously underrepresented in many corporate and professional positions. Being the only African American—or, at best, one of only a few—results almost by definition in feelings of loneliness. Such feelings may be heightened by maladroit professional and semi-social interactions with well-meaning white colleagues. An awkward remark ("blacks have a natural ability for basketball" or the traditional "some of my best friends are black") or a racist joke can be very painful. Insulting remarks can cause one to feel relegated to "solitary confinement" on the job.[9]

To survive in an environment that neither understands nor fully supports them, some African Americans adopt a policy of what the French call *soyez méfiant* ("be mistrustful").[10] This survival tactic—deeply rooted in the African American experience and more race- than class-based—inevitably intensifies loneliness. Leon Lewis reflects on *soyez méfiant* in this passage:

Everything is different when you're black. It's amazing how the quality of one's life can be changed by what might happen, by what you think might happen and by what other people think might happen.

Often I've been invited to cocktail parties, openings and other gatherings of a business or civic nature, and many times I've been the only black person in attendance. I can become very uncomfortable in that setting. My subconscious might start sending up smoke signals, and I think, say, "What if that lady standing near me should suddenly scream?" Every eye would be on me, and I could be in a world of trouble. Why should a thought like that enter my mind? The lady doesn't look as if she is about to scream, but it has happened and who is to say it will never happen again?[11]

Disaffection is another special problem for the African American middle class. Like V. S. Naipaul living in the garden of the oppressor, the African American corporate manager or professional, working in the same garden, can feel "unanchored and strange."[12] A feeling of alienation can intensify in the face of racial hypocrisy within the work environment. Disgust and disillusionment can take hold when, in spite of an institution's professed concern for fair employment and meritocracy, qualified minorities are overlooked ("they can't be found"), less demanding standards are applied to white "favored sons," African Americans are paid less than comparably educated whites, and minority employees must cope with a work environment in which policy making and attitudes are shaped by whites who are at best indifferent and at worst antagonistic to their needs.[13] Expectations of equal treatment with which employees might have entered the institution quickly wither under the harsh light of reality.

Some African American managers and professionals also suffer from hypertension caused by stressful attempts to adapt to a white-dominated work environment. Recent studies have validated this slice of racial experience, long recognized by African Americans themselves, and have also concluded that African Americans overall suffer more hypertension than white Americans. High blood pressure strikes nearly twice as many African Americans as whites, and with more devastating consequences: "Black hypertension victims suffer heart failure at twice the rate of white victims and have 12 to 18 times the kidney-failure rates. Hypertension also gives American blacks the world's second highest death rate from strokes, after the Japanese."[14]

"John Henryism," a description taken from the fictional African American laborer of legendary strength who died while pitting his sledgehammer against a steam drill, is the term frequently used to define the syndrome of stress and hypertension within the African American middle class. "John Henryism is a manifestation of 'the struggle to get into the mainstream' and is characterized by a belief that one can triumph despite the odds"; unlike the aggressive "Type-A" personality, the John Henry personality "shows extreme patience and tends to suppress anger in order to deflect white hostility."[15] Roger Wilkins, an African American lawyer and social commentator, reflects on his personal struggle with John Henryism: "I had always to be careful never to break the unstated rules that minimized my difference, the unspoken inferiority that I hoped my [white] friends would ignore. So I was quiet for the most part, waiting for situations to develop before I reacted, always careful, always polite and considerate."[16]

One study traced John Henryism in a group of graduates of the Meharry Medical College in Nashville, Tennessee. Over a twenty-five-year period, 44 percent of the subjects developed hypertension, owing a large part, according to one observer, to the fact that African American physicians normally practice under more stressful conditions than those faced by their white counterparts. African American doctors have "traditionally practiced alone with limited finances and in situations where they were forced to struggle for patients and acceptance from peers."[17]

Complex racial discrimination, certainly a contributor to John Henryism, is one of the greatest obstacles facing the African American manager or professional. [18] Employment discrimination that is subtle, sophisticated, or unintentional is difficult enough to uncover, although its sting is as great as the old-fashioned overt brand of discrimination. Such employment discrimination is doubly difficult to recognize or prove when it is accompanied by a nonracial factor—an African American job applicant may in fact meet fewer of the traditional (though perhaps not critical) qualifications for a job than a white applicant, for example, or a discharged African American employee may have violated an inconsequential company policy. A neutral factor can provide a handy pretext for racial discrimination and can even blind an African

American applicant or employee as to the true reason behind a personnel action.

Disparity between African Americans and whites in the incidence of complex racial discrimination is manifested in several ways.[19] Among the most telling evidence is the percentage of all employment discrimination cases that are brought by African American plaintiffs and the percentage of judgments won in those cases. Legally, employment discrimination does not arise until a court issues a judgment to that effect. Drawing information from a computerized database, a recent survey of every employment discrimination case reported out of federal court in 1987 found that of the seventy-seven *strictly* racial discrimination cases reported, sixty-five (slightly more than 84 percent) were filed by African American plaintiffs alone, compared to seven (9 percent) filed by white plaintiffs alone. (Five cases were filed by other minorities.) Virtually all of these cases involved middle-class jobs: teachers, chemists, engineers, journalists, physicians, business managers, and the like.[20]

It is important to remember that these statistics represent only *reported* cases, not the total number of employment discrimination cases actually filed in the district courts or appealed to the circuit courts or the Supreme Court in 1987, to say nothing of the claims that never made it to court in that year. District court judges usually report only cases deemed "significant." (As a law clerk to a district court judge, for example, I was given considerable voice in deciding which of the judge's decisions would be submitted for publication.)

It should also be noted that, of the 1,248 employment discrimination cases (including sex, religion, age, national origin, and several other discriminatory bases as well as and in combination with race) filed in the district courts from July 1, 1986, to June 30, 1987 (the United States Courts Administrator's most relevant reporting period), only 11.7 percent ever reached trial. This is a relatively high percentage; on average, only 5 percent of all civil cases filed in the district courts during this period reached trial.[21] (Most civil cases are voluntarily or involuntarily dismissed or settled for a variety of reasons, both substantive and procedural.)

Although they represent only a small fraction of the employment discrimination cases appearing in 1987, the seventy-seven reported cases clearly reflect intra-class racial disparity in the experience of complex racial discrimination. Given that these cases survived the weeding-out process and were in fact reported (indicating that the discrimination claims were not shams), they suggest that middle-class African Americans are far more likely—nine times more likely—to encounter some degree of racial discrimination on the job than are middle-class whites. If we take the analysis one step further and compare the number of victories by African American plaintiffs with the number of victories by white plaintiffs, we get an even more definitive sense of the racial distribution of employment discrimination. African American plaintiffs won fourteen of the cases they brought; white plaintiffs won none of their cases.

The low percentage of plaintiff victories (slightly less than 22 percent for African Americans)—or, stated differently, the high percentage of *defendant,* or *employer,* victories—tells another important story. These statistics indicate how difficult it is for a plaintiff to win an employment discrimination lawsuit in federal court.[22] Arguably, the defendants have the edge, not solely because some plaintiffs lack meritorious claims, but also because the Supreme Court has stacked the procedural deck in favor of the employer. As the next section of this chapter explains, certain rules, policies, and practices developed in the context of Title VII litigation place the plaintiff at a decided disadvantage. Of the seventy-seven reported cases, plaintiffs won only eighteen, or about 23 percent. And, of course, "plaintiff" in employment cases means an African American litigant nearly 85 percent of the time (and African American or other minority 90 percent of the time).

Other legal reference sources support the claim that employment discrimination falls more heavily on African Americans than on whites. A perusal of all the federal employment discrimination cases reported between 1975 and 1989 reveals that a clear majority of cases involved African American plaintiffs and that far more African American plaintiffs won their cases than did whites.[23] The major casebooks are in accord.[24]

Litigation brought by the federal government's Equal Employment Opportunity Commission (EEOC) provides further evidence. Each EEOC annual report briefly describes the lawsuits the commission is authorized to file in federal court as a plaintiff.

Since at least 1980, the great majority of the cases based on race allege discrimination against African Americans or Hispanics.[25] The annual reports also list the number of complaints (in the thousands) filed with and processed by the EEOC, although these statistics do not indicate the complainant's race. In most cases, the EEOC finds no cause to believe that a Title VII violation occurred—which some might explain by pointing to the political composition of the EEOC and its staff, products of the Reagan administration. But when we look at the cases in which the EEOC does find cause and which eventually are filed in federal court and reported, we have already seen that African Americans are involved in most of them as plaintiffs and are also involved in most of the cases in which the plaintiffs are victorious.

At least two other indicators—racial wage gaps and the collective experiences and personal perceptions of individuals—offer compelling evidence that the complex racial discrimination faced by middle-class African Americans is more than an intermittent phenomenon. They provide at least prima facie proof that such discrimination is regular and systemic in places of middle-class employment, from corporations, law firms, law faculties, and newsrooms to the motion picture and television industries.[26]

In spite of dramatic improvements in the occupational status of African Americans since the 1960s—mainly as the result of improvements in education and affirmative action[27]—a wage gap still exists between African American and white males of comparable ages and with comparable education and experience. Farley and Allen report as an example that in 1979 young African American lawyers averaged about two dollars less per hour in earnings than young white lawyers.[28] Unfortunately, the authors do not indicate whether they took account of differences in type and size of law practice or even regional differences in the practice of law.

Other studies offer more cogent evidence of a racial wage gap. One, published by the Rand Corporation in 1986, found that African Americans earned 20 to 30 percent less than comparably educated whites in 1980. Another, published by *Money* magazine in 1989, reported that this gap had shrunk somewhat, to 10 to 26 percent, in 1987, the latest figures available. One important lesson to be drawn from these studies is that *"simply equalizing the number of years of schooling alone would [still] leave a sizable racial wage gap."*[29]

Along with statistics on wage gaps, personal observations made by individuals of both races clearly portray a situation of intraclass racial disparity. The numbers and the narratives reinforce each other, with the numbers supporting a suspicion of racial discrimination that African Americans have held for a long time.[30] Glegg Watson and George Davis, for example, co-authors of *Black Life in Corporate America: Swimming in the Mainstream* and former co-teachers of a course on multicultural management at the Yale School of Management, believe that complex racial discrimination is prevalent in corporate America and has had a considerable effect on African Americans. Watson asserts in an interview that "black advancement to the top of the corporate pyramid has moved beyond the preparation-and-qualification question and on to a team-acceptance question." Davis is more explicit: "Race is not mentioned much in corporate America, yet it has a big effect on people's careers because management is teamwork—and in teamwork you've got to have a high comfort level among the team members."[31]

Others share these views. "By and large, it's a matter of chemistry," says an African American partner at Heidrick & Struggles, the nation's largest executive search firm. "Most companies want a guy who is 6-foot-2, blue-eyed, and blonde—what we call the guy who steps out of the IBM catalog. Blacks generally just don't fit that description." The chairman of an African American management firm notes that "headquarters people, who have seen the black manager over time and know that he is competent and articulate, would have no problem, but what they're afraid of is how the guys in Kansas will take this black executive when he comes to town." Even white executives who themselves feel comfortable with African American managers are reluctant to place them in line positions that expose them to racist white managers, who may jeopardize the African American manager's success.[32]

A 1984 survey of corporate personnel executives by *Business Week* magazine confirms that even in companies with a strong commitment to affirmative action, African American managers are perceived as "different." "This 'difference,' " the study concludes, "raises questions about the unacknowledged cultural and racial barriers to the realm of senior management, which is largely white."[33]

The case is much the same in the nation's newsrooms. Max Robinson, the late co-anchor of ABC News and the first African American anchor of a national news program, recalls that on the day

Ronald Reagan was crowned and our hostages came home, I watched from the sidelines, because ABC chose not to include me in the coverage of either event, even though I [was] the national-desk anchor. . . . [I] looked around and found that . . . suddenly black people disappeared. In an orgy of white patriotism, black people would interfere with the process and point out the reality Americans didn't want to face.[34]

Other African Americans in network news concur in Robinson's general charges of racial discrimination. Some believe both that their careers have been damaged and that balanced network coverage of African American society suffers because African Americans are kept out of decision-making positions. As Richard Levine reports:

Although the overt racism that simply excluded minorities from network news jobs has long since ended, many blacks feel that an "unconscious racism" . . . on the part of their white superiors handicaps both the coverage of the black community and their own careers. . . . No matter how many black reporters appear on-camera, white producers and executives are running the show.[35]

The first major poll of minority journalists conducted by a news organization is also replete with findings of complex racial discrimination. Of those surveyed in 1982, 75 percent felt that they did not have "the same chances for promotion as white colleagues"; 51 percent reported that their editors believed "that minority journalists, as a group, are less skilled" than whites; and 10 percent had been "told openly that race was the reason they were refused certain assignments, notably on sensitive subjects including school desegregation." One respondent said: "I believe [white editors] expect less from minority staffers, and only if we do more will we be seen as equal."[36]

If the 1980s was the "Cosby Decade," it was also the decade of complex racial discrimination in the television and motion picture industry. There has always been employment discrimination in Hollywood. But "this new strain is more subtle and discreet," and some African American actors believe that it is more "dangerous" than the overt form experienced under Jim Crow, because "those who are guilty of [subtle] discrimination don't even realize it."[37] Even some of the performers in the hugely successful 1977 TV miniseries "Roots" have encountered racial barriers. Ben Vereen, for example, has experienced racial discrimination under the guise of artistic expression: "I'll want to read for a role I like, but they'll say, 'You can't play that, you have to play the janitor. We want a white actor for that part.' " Another star of "Roots" adds: "If you had been a white actor, and you were in the most popular show in television history, you would have had—at the very least—a job."[38]

It is difficult to find work environments in which complex racial discrimination is more pronounced than in American law firms and law schools. A 1987 survey by the Minority Employment Committee of the Los Angeles County Bar Association provides insights into the plight of African American lawyers in Los Angeles and other cities. The survey concludes that a "capable minority attorney might not be hired by some Los Angeles law firms, if the firms' partners believe their clients would not work with a non-white lawyer—or that a minority attorney would not fit in at the firm." A named partner of one firm stated that "the client is not always as interested in quality as with someone who fits the mode that they feel comfortable with. Rather than to have someone who might be sharp and a black, they would rather have someone who fits the profile."[39] Although it may not be prejudiced discrimination, refusing to hire or promote a minority person out of fear that biased clients may take their business elsewhere is at least discrimination about prejudice, which has the same result.[40]

A similar situation exists in law schools. Some white law professors are predisposed to assess the performance of African American law professors in a negative or hypercritical fashion, are intolerant of even small mistakes committed by these scholars, and tend to deny African Americans the deference or presumption of competence normally accorded to white male law professors—in short, they possess, whether consciously or unconsciously, a set of negative biases against African Americans.[41]

The existence of such a mindset is reflected in both statistics and personal observations. The percentage of minority teachers on law school faculties is extremely low: for example, of the 5,064 full-time law professors teaching at white-controlled law schools during the 1986–1987 academic year, only 3.7 percent were African Americans.[42] The turnover rate for minority law professors is also quite high.[43] Some minority law professors have concluded, based on years of experience, that their white male colleagues seem to believe that only a "superstar" minority should be hired, promoted, or given tenure. Female law professors, also subject to negative prejudging, have similarly noted that law faculties are "only looking for the [female] superstars."[44]

Some might be inclined to dismiss the problems of affluent African Americans as inconsequential, marginal, or "merely social." But the central point about racial discrimination remains: whether complex or Jim Crow–style, such discrimination harms African Americans by restricting opportunities and undercutting human dignity. In the following passage, Professor Derrick Bell, one of the nation's leading law professors, reflects on an incident of racism at Stanford Law School, which involved a series of faculty lectures offered to first-year law students in response to some student complaints about Bell's teaching. Bell was invited to participate but was not told the real reason. Later, the law school apologized to him, but the pain was not diminished:

The fact of my exclusion from the dialogues that must have taken place before so radical a remedy for student upset was adopted was a denial of my status as a faculty member and my worth as a person every bit as demeaning and stigmatizing to me as the Jim Crow signs I helped remove from public facilities across the South two decades ago.[45]

Along with complex racial discrimination, racial segregation in the top levels of the middle-class work force is one of the most serious intra-class disparities between the African American and white middle classes. Racially segregated, or underrepresented, work forces evoke strong images of an earlier racial hierarchy, images that harm both races in several ways. Such a picture can, for example, ignite latent racism in some whites, particularly the young or inexperienced. The racially imbalanced work forces at major white colleges and universities, which employ few African

American faculty members and many unskilled African American workers, may well have contributed to the upsurge of campus racism during the 1980s. Jim Crow images may also leave indelible doubts in the minds of whites about the caliber of work African Americans are capable of performing. Most important, however, these images create psychological barriers for African Americans themselves. White-only or white-dominated workplaces convey negative messages, especially to young African Americans: you are unwelcome; you can't perform at this level.[46] As Lance Morrow, essayist for *Time* magazine, puts it:

People become only what they can imagine themselves to be. If they can only imagine themselves working as menials, then they will probably subside into that fate, following that peasant logic by which son follows father into a genetic destiny. If they see other blacks become mayors of the largest cities, become astronauts, become presidential candidates . . . and, more to the point, become doctors and scientists and lawyers and pilots and corporate presidents—become successes—then young blacks will begin to comprehend their own possibilities and honor them with work.[47]

Finally, employment segregation, which isolates African Americans in predominantly white environments, can lead to feelings of loneliness, disaffection, and John Henryism, which can adversely affect performance.

Notwithstanding these deleterious social consequences, images of Jim Crow abound in places of high-level employment. Although the number of African American corporate managers and professionals has increased with the general rise in the occupational status of minorities since the 1960s, African Americans were still underrepresented in these vital occupations well into the 1980s. According to the EEOC, only 4.7 percent of all corporate managers and 4.5 percent of all professionals in 1985 were African Americans.[48] In individual professions, African Americans held fewer than 1 percent of the partnerships at the nation's largest law firms in 1987; 3.9 percent of the full-time teaching positions in the nation's law schools during the 1985–1986 academic year; 6.3 percent of investment banking jobs in 1985, two years before the Wall Street purge of African American investment bankers; and fewer than 5.5 percent of newspaper editorial posts in 1982.[49] These findings are in accord with the work of Farley and Allen, who conclude that "blacks are more concentrated at the bottom of the occupational hierachy than whites, and the only blacks who have attained occupational parity with similar whites are college-educated women."[50]

Complex racial discrimination and racial segregation in top-level jobs are the most important intra-class racial disparities within the American middle class. They are parents to the loneliness, disaffection, and John Henryism that many African Americans experience. Complex racial discrimination and a racially segregated work force do not exist in a vacuum. Rather, they are linked to the nation's current regime of interracial relations and, more particularly, to that regime's racially subordinating features.

Racial Subordination Through Formal Equal Opportunity

Through its tenet of racial omission, formal equal opportunity subordinates the civil rights interest of the African American middle class, a subordination that is most pronounced within the employment context. Both the strict scrutiny test and judicial treatment of statutory antidiscrimination law force middle-class African Americans to endure, relative to their white counterparts, a disproportionate amount of the employment hardships discussed in this chapter.

Strict Scrutiny Test. The strict scrutiny test can be found nowhere in the Constitution or in its legislative history. It is a legal doctrine invented entirely by judges. Developed as a means to facilitate close judicial review of Jim Crow and other "suspicious" legislative enactments, the strict scrutiny test applies to lawsuits brought under the equal protection clause of the Fourteenth Amendment or the equal protection component of the Fifth Amendment's due process clause. The former constitutional provision protects against state actions, and the latter against federal actions.[51]

Now a fixture in constitutional law, the strict scrutiny test is the legal system's primary means of implementing formal equal opportunity's racial omission tenet. It commands that race be omitted from the government's formulation of laws and public policies. More important, it operates to strike down, as a denial of equal protection of the laws, any governmental activity or legislation that either is predicated on an explicit racial or other "suspect classification" or violates a "fundamental personal interest."[52] An act under scrutiny is saved from judicial strangulation only if the government can meet a twofold burden. First, the classification must be justified by a "compelling governmental interest." Second, the means chosen to achieve the classification's purpose must be the least restrictive, most narrowly tailored means available.[53]

As applied by the Supreme Court, the strict scrutiny test sets up a standard of judicial review so rigorous as to be fatal to most of the legislation in question. The first burden is especially difficult to meet. Protecting national security and remedying past institutional or individual discrimination are among the few (if not the only) arguments the government has been able to use to demonstrate a compelling governmental interest to the Supreme Court's satisfaction.[54]

The Court, however, has attempted to balance the interventionist proclivity of the strict scrutiny test with a more deferential form of judicial review. Legislation not predicated on a suspect classification or violating a fundamental personal interest—which describes the great majority of legislative acts—does not offend constitutional equal protection if it can be rationally related to a legitimate governmental purpose. The "rational basis" test provides the widest degree of judicial comity to even speculative legislative judgments.[55]

Both the strict scrutiny test and the rational basis test are so predictable that the outcome of a judicial review is virtually determined by the type of legislation being reviewed. Legislation involving a suspect classification or a fundamental personal interest most likely will not survive constitutional scrutiny, whereas legislation not involving either of these categories is likely to be sustained. The Supreme Court's analysis for equal protection claims is in this sense outcome-determinative.[56]

Middle-class African Americans find the strict scrutiny test to be a problem because it quashes voluntary attempts to promote real equal employment opportunity. The test, in short, often commands the omission of race at the *wrong time*. Except in a very limited situation, it enjoins the public sector's use of race-conscious employment policies or practices that would promote racial inclusion. In so doing, it treats policies and practices that result in racial exclusion *pari passu* (on an equal footing) with those that are socially beneficial.

The limited circumstance under which the strict scrutiny test permits governmental bodies to use an explicit racial classification is clear: race can be used only if doing so achieves a compelling governmental purpose. Thus far, remedying a public employer's prior racial discrimination is the only purpose the Supreme Court has found compelling in the employment context. As the Court itself stated: "It is now well established that government bodies, including courts, may constitutionally employ racial classifications essential to remedy unlawful treatment of racial or ethnic groups subject to discrimination."[57]

But establishing prior racial discrimination by an employer is no easy task. Absent the unlikely event that an employer (even in connection with the voluntary use of a racial classification)[58] either admits that it discriminated or leaves behind "smoking-gun" evidence, the victim's only chance of proving prior discrimination is to prove that the employer violated constitutional or statutory antidiscrimination law. If the asserted violation involves the equal protection clause, the victim will most likely be defeated by the intent test, which requires the plaintiff to prove that an employer intended to discriminate. (The intent test is discussed in detail in Chapter 3.) If the asserted violation involves a federal statute rather than the Constitution, the victim will have to surmount enormous barriers created by Title VII of the 1964 Civil Rights Act.

Thus the strict scrutiny test—specifically, the Supreme Court's color-blind perspective and narrow interpretation of compelling governmental purpose—subordinates the interest of the African American middle class in equal employment opportunity. It does so by making it extremely difficult for a public employer to voluntarily use racial classifications for the purposes of assisting qualified African Americans in catching up with their white counterparts, dismantling psychological and institutional barriers erected by past employment practices, or otherwise overcoming the present-day effects of earlier subordinating systems. Making it difficult for employers or African Americans to use devices that could purge complex racial discrimination and segregation from the workplace perpetuates rather than diminishes these forms of intra-class racial disparity.

Given the difficulties of proving a violation of constitutional or statutory antidiscrimination law, voluntary racial preferences may be the only way to effectively counteract complex racial discrimination and segregation in employment. Even the Supreme Court recognizes that "affirmative race-conscious relief may be the only means available 'to assure [true] equality of opportunities and to eliminate those discriminatory practices and devices which have fostered racially stratified job environments to the disadvantage of minority citizens.'"[59] Reports issued since the 1960s by the Department of Labor, the U.S. Commission on Civil Rights, the Rand Corporation, and others support this conclusion and assert that racial preferences have launched many qualified African Americans on successful careers they otherwise would not have entered or dared to pursue.[60] Placing barriers in the path of voluntary efforts to promote racial inclusion necessarily accommodates, extends, and perhaps even intensifies racial exclusion—the very condition these voluntary efforts are so capable of reversing.

Title VII.   Title VII of the 1964 Civil Rights Act is the nation's major antidiscrimination law in the employment context.[61] Its key antidiscrimination section, Section 703 (a), provides a classic illustration of how Congress has decided to implement the racial omission tenet in federal civil rights laws:

It shall be an unlawful employment practice for an employer—
   (1) to fail or refuse to hire or to discharge any individual, or otherwise to discriminate against any individual with respect to his compensation, terms, conditions, or privileges of employment, because of such individual's race, color, religion, sex, or national origin; or
   (2) to limit, segregate, or classify his employees or applicants for employment in any way which would deprive or tend to deprive any individual of employment opportunities or otherwise adversely affect his status as an employee, because of such individual's race, color, religion, sex, or national origin. . . .[62]

Although Congress made employment discrimination on the basis of race, color, sex, religion, or national origin illegal under Title VII,[63] it did not define the word *discrimination*. This omission may have been deliberate; Congress might have believed that the task of defining such a complex term was better left to the courts.

Responding to this challenge, the Supreme Court devised two distinctly different definitions of employment discrimination: disparate treatment (requiring proof of racial motivation) and disparate impact (requiring no such proof).[64] Both concepts were defined succinctly by the Court in *Teamsters v. United States:*

'Disparate treatment' such as is alleged in the present case is the most easily understood type of discrimination. The employer simply treats some people less favorably than others because of their race, color, religion, sex, or national origin. Proof of discriminatory motive is critical, although it can in some situations be inferred from the mere fact of differences in treatment. . . . Undoubtedly disparate treatment was the most obvious evil Congress had in mind when it enacted Title VII. See, e.g., 110 Cong. Rec. 13088 (1964) (remarks of Sen. Humphrey) ("What the bill does . . . is simply to make it an illegal practice to use race as a factor in denying employment. It provides that men and women shall be employed on the basis of their qualifications, not as Catholic citizens, not as Protestant citizens, not as Jewish citizens, not as colored citizens, but as citizens of the United States").

Claims of disparate treatment may be distinguished from claims that stress "disparate impact." The latter involve employment practices that are facially neutral in their treatment of different groups but that in fact fall more harshly on one group than another and cannot be justified by business necessity. . . . Proof of discriminatory motive, we have held, is not required under a disparate-impact theory. . . . Either theory may, of course, be applied to a particular set of facts.[65]

It is difficult to prosecute a disparate-impact claim of racial discrimination in the top levels of the work force, such as law firms and medical corporations. In order to state a claim of such employment discrimination under Title VII, one must rely on sufficient statistical evidence.[66] Ordinarily, in places of high-level employment, too few African Americans apply for a specific position with a particular employer within a given time frame to create an applicant pool large enough to be statistically significant.[67] The even smaller numbers of African American employees who work in these settings engender an even greater statistical problem in promotion cases. Hence, as a practical matter, an African American denied a position or promotion within such select areas of the work force will probably have to seek legal redress under a disparate-treatment theory of employment discrimination.

Other middle-class African Americans often have the option of proceeding under either a disparate-treatment or a disparate-impact theory. African Americans working as teachers, as police officers, as firefighters, or in similar lower-paying middle-class jobs usually have the numbers to sustain the statistical analysis required in disparate-impact cases.[68] Because the problems involved in disparate-treatment cases can present obstacles to employees at all levels of the African American middle class, the following discussion focuses only on the issue of disparate treatment.

Proceeding under a disparate-treatment theory of employment discrimination will be difficult at best for any middle-class African American. This difficulty has less to do with the fact that Title VII was created when most forms of racism were overt and less to do with the transaction costs that accompany complex litigation than it does with federal case law.[69] Federal courts have made it extremely burdensome for Title VII plaintiffs to win individual disparate-treatment cases. Proving discriminatory motivation, establishing causation, use of both the unitary litigation model and a less stringent evidentiary standard for defendants in mixed-motive cases, and judicial hostility toward even applying Title VII to high-level jobs are among the most serious obstacles to successfully litigating individual disparate-treatment cases. These obstacles help to explain, at least in part, the low percentage of plaintiff victories in Title VII cases, discussed earlier in this chapter.

The Supreme Court has developed a system of proof for individual, nonclass disparate-treatment cases of employment discrimination.[70] The plaintiff is given the initial burden of proving a prima facie case of disparate treatment. The central issue addresses the defendant's motivation: was the defendant motivated by a discriminatory animus? The plaintiff can prove the requisite state of mind by using direct, smoking-gun evidence (which is rarely available today) or, inferentially, using circumstantial evidence.[71] If the plaintiff succeeds, the defendant is given an opportunity to rebut the plaintiff's prima facie case by showing a "legitimate, nondiscriminatory reason" for the treatment of the plaintiff. If the defendant meets its burden of proof, the plaintiff is then given an opportunity to show that the defendant's stated reason is nothing more than a pretext for intentional discrimination.[72]

In *Texas Department of Community Affairs v. Burdine*, the Supreme Court let stand a devastating problem of proof for Title VII plaintiffs by reaffirming earlier Court rulings that a defendant's burden of proving a legitimate, nondiscriminatory reason for a plaintiff's treatment is a burden of production only, not one of persuasion.[73] In the absence of smoking-gun evidence or an unsophisticated defendant, the Court's holding makes it easy for a defendant to win a disparate-treatment case. The defendant can rebut the prima facie case on the basis of admissible but untrue evidence as to its actual motivation. The plaintiff, not being privy to the defendant's thinking, is left with the near-impossible task of persuading the trier of fact that the defendant's stated motivation is untrue.[74] Given that the defendant is in the best possible position to know the true reasons for the action taken against the plaintiff, that the alleged discrimination may have left the plaintiff without a job and hence without ready access to employment records, and that courts normally allow the use of subjective reasons in articulating a "legitimate, nondiscriminatory reason,"[75] placing the burden of persuasion on the plaintiff not only is exceedingly unfair to the plaintiff, but also is a sure way to smother the truth.[76] It is unrealistic to expect many African American applicants or employees to be able to prove discriminatory intent under these circumstances.

Even if discriminatory intent can be proven, a plaintiff will also have to face the problem of proving causation. In understanding the discussion of causation, it may help to remember that Title VII prohibits discrimination "because of" race, color, religion, sex, or national origin. The key question is simply this: what does the causal connector "because of" mean?

Unfortunately, the law provides no clear answer. Title VII does not define the term. The Supreme Court has not conclusively decided the causation issue. Lower federal courts have ruled on it but have gone in different directions.

Although Title VII does not define the causal connector "because of," it does suggest two standards. The first is presented in Section 703(a)(2), quoted above, which prohibits acts that "tend to deprive" individuals of employment opportunities. This section seems to suggest that an impermissible factor (such as racial prejudice) cannot be among the factors motivating an employer's action. This standard of causation is called the "taint" standard: if an employer's action is based even in part on, or is tainted by, an impermissible factor (specifically, race, color, sex, religion, or national origin), then it is unlawful employment discrimination under Title VII.

Using Section 703(a)(2) as textual support for a theory of causation in disparate-treatment cases is problematic. This section provides statutory support for disparate-impact litigation, which has its own definition of causation;[77] disparate-treatment litigation derives its authority from another section of Title VII, Section 703(a)(1), also quoted earlier. Recent Supreme Court opinions tend to blur the distinction between disparate-impact and disparate-treatment analysis, however,[78] and it thus does not seem totally wrong-headed to borrow from disparate-impact authority to make a point regarding the definition of causation in disparate-treatment litigation. Furthermore, the taint standard, also called the "discernible-factor" standard (a personnel decision is unlawful if race, for example, was a discernible factor in the decision),[79] seems to enjoy textual support beyond Section 703(a)(2). As Brodin correctly argues, the taint standard is consistent with the broad congressional design of Title VII—namely, "to eliminate . . . discrimination in employment based on race, color, [sex,] religion, or national origin."[80]

Another section of Title VII, suggests a different approach to causation. Section 706(g), patterned after the National Labor Relations Act's remedial provisions,[81] sets forth the type of relief a victorious plaintiff may receive under Title VII. The last sentence reads:

No order of the court shall require the admission or reinstatement of an individual as a member of a union, or the hiring, reinstatement, or promotion of an individual as an employee, or the payment to him of any back pay, if such individual was refused admission, suspended, or expelled, or was refused employment or advancement or was suspended or discharged for any reason other than discrimination on account of race, color, religion, sex, or national origin or in violation of section 704(a).[82]

This sentence would seem to address only the question of remedy. But the entire Section 706(g) actually resulted from an amendment to Title VII, an amendment whose purpose was to specify to a federal district court that a Title VII violation can be found only when race, color, sex, religion, or national origin is the sole motivation behind an employer's action.[83] This is sometimes called the "sole-factor" standard: causation is established in a Title VII case only when the employment decision is based *solely* on one of the impermissible criteria.[84]

There is, however, legislative history that clearly contradicts this reading of the statute. Congress, for example, rejected another amendment to Title VII that would have reworded "because of" in Section 703(a) to read "solely because of."[85]

Federal courts have been no more decisive than Congress in resolving the causation issue. In *McDonnell Douglas Corp. v. Green*, the Supreme Court seemed to adopt the taint standard suggested in Section 703(a)(2). The Court stated that "[i]n the implementation of . . . [personnel] decisions, it is abundantly clear that Title VII tolerates *no* racial discrimination, subtle or otherwise."[86]

In *McDonald v. Santa Fe Trail Transportation Co.*, the Supreme Court suggested that the proper causation standard might be somewhere between the liberal taint standard and the stricter sole-factor standard. Responding to the plaintiff's claim that the "legitimate, nondiscriminatory reason" offered by the employer discharging workers was mere pretext, the Court said:

The use of the term "pretext" in this context does not mean, of course, that the Title VII plaintiff must show that he would have in any event been rejected or discharged solely on the basis of his race, without regard to the alleged deficiencies . . . [N]o more is required to be shown than that race was a "but for" cause.[87]

McDonald thus adopts a "but-for" causation standard: Title VII is violated when the plaintiff shows that but for the use of an impermissible criterion (race, color, sex, and so on), the adverse personnel decision would not have been made.

A recent Supreme Court plurality opinion, *Price Waterhouse v. Hopkins*, provides important dicta on the causation issue. Justice O'Connor and the three dissenting justices (Rehnquist, Scalia, and Kennedy) ruled that the but-for standard of causation applies to whoever bears the burden of persuasion in disparate-treatment litigation under Title VII.[88] The four-justice plurality opinion (Brennan, Marshall, Blackmun, and Stevens), in contrast seemed to suggest that something less than but-for causation applies to at least the plaintiff's burden of persuasion. As the plurality stated: "To construe the words 'because of' as colloquial shorthand for 'but for causation' . . . is to misunderstand them. . . . We conclude instead, that Congress meant to obligate . . . [Hopkins] to prove that the employer relied upon . . . [impermissible] considerations in coming to its decision."[89] Justice White, the swing vote, saw only a semantic difference between the formulations offered by the two camps.[90] Obviously, however, both camps saw more than a semantic difference between their positions.

There is nevertheless some indication that a majority of the justices in fact agree on a single standard. Five of the justices (the plurality opinion and Justice White's concurring opinion) expressly point with approval to the Court's opinion in *Mt. Healthy City School District Board of Education v. Doyle*,[91] a First Amendment case that applied the "substantial-factor" standard (the impermissible criterion must be a substantial motivating factor behind the personnel action). Justice O'Connor also seems to accept the substantial-factor standard,[92] but it is unclear precisely how this standard differs, at least in the eyes of the plurality, from the but-for standard clearly favored by Justice O'Connor and the three dissenting justices. Thus, at the Supreme Court level, the standard of causation remains fuzzy.

The lower federal courts have joined the Supreme Court and Congress in failing to agree on a causation standard. The Eighth Circuit has used the taint standard, sometimes calling it the discernible-factor test. The Third, Fourth, Fifth, and Seventh Circuits have adopted the but-for standard. The First, Second, Sixth, Ninth, Eleventh, and D.C. Circuits have embraced the substantial-factor standard, using various terms such as "significant," "motivating," "determinative," "dominant taint," or "dominant factor" to refer to it.[93]

In short, assuming that the employer can meet its burden of

production under *Burdine,* the success of the plaintiff's disparate-treatment case may depend on which causation standard the court applies. A plaintiff will have an easier time establishing a Title VII violation in jurisdictions employing the taint standard than in jurisdictions employing the stricter but-for or substantial-factor standards. No jurisdiction can legally use the sole-factor standard.

If the plaintiff in the Title VII disparate-treatment case succeeds in proving intent and establishing causation, he or she faces two more hurdles, should the case proceed to the mixed-motive stage. This is the stage of disparate-treatment litigation that goes beyond the pretext stage discussed earlier in this chapter. The issue in a pretext case is whether *either* a permissible or impermissible factor—but not both—motivated the adverse employment decision. The issue in a mixed-motive case is which of two or more proven factors, one of which is impermissible, played the dominant role in the decision. Thus, in a mixed-motive case, there is no single "true" motive behind the decision.[94] Both of the hurdles a plaintiff faces at this stage arise from the Supreme Court's opinion in *Price Waterhouse v. Hopkins.*

The first obstacle is engendered by the Court's adoption of a unitary litigation model in mixed-motive cases. Six of the nine justices (Brennan, Marshall, Blackmun, and Stevens, who formed the plurality, and White and O'Connor, who wrote separate concurring opinions) held that the employer's burden of proof in a mixed-motive case is part of the liability phase of the litigation, enabling the employer to avoid not only the imposition of a remedy but also a finding of liability if it should meet the burden of proof. The Court based its holding on the argument that, because Title VII clearly seeks to preserve a measure of freedom of choice for the employer by authorizing it to make employment decisions against an employee on the basis of permissible criteria, the employer must be given the opportunity to meet its mixed-motive burden of proof (showing dominant reliance on a permissible criterion) before a finding of liability is made.[95]

The Court expressly declined to follow the model used in the Eighth and Ninth Circuits and in the *Hopkins* district court opinion by Judge Gerhard Gesell, in which a distinction is drawn between liability and remedy in mixed-motive cases.[96] Under this litigation model, the plaintiff's burden of proof goes to the issue of liability and the defendant's to the issue of remedy. If the plaintiff proves that the employment decision was motivated by an impermissible criterion, the plaintiff proves disparate-treatment discrimination and, in the absence of an affirmative defense, a violation of Title VII. At this point, the employer can avoid the imposition of certain Title VII remedies (mainly back pay and reinstatement) by proving that it would have reached the same decision in the absence of the impermissible motive.[97]

The bifurcated litigation model does not provide relief for the plaintiff if the employer meets its burden. But it does serve Title VII's goal of promoting racial inclusion to a greater extent than the unitary model does, because the bifurcated model makes it easier for the plaintiff to prove employment discrimination. This in turn augments the deterrence value of Title VII in at least two ways. First, a finding of liability allows a judge to issue an injunction against future acts of discrimination in the workplace.[98] Should the employer violate this injunction, it could be cited for contempt of court. Second, a finding of liability entitles the victorious Title VII plaintiff to receive attorneys' fees—the real deterrent feature of Title VII, because the monetary amounts of Title VII remedies are so small.[99] Shifting the plaintiff's attorneys' fees to the defendant helps to deter future acts of discrimination by the defendant and other Title VII defendants.

The second ruling in *Hopkins* that will surely hurt plaintiffs' chances of winning mixed-motive cases is the acceptance of the preponderance of evidence standard. The plurality and concurring opinions held that the employer's burden of persuasion in a mixed-motive case requires the employer to show by a preponderance of evidence—rather than by clear and convincing evidence—that it would have reached the same decision even if it had not relied on the impermissible criterion. The Court reasoned that the preponderance of evidence standard, which is easier to meet than the clear and convincing evidence standard, is applicable because it is part of the conventional rules of evidence that generally apply in civil litigation.[100] But given that the employer, as even Justice O'Connor recognizes in her concurring opinion, "has created the uncertainty as to causation by knowingly giving substantial weight to an impermissible criterion,"[101] it seems fair to place the responsibility on the employer to clarify the issue of causation convincingly.

Mixed-motive litigation matters little in some federal courts. Some federal judges have relaxed Title VII's protections in relation to high-level jobs, and others have taken a "hands-off" attitude.[102] As the Second Circuit observed, these courts have rendered employers controlling high-status jobs "virtually immune to charges of employment bias, at least when the bias is not expressed overtly."[103] This judicial policy of self-abnegation was actually more widespread in the 1970s than it is today. It began with cases challenging the employment practices of colleges and universities regarding faculty. Many judges felt strongly that the judiciary was unqualified to second-guess faculty personnel decisions and hence that "the federal courts should hesitate to invade and take over . . . education and faculty appointments at a University level."[104]

Congress may have agreed with this rationale in 1964 when Title VII, as originally passed, exempted from its coverage faculty employment practices in all educational institutions.[105] The express reason for the exemption is unknown, however, because it has virtually no legislative history.[106] But by removing the exemption in 1972, Congress made it clear that judges must scrutinize college and university employment with the same degree of care given to blue-collar employment.[107] More important, the legislative history of the 1972 amendments to Title VII expressly states that all employers covered by the act are to be governed by the same standards.[108]

These judicially created obstacles to successful litigation of individual disparate-treatment cases—allocation of the burden of proof, the but-for or substantial-factor standard of causation, the unitary litigation model and the relaxed evidentiary standard in mixed-motive cases, and poor judicial attitude—may exist in spite of, rather than because of, the civil rights interest that is at stake for African Americans. There may even be "compelling" countervailing interests underpinning these laws and policies. But it cannot be gainsaid that these laws and policies deny priority to a crucial civil rights interest of the African American middle class—namely, equal employment opportunity. The fact that academic institutions won all but one of the twenty-three racial discrimination cases brought in federal court against them between 1971 and 1984,[109] to say nothing of the low percentage of plaintiff victories in race-based employment cases generally, is indicative of the lack of regard Title VII now shows to middle-class African Americans.

By subordinating the interest of the African American middle class in employment, Title VII contributes to the problem of complex racial discrimination. The existing judicial interpretations and applications provide little protection against such discrimination and may even encourage would-be discriminators. Required only to produce evidence probative of a legitimate, nondiscriminatory reason for disparate treatment and protected by the but-for or substantial-factor standard, as well as by the unitary litigation model and the preponderance of evidence standard in mixed-motive cases, an employer has a real opportunity to discriminate—whether the motivation is racism or some perceived economic benefit—and to get away with lying about it. Judicial disdain for Title VII also provides such an opportunity, without requiring even the effort of lying.

Title VII's racially subordinating features also contribute to conspicuous racial stratification in high-level jobs. The burden of proof and the causation standards are so onerous for plaintiffs, the unitary litigation model and the preponderance of evidence standard so favorable to defendants, and the judicial attitude so obvious that the chances of winning a Title VII lawsuit are remote. These obstacles also undoubtedly discourage many African Americans from even filing a Title VII charge with the EEOC or from pursuing the matter all the way to federal court. If African Americans do not win Title VII cases or file Title VII lawsuits, Title VII is obviously less effective in doing what Congress intended it to do. As the Supreme Court itself has stated: "[I]t was clear to Congress that '[t]he crux of the problem [was] to open employment opportunities for Negroes in occupations which have been traditionally closed to them,' . . . and it was to this problem that Title VII's prohibition against racial discrimination in employment was primarily addressed."[110]

Summary

One of the largest segments of African American society, the middle class is also the most assimilated into mainstream American

society. A typical African American middle-class household consists of a nuclear family in which both parents work, with one of
them likely to be a manager or professional. The family is likely
to own the home in which it lives and to possess a late-model
automobile, a complete line of household appliances, and investments or savings. Annual household income ranges from \$25,000
to \$75,000 (reaching \$100,000 or more when the upper class is
included). Like its white counterpart, the average African American middle-class household is relatively stable and comfortable.

Unlike the white middle class, however, the African American
middle class faces hardships caused by race that in some instances threaten the success members of this class have achieved.
Long after the death of Jim Crow, color remains a significant factor affecting a skilled and talented person's chances for personal
happiness and material success. Loneliness, disaffection, stress
and hypertension, complex racial discrimination, and conspicuous
racial stratification in high-level employment are the major features of intra-class racial disparity within the American middle
class. Complex racial discrimination and racially segregated top
jobs are the most serious employment disparities; they fuel the
other racial disparities and have serious negative social consequences. The high percentage of employment discrimination
cases filed and won by middle-class African Americans, in contrast to middle-class whites; the high percentage of cases filed by
the EEOC on behalf of middle-class African Americans; racial
wage gaps; and the collective experiences of African Americans
pursuing middle-class careers—all offer evidence of the depth
and continued existence of the American race problem.

Complex racial discrimination and racial segregation in high-
status jobs are perpetuated in part through the racial subordination engendered by formal equal opportunity. Civil rights laws
and practices fully sanctioned by the federal government and ultimately designed to vindicate the racial omission tenet—the
strict scrutiny test in racial preference law, the burden of proof
and the standard of causation in disparate-treatment litigation,
the unitary litigation model and evidentiary standard in mixed-
motive cases, and poor judicial attitude in antidiscrimination
law—fail to give priority to the civil rights interest of the African
American middle class in equal employment opportunity. These

judicially created features of formal equal opportunity subordinate this important civil rights interest, in the case of the strict scrutiny test, by enjoining or discouraging public-sector employers from using the only proven means of promoting racial inclusion and, in the case of other features, by decreasing the odds of a plaintiff winning an individual disparate-treatment case under Title VII. Such racial subordination depletes the arsenal of weapons that can be used to combat complex racial discrimination and segregation in employment; it undercuts the defenses of the African American middle class against racial exclusion. The strict scrutiny test's rejection of racial inclusion and Title VII's inability to unearth complex racial discrimination on an individual basis leave these African Americans more, not less, vulnerable to employment discrimination, underrepresentation, and other employment hardships.

Racial subordination in this area of the law may also contribute to intra-class racial disparity in a more active way. It may in fact actually encourage employment discrimination or segregation. When the courts show such little regard for the employment interests of the African American middle class, this situation provides a would-be discriminator with the opportunity to discriminate and with encouraging signals about the possibility of getting away with it. Some employers may read the courts' construction of Title VII, particularly the reluctance to apply Title VII to top jobs, as a green light to engage in subtle forms of employment discrimination, a sign that it is permissible to discriminate, as long as you do so discreetly or cleverly.

Chapter Three

The African American
Working Class

Defining Characteristics

Using the income approach discussed in Chapter 2, we can define the African American working class as those individuals and
families with an annual household income ranging from $10,000
(or, roughly, the poverty line) to $25,000, the income floor for
middle-class households. A family in this income range is likely to
rent a house or apartment rather than owning its own home. Relative to a middle-class household, this family probably "eats less
meat and more potatoes, drinks less wine and liquor but more
beer." Despite income limitations, however, the working-class
family does not usually live on a subsistence budget; households
in this category are able to function with "a sense of self-respect
and social participation."[1]

Based on the $10,000–$25,000 income range, approximately
33 percent of African Americans belong to the working class,
compared to slightly more than 28 percent of white Americans.
With approximately 34 percent of African Americans falling below
the poverty line, compared to approximately 15 percent of
whites, the various socioeconomic classes in African American society are roughly the same size. (See the table and the chart on
pp. 37 and 38.)

A more detailed profile of African American working-class
households reveals specific characteristics:

• Thirty-seven percent of these households consist of family
  units headed by both husband and wife. Among this group,

roughly 33 percent of the men are semi-skilled or unskilled blue-collar or service workers; the other 67 percent are divided, approximately equally, into four groups: clerical workers, farmers (farm laborers or farm owners), those not in the labor force (a term describing individuals who are not working and are not actively looking for work—for example, "discouraged workers" who have stopped looking or those who are disabled, on public assistance, or between jobs), and retired persons. About one-third of the women in this group are employed as semi-skilled or unskilled blue-collar or service workers, and another one-third work in clerical positions; about 17 percent are homemakers (not employed outside the home), and an equal percentage are not in the labor force.

- Twenty-five percent of the households are headed by women. About one-fourth of these female heads of household are semi-skilled or unskilled blue-collar or service workers, and another one-fourth are clerical workers. The remaining 50 percent are either currently unemployed or not in the labor force. Rose suggests that those in this group are likely to be disabled or receiving public assistance in a large urban setting.[2]

- Nineteen percent of the households consist of individual men. About one-third of these men are clerical workers, another one-third are semi-skilled or unskilled blue-collar or service workers, and one-third are not in the labor force.

- Nineteen percent of the households consist of individual women. These women can be divided into three approximately equal groups: clerical workers, professionals, and retired persons.[3]

Some working-class African Americans live in constant fear of slipping into poverty. Many who have crossed the line out of poverty nevertheless remain perilously close to the world of hunger and homelessness. Others who have never experienced poverty live but a misstep away from its open doors—a divorce, the untimely death of a spouse, the unemployment of a working spouse, a catastrophic illness in the family, old age, or retirement can result in dramatic changes for the worse. Indeed, between 1978 and 1986, 5.2 percent of the nation's working class fell below the poverty line or into the low end of the working class. And, during this same period, a shocking seven million Americans were added to the ranks of the poor.[4]

Several factors explain why many in the American working class, regardless of race, are financially unstable. Irrational economic behavior, expediency, and a lack of long-term planning are certainly destabilizing forces within this segment of society.[5] But income itself is the crucial factor. With incomes below the national average (which was approximately $25,000 in 1986),[6] members of the working class simply have little margin for error. Thus, working-class households have to be smarter consumer spenders, more careful financial planners, and better disciplined in general than middle-class households. These characteristics are not easy to sustain when one lives under the stress of a job that may be low-paying, uninteresting, physically demanding, or closely supervised—circumstances that diminish one's ability to shape the events in one's life.[7]

Although working-class African Americans suffer class subordination neither more nor less than their white counterparts, the African American working class, unlike the white working class, must contend with certain other societal hardships that can be more destabilizing and demoralizing than the racially neutral factors. These societal barriers to a better life constitute the American race problem, or intra-class racial disparity, within the American working class.

The Subordination Question
Intra-Class Racial Disparity

Working-class African Americans encounter particularly serious racial disparities in two areas of American life: housing and education. Housing discrimination and segregation, often accompanied by violence, are the primary problems in the first area. Two sets of problems are dominant in education: forms of discrimination and segregation in primary schools, on the one hand, and the low enrollment of African American students in colleges and graduate schools, on the other hand. The disparities in housing and higher education also adversely affect the African American middle class, particularly at the low- and middle-income levels, and, to that extent, the discussion in this chapter is also applicable to the middle class.

Choosing to focus this chapter on housing and education does not imply that the employment disparities within the American working class are insignificant—clearly, these problems are serious. For example, racial wage gaps still exist in several sectors of the working class, and African American workers—last hired, first fired, and less protected by unions—have borne the brunt of plant shutdowns and relocations during the 1970s and 1980s and face greater career instability in many occupations.[8] Collective experience and personal perceptions also support assertions that racial disparities exist on the job. A recent survey shows that 80 percent of African Americans (compared to 37 percent of whites) believe that if equally qualified persons compete for the same job, an African American is less likely than a white to be hired. And 62 percent of African Americans (versus 41 percent of whites) believe that their chances of advancing to managerial or supervisory positions are generally not as good as those for whites.[9]

Thus, many of the problems of employment discrimination faced by working-class African Americans are similar to those discussed in Chapter 2. But unlike middle-class individuals, most working-class people lack the time, money, and flexibility to pursue Title VII litigation, which is both expensive and protracted. African American workers who are unionized can sometimes choose to file a grievance over employment discrimination, a procedure that is less expensive and more efficient than a Title VII case. But in many instances there is no adequate mechanism for redress.

Despite the seriousness of these employment hardships, this chapter will not analyze them in detail and will instead focus on intra-class racial disparities in housing and education. It is in these two areas that the impact of formal equal opportunity and its tenets—as interpreted and applied by Congress and the courts—is most clearly seen.

Housing.   Housing discrimination and segregation, sometimes buttressed by acts of violence, are rooted in the overall history of racial segregation in American society.[10] The style of residential segregation has varied throughout the centuries in this country. During slavery, free African Americans, who needed to be within walking distance of white residential and business areas, lived interspersed among whites. Ironically, the demand for their inexpensive labor and the primitive state of transportation brought African Americans in closer proximity to whites than is the case today. After slavery, most African Americans were concentrated in low-income pockets that dotted metropolitan areas; those few who could afford it and who wanted to do so, however, could live in virtually any part of town. At the turn of the century, Jim Crow laws, real estate practices, and personal intimidation began to isolate African Americans to the least desirable sections of town, and residential areas became heavily segregated.

Present-day residential patterns have evolved directly from this style of housing segregation. African Americans today are primarily isolated in inner-city ghettos, rural areas, or suburban communities that form segregated rings around cities. Despite the increasing number of minorities moving to the suburbs and the decreasing rate of segregation overall since the 1960s (a decrease so small that it will still leave cities "highly segregated in the foreseeable future"), many of our communities remain nearly as segregated today as they were in the 1960s.[11] In a recent poll, 69 percent of the whites questioned guessed that fewer than 5 percent of the people in their neighborhoods were African Americans, whereas 45 percent of African Americans guessed that more than 75 percent of their neighbors were members of their own race.[12]

Most African Americans prefer to live in racially integrated communities,[13] for numerous reasons. Segregation limits the housing market for African Americans, which may increase their housing costs; it also typically relegates them to low-quality, older housing, which families are more likely to rent than to buy.[14] These segregated residential areas usually experience poor community services (erratic garbage collection, lack of snow removal and street or other structural repairs). Some also argue that, by confining African Americans to the inner city, segregated housing puts them at an employment disadvantage, because job opportunities are growing more rapidly in the suburbs than in the inner city (although others claim that unemployment rates for African Americans in the suburbs are almost as high as the rates for those in the cities).[15] Residential segregation is, however, unquestionably a major contributor to segregation in the public schools. By engendering racial isolation, housing segregation also helps to perpetuate stereotypes and to reinforce Jim Crow beliefs in the inferiority and "invisibility" of African Americans—the notion, elegantly explored in Ralph Ellison's *Invisible Man*, that African Americans are devoid of substance, flesh and bone.[16]

The disproportionality of housing discrimination within the American working class, reflected to at least some extent by the existence of such obvious and extensive residential segregation, is evidenced in several ways. Although the great majority of the plaintiffs in housing cases filed in federal court since 1975 were African American or Hispanic,[17] the record of housing discrimination judgments is probably not the best source of information; in 1987, at least, the number of race-only housing discrimination cases decided by the federal courts was too small to be statistically significant.[18] Evidence is readily available, however, in the dozens of fair housing studies conducted periodically by local and regional offices of the Department of Housing and Urban Development (HUD).[19] These studies are designed to test the rental housing market for housing discrimination. A typical study begins with a telephone survey of advertised apartment vacancies, followed by a site survey conducted by both minority and white teams. Each test team usually consists of two or three "apartment hunters" (a couple and an individual), one of whom would normally be identified by telephone voice either as white or as an African American or other minority. Usually, after one team has inquired about a vacancy by telephone and made a follow-up visit to the site, the other team duplicates this procedure. The teams do not exchange information during testing.

In such a study in Boston, forty-two tests were conducted on eighteen apartment houses. The white team was invited to the apartment complex to see a unit in every test, whereas in thirty-one of the tests the minority team was told *not* to come to the apartment building, because no units were available. A Detroit study of eleven rental complexes, each of which was tested four times, yielded similar results: white teams were treated more favorably than minority teams in thirty of the forty-four tests. According to HUD, these and other studies conducted in cities throughout the nation "produced firm evidence" of housing discrimination.[20]

For a sense of the human dimension of housing discrimination, one can turn to the popular media. In 1986, after enduring months of racial taunts and vandalism, an African American family was forced to move out of its home in a working-class neighborhood on Cleveland's West Side. A year earlier, an interracial couple and their two children had been subjected to numerous threats, racial slurs, and acts of vandalism by angry white neighbors demanding that they and an African American family leave a working-class Italian enclave in southwest Philadelphia. Earlier that same year, an African American woman living alone in a Chicago apartment building—the only African American in that complex—walked out of her apartment to find her car resting on slashed tires. The act was repeated later, and this time her headlights were also smashed. On other occasions, she returned home to find her telephone line snipped, her apartment ransacked, and an unsigned letter containing racial slurs and a threat: "Last chance, get out." The letter was the final blow; she moved out of her apartment.[21]

Housing discrimination today can also be more subtle. In fact, like much discrimination in the post-1960s, it often takes the form of complex racial discrimination, which is subtle in the sense that it may be sophisticated, unconscious, or institutionalized and is sometimes accompanied by nonracial factors.[22] In contrast to those who suffer from the "Al Campanis syndrome," practitioners of complex racial discrimination are usually clever enough to hide racist feelings.[23]

Housing officials have noted, for example, that African Americans "often encounter discrimination with a smile." As one official describes: "Many times people are denied [housing] and know they've been denied, but don't know it's discrimination. . . . The person may be very nice and may never directly say anything that leads [prospective tenants or homeowners] to know it's something about them . . . but [they are] told that a unit is not available." The Kentucky Human Rights Commission cites another common example of "smiling discrimination" in housing: a rental agent tells an African American family, "I'm very sorry, but we don't have a vacancy today"; later, the same agent tells a white family the same thing but adds, "I expect we'll have one tomorrow."[24] Numerous examples of smiling discrimination in other areas of interracial relations appear daily in the news media.[25]

Smiling discrimination is not the only form of complex racial discrimination encountered in the area of housing. One observer claims that "the ploys are endless." In Atlanta, for example, "one ruse is to demand earnest money in cash from a black prospect. When the would-be-buyer returns from the bank, he is told, 'Sorry, the property has been taken.' " Another maneuver allows rental and sales agents to tip off one another "by writing the names of white applicants in script." "Steering"—real estate agents deliberately directing African Americans to minority or mixed neighborhoods and whites to predominantly white neighborhoods—is yet another example. According to University of Chicago urbanologist Gary Orfield, steering is "one of the driving engines of resegregation. . . . If you can stop that, you've solved a big part of the problem."[26]

Redlining and blockbusting are two additional forms of housing discrimination. Redlining is the refusal to lend mortgage money to persons residing in predominantly minority (usually African American) neighborhoods. Blockbusting involves real estate agents warning white homeowners of a minority group "invasion" (and a presumed decrease in property values) to frighten them into selling their houses to an agent at below-market prices. The agent then resells the houses to minorities at inflated prices. Blockbusting is especially pernicious, not only because it is discriminatory and segregative but also because it is a primary cause of overpriced housing for minorities.[27]

Education.   In examining intra-class racial disparity within the context of primary education (by which I mean kindergarten through high school), it is useful to keep in mind the historical relationship between African Americans and public schools. Despite the fact that African American students today are more likely than any other racial or ethnic group to attend public schools,[28] this relationship has been an unkind one, not unlike that of a badly abused child struggling to escape ubiquitous parental mistreatment, neglect, and violence, both physical and psychological. The story unfolds within the radius of an intellectual and emotional swing between desegregated and segregated schools on the part of African Americans. From the days of slavery to today, the pendulum has swung first from desegregated to segregated schools and then back toward desegregation, with now perhaps another swing in the direction of separate schools.

The first American public schools were desegregated, as early as the 1640s in Massachusetts and Virginia. African American children could attend these schools and were educated alongside white children. They had to pay a high price for the "privilege" of sitting next to a white child, however, for mistreatment and racial insults by white pupils and teachers alike were part of the regular curricula throughout colonial America.[29]

After the Revolutionary War, African Americans took steps to establish separate schools for their children. In Massachusetts, for example, Prince Hall, a prominent war veteran, petitioned the legislature for an "African" school so that African American children could have a safe and supportive environment in which to learn. The petition was rejected, but in 1798 a white teacher founded such a school in the home of Primus Hall, the son of Prince Hall. Two years later, African Americans petitioned the city of Boston to fund a separate school. Although this petition was also rejected, African Americans proceeded to set up their own schools, hiring two Harvard-educated men as instructors. In 1818, the city of Boston began funding these existing schools and even opened another separate school in 1820, ten years before the modern system of public education (with state support, compulsory attendance, and so forth) became a fixture throughout the country. With the change from desegregated to segregated schools, many African Americans thought they had won their struggle for quality education.[30]

But hidden costs came with public support of African American schools—costs such as second-class treatment and loss of control. The Boston School Committee, for example, dismissed the school master at one of the schools it had begun funding, even though he had been selected by the African American parents. Worse, the committee then ignored the complaints of incompetence and sexual misconduct that were lodged against the man it installed to replace the schoolmaster. Parents also complained about the quality of education at the African American schools, believing it inferior to the education white children were receiving at their schools. Having lost control with the advent of state funding, African Americans felt entitled at least to education of a quality equal to that found in white schools. Lacking that, they supported a lawsuit filed to desegregate the Boston public school system.[31]

The suit was brought in a Massachusetts court under the constitution and laws of Massachusetts, and eventually it reached the state's highest court. In 1850, the case was decided against the plaintiffs. The court, in *Roberts v. City of Boston*, held that the Boston School Committee's segregation policy was reasonable and that there was no principle of state law guaranteeing African Americans treatment from government equal to that accorded whites.[32] After the adoption of the equality amendments to the federal Constitution between 1865 and 1870, the general issue presented in *Roberts* came before the U.S. Supreme Court in *Plessy v. Ferguson*. In that case, the Court gave the federal Constitution's imprimatur to the separate-but-equal racial policy. Segregation remained the law until the Supreme Court overturned *Plessy* in *Brown v. Board of Education* in 1954.

Although *Brown* swung the pendulum back to desegregation, where it had been originally, millions of minority children today, more than a generation after *Brown*, still receive an inferior ("unequal") education. Even with the decline of segregated schools since the 1960s, a substantial number of African American children still attend racially isolated and educationally inferior schools.[33] But equally troubling is what Jennifer L. Hochschild calls the "second-generation discrimination" and "resegregation" that occur within integrated schools, practices that have a negative effect on the quality of education African American students receive in these schools.[34]

These practices take a variety of forms. One involves the tendency of administrators and teachers to automatically place African American students in classes for the educable mentally retarded (EMR) without careful attention to what may in fact be other, simpler problems of learning or development. Although such classes are intended to help rather than to harm students, the effect is to resegregate the school internally. At best, such policies associate African American students with slow learning; at worst, they reflect the avowed or unconscious prejudice of those responsible for the placements. Hochschild reports that "in the South, blacks were overrepresented in EMR classes by a factor of 330 percent in 1968; overrepresentation increased to 540 percent by 1974."[35]

Tracking (grouping students by supposed ability) is another form of second-generation discrimination and resegregation. Among students from the same socioeconomic class, African Americans are more likely than whites to be tracked in compensatory education classes and less likely to be placed in gifted or college preparatory programs. "About half of all black students are in low-achievement reading groups, compared to one-fifth of whites; over one-quarter of whites but fewer than one-tenth of blacks are in high-achievement reading groups"; such racial disparity in tracking "isolates students, associates skin color with skill, and leads parents, teachers, and students alike to expect little and demand less from blacks."[36]

Second-generation discrimination also occurs in the disciplining of students, including suspension, expulsion, and other punishment. African American students on average are suspended "at a younger age, for a longer time, and more often than whites." In some districts, African American students are punished five to ten times more often than white students.[37]

Racial disparity also exists in the techniques used to desegregate or integrate schools. African Americans are often asked to shoulder the burden of mandatory student busing. Mandatory busing is usually considered "successful" (that is, acceptable to whites, as evidenced by minimizing "white flight" to the suburbs or to private schools) when it is one-way (African Americans are bused to white schools rather than the reverse), when the percentage of African American students in white schools remains below 33 percent, when whites keep control of the school system, and when mandated decreases in the rate of racial isolation in segregated schools are relatively slight and very gradual. Short of mandatory busing, whites are most inclined to accept integration techniques tied to educational components that are particularly beneficial to white students (such as magnet schools with programs for gifted or academically successful students) or that involve tracking. These techniques, in effect, use African American children as stepping-stones for the academic success of white children.[38]

School integration has also been a painful experience for African American administrators and teachers. In the South, for example, thousands of African American principals, teachers, and other personnel were fired, demoted, or not rehired when the public schools were integrated. (Some government officials claim that the problem of such discrimination against administrators and faculty "has been largely solved.")[39]

Dissatisfied with racial disparity in integrated schools, many African American leaders, including some of those who participated in the long battle for school desegregation and in the enforcement of *Brown I*'s mandate, have followed the path taken by Prince and Primus Hall two hundred years ago and have begun to argue for separate schools. For example, federal judge Robert Carter, who helped to argue *Brown I* before the Supreme Court in 1954, believes that the *Brown I* plaintiffs and the Supreme Court may have been mistaken to equate equal (or quality) education with integrated education or to think that the former could be derived from the latter. He is, however, certain that by pursuing desegregation or racial mixing without regard to the quality of education it produces for African Americans, we run the risk of becoming "prisoners of dogma."[40] Derrick Bell, who edited a volume titled *Shades of Brown: New Perspectives on School Desegregation,* has been an assiduous critic of integrated schools, arguing, as Judge Carter does, that they may not be in the best educational interest of African American children and, for that reason, "may not be the relief actually desired by the victims of segregated schools."[41]

Bell's reading of the African American community may not be far off the mark, for at least one opinion poll shows that support for integrated schools among African Americans declined from 78 percent in 1964 to 55 percent in 1978. In 1964, 75 percent believed that the government should enforce school integration; by 1978, only 60 percent felt this way.[42] This poll, of course, is more than a decade old, and it also shows that a (slight) majority of African Americans still supported integrated schools; nevertheless, it may be indicative of a trend—or at least of the serious questions being raised.

Separate, or African American, schools can in fact resolve certain of the historical and modern problems that have been encountered with integrated schools. Specifically, in a separate school, African American teachers and administrators are in charge; and the predominance of African American students allows the staff to make EMR placements, to track students, and to mete out discipline in a nonbiased and nondiscriminatory manner and without stigmatizing a racial group as slow, insufficiently motivated, or troublemakers. African American culture and awareness are taken seriously by teachers and administrators; role models are created and leadership is nurtured by the presence of African American class presidents, cheerleaders, and other student leaders; and minority students are no longer used as pawns to win white support for integration.[43]

Although separate public schools may be able to resolve some of the problems of control and mistreatment that have plagued integrated schools, it is nevertheless true that racially isolated schools alone cannot provide a quality education. Without the financial resources to pay for excellent staff, state-of-the-art equipment, a rich collection of classic and modern books, and other essentials, children will not receive good basic schooling in reading, science, mathematics, history, and other fundamentals. Because "green follows white"—that is, whites usually control financial resources—"black schools are in grave danger of being short-changed."[44]

Racially isolated schools also lack cultural diversity. African American children, many of whom live in segregated housing, run the risk of growing up without learning how to deal effectively either with racism or with other races and cultures. The importance of cultural diversity in education was recognized more than a century ago by a Kansas court:

At the common schools, where both sexes and all kinds of children mingle together, we have the great world in miniature; there they may learn human nature in all its phases, with all its emotions, passions and feelings, loves and hates, its hopes and fears, its impulses and sensibilities; there they may learn the secret springs of human actions, and the attractions and repulsions, which lend with irresistible force to particular lines of conduct. But on the other hand, persons by isolation may become strangers even in their own country; and by being strangers, will be of but little benefit either to themselves or to society. As a rule, people cannot afford to be ignorant of their society which surrounds them; and as all kinds of people must live together in the same society, it would seem to be better that all should be taught in the same schools.[45]

The benefits of cultural diversity are not lost on African Americans. Although only a slight majority may favor integrated schools, those who speak in favor of separate schools clearly do so only out of disdain for the discrimination and segregation that occur within integrated schools—an indication that most African Americans do, under acceptable circumstances, favor integrated schools, just as they favor integrated housing.

The hardships that arise within the context of public primary education fall most heavily on those African American families who lack the resources to avoid or escape the harmful effects of inner-city schools. Such families cannot afford private schools, private tutorial services that supplement public education, or a house in the suburbs where the public schools, even those in predominantly African American suburban communities, provide better basic education than that found in inner-city schools.[46] Thus, students from poor, working-class, and perhaps some lower-middle-class households are more likely than students from wealthier households to be denied good basic schooling.

Working-class African Americans are probably hit the "hardest" in the sense that individuals in the poverty class may have concerns more immediate than schooling, notwithstanding the importance of education to this class. Members of the lower middle class have more resources (income, flexibility, and greater control over their lives) that might allow them to move to the suburbs, to arrange for professional tutoring, or to intervene in the inner-city school's educational process. Such intervention might include spending more time helping a child with homework, traveling to libraries around the city to find a new array of books for the child, exposing the child to museums and cultural events, or simply pushing the school to direct more of its limited resources toward the child. Some African American children have been able to emerge from inner-city schools with strong academic skills as a result of such parental intervention. These options, however, are often not quite as available to the working class.

Those children who are able to successfully navigate the primary school system continue to face problems of racial disparity as they look ahead to higher education. If intergenerational upward mobility in American society increases steadily with education, and if college and postgraduate education are the real keys to improving the socioeconomic status of African Americans,[47] then the future for the African American working and middle classes does not look promising. In 1980, whites were more than twice as likely as African Americans to have completed college or earned an advanced degree.[48] Since 1980, matters have gotten worse, not better.

A study conducted by the American Association of State Colleges and Universities shows that although the number of African American high school graduates grew by 29 percent between 1975 and 1982, the number of these students enrolling in college declined by 11 percent during this period. In contrast, the number of white high school graduates increased by 7 percent, and white college enrollment decreased by less than 1 percent during the same period. The decline in African American college enrollment at some schools far exceeded the national average; at Oberlin College in Ohio, for example, enrollment of African American students fell 39 percent in a twelve-year period ending in 1985.[49]

The American Council on Education tells the same story. Focusing on eighteen-to-twenty-four-year-old whites and minorities, the council's most recent report states that the general trend in college enrollment from 1976 to 1988 is unmistakable: "Whites have increased their college attendance rates while college participation by African Americans and Hispanics has declined." About 68 percent of all African Americans in this age range graduated from high school in 1976 (compared to approximately 82 percent of whites), and slightly more than 33 percent of these high school graduates enrolled in college that same year (compared to 33 percent of whites). Thus, the college enrollment rate of African Americans was slightly *better* than the rate for whites in 1976. In 1988, however, both the high school graduation and college enrollment rates for African Americans were lower than those of whites: the high school graduation rate for African Americans was about 75 percent (compared to approximately 82 percent for whites, virtually unchanged since 1976), and the college enrollment rate for African Americans was roughly 28 percent, lower than the rate in 1976 and in at least five other years since 1976. (The college enrollment rate for whites had risen to 38 percent in 1988, the highest ever.)[50]

Likewise, the number of African Americans receiving degrees fell sharply between 1976 and 1987, especially for African American males. During this period, the number of African Americans earning bachelor's degrees fell about 4 percent overall and about 12 percent for African American males (compared to an increase of approximately 4 percent for whites overall and a decrease of roughly 9 percent for white males). The number of master's degrees earned by African Americans decreased by almost 32 percent overall and 34 percent for African American males (compared to decreases of about 13 percent for whites overall and approximately 24 percent for white males). The number of Ph.D.s earned by African Americans declined by about 22 percent overall and roughly 47 percent for African American males (compared to about a 5 percent decline for whites overall and a 21 percent decline for white males). Although African American females earned 30 percent fewer degrees at the master's level by the end of this period, they, like their white counterparts, earned more bachelor's degrees and Ph.D.s in 1987 than they did in 1976. In terms of degrees conferred during these years, it can be concluded that African Americans sustained "the greatest losses among all racial/ethnic groups, and [that] these losses have been accelerated by the disappearance of African American males from college campuses."[51]

It is impossible to overstate the importance of college and postgraduate education for African Americans. The dearth of highly educated individuals not only affects the social and economic status of African Americans overall; it also limits both the supply of African American educators needed to improve the quality of education in predominantly minority inner-city schools and the supply of role models and community leaders who are indispensable in any prescription for solving the American race problem. Increasing the ranks of college-educated African Americans must become a top priority of the nation.

Certainly, many factors account for the problems African Americans face in both housing and education. The next section of this chapter tries to demonstrate that a nexus exists between these intra-class racial disparities and our civil rights laws and policies. Through its tenets of racial omission and racial integration, formal equal opportunity subordinates working-class African Americans—racial subordination that exacerbates, accommodates and even encourages complex racial discrimination and de jure or de facto segregation in housing, poor or ineffective public schooling, and low enrollment in higher education.

Racial Subordination and Housing

Working-class African Americans have a legitimate civil rights interest in equal housing opportunity. They demand the right to seek housing wherever it is available, the right to live wherever they choose. Some argue that nonlegal factors explain housing segregation in today's society, factors such as the desire for ethnic homogeneity and the inability of African Americans to afford expensive housing. Although it is true that ethnic groups tend to cluster in isolated sections of metropolitan areas, it cannot be denied that African Americans are more isolated from whites than any other major racial group is; nor can it be denied that such segregation has persisted at high levels for decades while segregation between whites and other minorities has declined much faster. Even ethnic groups who have only recently emigrated to the United States are less segregated from whites than are African Americans.[52] It is also true that African Americans as a group may find it difficult to afford expensive housing, but this does not completely account for segregation, for, as research has shown, "blacks of every economic level are highly segregated from whites of the same economic level."[53]

I believe that defects in our civil rights regime provide a better explanation. Several features of the legal apparatus designed to implement the racial omission tenet deny priority to the interest of working-class African Americans in fair housing and hence contribute to housing discrimination and segregation within this segment of society. The intent test, the strict scrutiny test, the paper-tiger statutory scheme of the Fair Housing Act of 1968, low

damage awards, and protracted litigation are the major subordinating features of civil rights law since the 1960s.

Intent Test.   The intent test comes into play when a federal
constitutional challenge is made—usually under the equal protection clause of the Fourteenth Amendment[54]—against a state,
city, or municipal land-use law, policy, or practice having an exclusionary effect on African Americans or other minorities. Limited only by human imagination, land-use devices that preclude
minorities from obtaining affordable housing in desirable areas
come in a variety of configurations: a new state constitutional provision requiring prior voter approval in a local referendum before
any municipality can develop a federally funded low-rent housing
project; a suburban township's charter provision requiring prior
voter approval of all zoning changes within the township by a 55
percent referendum vote, the effect of which is to preclude rezoning for low-income housing; a city's decision to rezone property that a private group had targeted for a low-and-moderate-
income housing project; or a city's denial of a religious order's
request to rezone a segment of its own land from single-family
to multiple-family housing, the effect of which is to prevent
the owner from constructing low-and-moderate-income housing
on its land.

The U.S. Supreme Court and the lower federal courts have
given constitutional clearance to these and other land-use manip-
ulations, in spite of their obvious exclusionary effect on working-
class African Americans. According to the federal courts, these
tactics are permissible under the Constitution's equal protection
clause because they are "facially-neutral" as to race—they do not
contain an explicit racial classification like those prevalent in the
days of Jim Crow; there is no "whites only" or "niggers stay out"
language of the face of these laws. They are not, therefore, racially discriminatory.[55]

The fact that these laws do have a visible effect on most African
Americans may, the Supreme Court concedes, indicate the existence of racial discrimination. But the Court has placed a burden
on plaintiffs that is more difficult to scale than the property barriers themselves. A plaintiff must prove that the legislative body
enacting the land-use barrier actually intended to exclude minori-

ties. No matter how outrageous the exclusion, the intent test remains the standard of liability for a civil rights claim brought under the Constitution.

Washington v. Davis is the seminal case on the intent standard of liability. This 1976 Supreme Court case was filed by African Americans applying for jobs with the police department in Washington, D.C. Their rate of failure on a written examination was significantly higher than that of white applicants. The lawsuit claimed that the exam was racially discriminatory, in violation of the Fourteenth Amendment's equal protection clause. Disagreeing with lower federal courts, which at that time had held that disproportionate effects standing alone suffice to prove racial discrimination, the Supreme Court said that "to the extent that those cases rested on or expressed the view that proof of discriminatory racial purpose is unnecessary in making out an equal protection violation, we are in disagreement."[56] The intent standard has been upheld in subsequent Supreme Court decisions.[57]

Effects are not, however, entirely irrelevant to an equal protection claim. They can be used as a basis for proving discriminatory purpose. They are among a panoply of factors probative of a discriminatory state of mind. As the Court stated in *Village of Arlington Heights v. Metropolitan Housing Development Corp.*, proof of discriminatory intent requires "a sensitive inquiry into circumstantial and direct evidence of intent."[58] In a more recent case, *Rogers v. Lodge,* which dealt with voting rights under the equal protection clause, the Supreme Court was even more direct: "[Discriminatory motive] may often be inferred from the totality of the relevant facts, including the fact, if true, that the law bears more heavily on one race than another."[59]

Although systemic disparate effects constitute a relevant area of inquiry—if only as a means of probing discriminatory intent—the Supreme Court has not really lightened the plaintiff's heavy burden of reading the defendant's state of mind. Because the defendant in land-use and other equal protection cases is normally an institution of government, the plaintiff's burden can at times be nearly impossible to satisfy. The Supreme Court itself in *Personnel Administrator v. Feeney* has indicated, albeit inadvertently, just how difficult the plaintiff's task can be.[60]

This case concerned a law passed by the Massachusetts legislature that granted military veterans absolute preference for state
jobs. Because 98 percent of the veterans were males, this law had
the foreseeable and natural effect of excluding females from state
jobs, and it was challenged on equal protection grounds. Reversing the lower court, which found the law's adverse impact on
women too inevitable to have been "unintended," the Supreme
Court ruled that discriminatory purpose "implies more than intent as volition or intent as awareness of consequences. . . . It
implies that the decisionmaker, in this case a state legislature,
selected or reaffirmed a particular course of action at least in part
'because of,' not merely 'in spite of,' its adverse effects upon an
identifiable group."[61] How can a plaintiff realistically meet this
incredible burden of proof ? How useful are such "relevant facts"
as foreseeability and magnitude of disparate impact in probing
discriminatory intent? When can it objectively be said that these
inferences of intentional discrimination have ripened into proof ?

Some of these concerns have been raised even by justices of
the Court itself. No justice has been a more thoughtful critic of
the Supreme Court's approach to the equal protection clause
than Justice John Paul Stevens. He criticizes the intent test on
the grounds that it lacks a "judicially manageable standard for ad-
judicating cases of this kind," and he also observes:

[I]n the long run constitutional adjudication that is premised on a case-
by-case appraisal of the subjective intent of local decisionmakers cannot
possible satisfy the requirement of impartial administration of the law
that is embodied in the Equal Protection Clause. . . . The costs and the
doubts associated with litigating questions of motive, which are often
significant in routine trials, will be especially so in cases involving the
"motives"of legislative bodies.[62]

With his usual perspicuity, Justice Stevens points out the utter
nonsense of the intent test: "[I]t is incongruous that subjective
intent is identified as the constitutional standard and yet the persons who allegedly harbored an improper intent are never identified or mentioned."[63]

The intent test, in short, makes the task of winning an equal
protection case against a legislative body extremely difficult, if not
impossible. By holding on to the intent test—which is mentioned

nowhere in the equal protection clause—the Supreme Court refuses to give priority to the civil rights interest of working-class African Americans in housing cases. The Court is telling these African Americans that "in spite of" their legitimate interest in breaking through land-use barriers that limit where they can seek affordable housing—and "in spite of" the absolute illogic of the intent test—the Supreme Court will not abandon or modify the current standard of liability under the equal protection clause.[64]

It is true that all those who make claims under the equal protection clause are subject to the limitations of its standard of liability. But the promise and the agony of equal protection litigation are not evenly distributed between African Americans and whites. The Fourteenth Amendment was "passed in large part to protect" African Americans.[65] Since *Brown v. Board of Education*, equal protection under the Fourteenth Amendment has been a critical tool in the struggle for racial equality in this country. The equal protection clause has special meaning and consequence to a vulnerable people.

Some of that consequence is apparent in the housing area, where the intent test necessarily contributes to the special housing problems of working-class African Americans. This test accommodates, and may even encourage, complex racial discrimination and segregation, for the standard of liability is so difficult to meet that many instances of housing discrimination and segregation simply cannot be redressed. Municipalities bent on maintaining a racially exclusionary way of life are virtually assured of prevailing in a private lawsuit if they are smart enough to keep their true motives hidden. This naturally discourages victims of housing discrimination and segregation from even attempting to bring lawsuits under the equal protection clause. The low probability of being successfully sued also provides little incentive for municipalities to change exclusionary land-use laws, policies, or practices. In fact, the intent test is so predictably onerous that would-be discriminators or segregationists may read it as a signal from the federal government that, in the final analysis, housing discrimination and segregation are permissible as long as true motives are kept private and everything is done with a smile.

Strict Scrutiny Test.   One of the most effective ways—some might say the only effective way—to counteract complex discrimination and segregation in housing is through the remedial use of racial preferences. Voluntary rather than court-imposed or other involuntary use of racial preferences can play a crucial role in resolving issues of racial discrimination and segregation. In the area of housing, racial occupancy controls, or "benign quotas," are the most common form of voluntary racial preferences.[66]

Racial occupancy controls are housing policies or practices that manage desegregation through the use of racial quotas. Mainly used in public housing, racial occupancy controls seek to create stable, desegregated communities by regulating residency on the basis of race.[67] Thus, depending on the racial composition of a particular neighborhood or housing development, a housing authority may give preference to an African American or to a white family so that the percentage of both racial groups will remain roughly constant.

The necessity for such racial management is predicated on social science data showing that as a predominantly white community becomes poor and more African Americans move in, whites gradually abandon the community. The loss of white residents, resulting in the transition to a predominantly African American population, is commonly referred to as "tipping." Architect and city planner Oscar Newman has testified that the "tipping point is a quantity that is difficult to predict with precision. It has been variously estimated, in different factual contexts, as ranging from a low of 1% black to a high of 60% black. Most social scientists and housing experts agree that under normal circumstances tipping begins to occur at between 10% and 20% black occupancy."[68] Economist Anthony Downs states the case for racial occupancy controls by observing that "almost all racially integrated neighborhoods and housing developments that have remained integrated for very long have used deliberate management to achieve certain numerical targets as to the proportion of minority-group occupants."[69]

Although some lower federal courts have upheld the use of racial occupancy controls, others have not.[70] In addition, the Reagan Justice Department won an important case against such controls.[71] The reason for the problems these controls have encountered is clear: racial occupancy controls—a most intense and blatant form of race-conscious social engineering—strike at the very heart of the racial omission tenet. In so doing, they violate the strict scrutiny test, which dictates that race must be omitted from the formulation of laws and public policies.

Racial occupancy controls cannot survive faithful application of the strict scrutiny test's two-tier analysis. Heavily predicated upon a racial (and hence suspect) classification, such controls invoke strict judicial review. Without evidence of prior racial discrimination perpetrated by the housing authority or the municipality imposing the controls (such as an admission of guilt), a governmental purpose compelling enough to justify use of controls seems lacking. Other governmental interests—such as nurturing positive interracial relations and preventing the resegregation of communities—should be, but are not, compelling enough to trigger a favorable ruling under the strict scrutiny test.

The strict scrutiny test's treatment of racial occupancy controls highlights its fundamental defect: the inability to distinguish between race-conscious policies that engender *racial exclusion* and those that promote *racial inclusion*. Applied to the former— to Jim Crow laws, for example—the strict scrutiny test is commendable; it promotes racial progress. But applied to the latter— to racial occupancy controls or other forms of affirmative action in the public sector—the test is reprehensible; it enjoins racial progress.

This paradox is perhaps inevitable. The fundamental purpose of the strict scrutiny test is to implement the tenet of racial omission, to prohibit the government's use of race as a factor in the formulation of laws and public policies. But dogged adherence to this perspective is bound to have a negative effect on those who continue to suffer from the government's conscious use of race in the past. Sometimes, the conscious use of race in the reverse direction is needed.

It is true that some African Americans could themselves be denied housing in a community or project utilizing a racial quota. But it is clear that this form of racial discrimination is vastly different from traditional discrimination for several reasons. First, racial occupancy controls seek to foster racial inclusion; traditional racial discrimination attempts to stigmatize and exclude

African Americans. Second, these controls are limited in scope and duration. Third, most working-class African Americans denied housing in such a case would probably be willing to move on to desegregate or integrate another community or would consider their temporary denial of housing a small price to pay for racial progress; these same individuals, however, would probably not tolerate the old brand of discrimination.

The strict scrutiny test, in short, commands the *omission* of race in the government's formulation of laws and policies regulating access to housing, except under a most compelling circumstance (as a remedy for prior racial discrimination by the housing authority or municipality, for example). Given the difficulty of proving such prior discrimination under the intent test, it is clear that unless there is an actual admission of prior discrimination, the compelling circumstance that allows the government to use racial occupancy controls may never materialize. This application of the strict scrutiny test realistically denies working-class African Americans the use of a proven means of counteracting widespread, institutionalized discrimination and segregation in housing.

Fair Housing Act.   The Fair Housing Act of 1968, also known as Title VIII of the 1968 Civil Rights Act,[72] provides minorities with an alternative to a constitutional challenge against housing discrimination and segregation. Unlike equal protection law, the Fair Housing Act is free of the constraints imposed by the intent test and the strict scrutiny test.[73] It is also unfettered by the Constitution's governmental-action requirement, which means that the act applies to private parties—homeowners, realtors, lending agencies, and others.[74] In spite of these benefits, the act is virtually useless in the fight against housing discrimination and segregation. Its effectiveness was strangled years ago by Congress, and other branches of government have inhibited all attempts to breathe new life into the legislation.

No other conclusion seems fair or accurate: the Fair Housing Act is poorly structured and administered. The 1988 amendments to the act, discussed in Chapter 6, constitute a belated official confession of the act's impotence. Unfortunately, the amendments do not fully solve the problems. In any case, the pre-amended

Act is more pertinent to a discussion of intra-class racial disparity, because it was in force in that form during every year from the late 1960s until 1988.

The Fair Housing Act prohibits discrimination on the grounds of race, color, religion, or national origin in the sale or rental of housing. Redlining is expressly proscribed. These prohibitions are designed to promote "the policy of the United States to provide, within constitutional limitations, for fair housing throughout the United States."[75] This policy, however, is a toned-down restatement of the 1949 Housing Act's policy that "every American family" should be provided "a decent home and suitable living environment . . . as soon as feasible."[76]

The watered-down policy statement presages other anemic features of the 1968 act. For example, its antidiscrimination provision was and continues to be vitiated by several statutory exemptions. One exempts a single-family house sold or rented by a person who owns fewer than four single-family houses. Another is called the "Mrs. Murphy's boardinghouse" exemption, a provision that exempts any owner-occupied building "containing . . . no more than four families living independently of each other."[77] These exemptions have not been eliminated by the 1988 amendments.

These statutory exemptions promote racial exclusion by providing government sanction for housing discrimination in certain contexts. More than that, they may be seen as actually *encouraging* discrimination and segregation, especially in the heavily segregated single-family housing market. For this reason, these exemptions are arguably unconstitutional under the Supreme Court's holding in *Reitman v. Mulkey.*[78] In this case, the Court held that California's famous Proposition 14, which amended the state's constitution to give all persons the "absolute discretion" to sell or rent their property as they saw fit, violated the U.S. Constitution because it had the effect of nullifying fundamental state policies against racial discrimination, of involving the state in such discrimination, and hence of "encouraging" private housing discrimination.

Sanctions provided in the pre-1988 Fair Housing Act were seriously defective—in fact, they were so impotent as to be an embarrassment. Actual damages were often meager ($500, $1,500, $3,500), and punitive damages, which are designed to deter prospective wrongdoers, were limited to $1,000.[79] Clearly, these paper-tiger sanctions neither compensated victims not discouraged discriminators. Fortunately, the 1988 amendments significantly increased these sanctions.

Governmental administration of the pre-amended act was also flawed. Although the Department of Housing and Urban Development was (and remains) largely responsible for administering the act, it lacked a crucial administrative tool: enforcement powers. Only the Justice Department or an injured private citizen could initiate a civil complaint.[80] Prosecutors were frequently overburdened. During the Reagan administration, they also became ideologically resistant to prosecuting many of the cases that arose.[81] Typically, an injured party is in a poor position to initiate litigation, usually lacking the time or resources. The 1988 amendments provide a much better enforcement scheme—twenty years too late.

The Fair Housing Act thus subordinated and continues to subordinate the civil rights interest of the African American working class. It forces members of this class to endure any form of housing discrimination—old or new—an exempted discriminator can envision. Even apart from its exemptions, the pre-amended act, rather than being a deterrent, for years conveyed to would-be discriminators and segregationists in words and by deeds that the federal government was not terribly interested in opposing housing discrimination or segregation.

Damages and Protracted Litigation.   The low monetary relief awarded in housing litigation, as well as the time and effort required to successfully prosecute a lawsuit, also frustrates the interest of working-class African Americans in equal housing opportunity. Such subordination is not limited to constitutional or pre-1988 Title VIII litigation but also arises in the context of what is called "Section 1982" litigation.

Section 1982 is derivative of the Civil Rights Act of 1866.[82] Its name is taken from its current codification in the U.S. Code. Section 1982 is a short provision, which reads in full: "All citizens of the United States shall have the same right, in every State and Territory, as is enjoyed by white citizens thereof to inherit, purchase, lease, sell, hold, and convey real and personal property."[83]

The provision was little used until 1968. In that year, it experienced a kind of judicial resurrection in the landmark case of *Jones v. Alfred H. Mayer.* The Supreme Court held in this case that Section 1982 "bars *all* racial discrimination, private as well as public, in the sale or rental of property, and that the statute, thus construed, is a valid exercise of the power of Congress to enforce the Thirteenth Amendment."[84] Significantly, the link to the Thirteenth Amendment is based on the Court's realization that "when racial discrimination herds men into ghettos and makes their ability to buy property turn on the color of their skin, then it too is a relic of slavery."[85]

Section 1982's usefulness in fighting housing discrimination and the herding of men and women into ghettos is severely limited, however, by the amount of monetary relief traditionally awarded in housing litigation. Punitive damages were frequently and may continue to be limited to the $1,000 ceiling prescribed in the pre-1988 Fair Housing Act.[86] And, rather than the five- to seven-figure awards plaintiffs routinely receive in some tort cases for such things as emotional distress, victorious plaintiffs in housing cases frequently receive negligible compensatory damages— as low as $500, $1,500, or $3,500.[87] As the California Attorney General stated, these awards "barely cover the costs of difficult, time-consuming civil rights litigation."[88] Bell offers an explanation for this extraordinary situation:

There is seldom a major out-of-pocket loss in a housing discrimination case. Usually the real injury suffered by the plaintiffs is the deep humiliation of racial rejection that is no less painful because it is deemed to be an intangible harm. Some courts have recognized this form of injury as a compensable type of damage through awards for emotional distress or embarrassment. . . . It is possible that the generally low level of these damages is in part due to the fact finder's lack of personal experience with this type of injury. It may also be due to an effort to find middle ground between the progressive legislation which is in some ways in advance of social realities, and the residual racism which makes it difficult to enforce such legislation fully.[89]

All civil rights litigation is protracted. It takes years to go from the filing of a complaint to the rendering of a judgment by a court.[90] Working-class African Americans simply lack the time and resources to commit themselves to such an ordeal. Even if

damages could cover the cost of litigation, it would still be difficult for many to take extensive—or even any—time out from
work and family to participate fully in complex litigation. The
wait itself may be enough to discourage the most ardent civil
rights plaintiff.

Meager damages and protracted litigation place the African
American working class in a poor position to defend itself from
housing discrimination and segregation. Regardless of how complex or simple the discrimination, litigation would not be cost-
efficient, in terms of either money or time. Knowing this, prospective discriminators or segregationists are not deterred and
may even feel that the law, being so accommodating, provides
them with tacit permission to discriminate.

Racial Subordination and Education

Primary Education.   Formal equal opportunity contributes to
intra-class racial disparities in primary education through the implementation of the racial omission and racial integration tenets
by school systems and the courts. These tenets are applied in a
manner that, intentionally or not, denies priority to the civil
rights interest of the African American working class in quality
education. Such racial subordination in turn contributes to
second-generation discrimination and resegregation in integrated
schools and to a lack of cultural diversity and adequate educational resources in racially isolated schools.

The tenet of racial integration fosters this subordination when
it is used as the basis of integration plans that allow teachers and
administrators to give less attention to the educational needs of
African American students (including the need for racial pride
and self-esteem) than to the educational needs of white students.
This results in the unequal treatment and placement of African
American children, discussed earlier in this chapter. Particular
techniques used to implement school integration, from one-way
busing to less coercive methods such as magnet schools in which
the best resources are distributed to white students, also place a
disproportionately heavy burden on African American children.

The intent test is the principal civil rights doctrine implementing the racial omission tenet in primary education. It prohibits a

school board or a state government from intentionally operating dual school systems, one white, the other minority. As a precondition of invoking the remedial power of a federal court, however, plaintiffs must prove that the defendant school board or state government intentionally established or maintained the dual school systems in question. Proof of segregative intent is required because, as in the case of exclusionary land-use laws, the equal protection clause is the relevant source of judicial authority. But, once again, the intent standard of liability is nowhere to be found in the Fourteenth Amendment or its legislative history; it is simply a judicial invention.[91]

Once segregative intent is established, a court has broad "inherent equitable" discretion to order new taxes or approve a wide variety of other desegregative measures tailored to the constitutional violation. Racial balancing is one such measure. Mandatory or voluntary busing, magnet schools, pupil or faculty quotas, and school district rezoning are typical examples of racial balancing. In the parlance of civil rights lawyers, this cluster of racial balancing measures is often referred to as "*Swann* remedies," because the Supreme Court approved their use in the famous case of *Swann v. Charlotte-Mecklenburg Board of Education.*[92] Judicial authority to order *Swann* remedies was confirmed in a companion case, *Davis v. Board of School Commissioners,* in which the Supreme Court ruled: "Having once found a violation, the district court or school authorities should make every effort to achieve the greatest possible degree of actual desegregation . . . [and consider the use of] all available techniques." Significantly, the Court also stated: "The measure of any desegregation plan is its *effectiveness.*"[93]

Racial balancing fosters two ingredients necessary for quality education. The first is cultural diversity. There simply is no other sure way to provide cultural diversity within segregated school districts than to use some form of racial balancing. The second involves good basic schooling. Although it would be wrong to think that predominantly African American schools necessarily provide poor schooling, it cannot be denied that many of these schools lack sufficient educational resources to do the job that is needed. To the extent that a predominantly white school district provides better education than a predominantly African American one, racial mixing between the two will give African American children better exposure to quality instruction. Indeed, in spite of second-generation discrimination and resegregation, studies show that the academic achievement of African American children improve in integrated schools, with no effect on the academic performance of white students.[94]

The phenomenon of "white flight" is a serious problem in school desegregation and has defeated many attempts to achieve racial balancing within single school districts, for it depletes the number of white pupils available for racial mixing within a particular district. White flight occurs when white parents send their children to private or religious schools or, most often, move to the suburbs, where exclusionary zoning ordinances erect economic and racial barriers for African Americans with low and moderate incomes.

Current school desegregation law has created its own barriers for those attempting to deal with this problem. In what is now known as *Milliken I,* the Supreme Court ruled that the intent test applies to every independent school district included in a desegregation plan. Segregative intent on the part of each autonomous school district must therefore be established before that district can be forced to participate in a school desegregation plan.[95]

Although it is the most widely attempted desegregative measure, racial balancing is not the only response to school segregation. In some cases, racial balancing may not even be a feasible remedy, given the racial composition of the area. Provided that segregative intent is established, a school desegregation plan can, alternatively, allow racially isolated schools to tap into public funds to pay for educational enrichment programs. These programs emphasize good basic schooling more directly and intentionally than racial balancing does. Some instructional programs may also focus on racial pride, African American history and culture, and other subjects dealing with the special educational needs of African American children. These remedial programs do not, however, attempt to tackle the problem of racial isolation, for they cannot create cultural diversity.[96]

Milliken II is the seminal case on educational enrichment programs. In that case, the Supreme Court held that a district court may order state officials to share in the future cost of educational enrichment programs. The Court reasoned that these programs respond to a constitutional violation and are designed to restore injured parties to a position they would have occupied had there been no constitutional violation.[97]

Educational enrichment components can stand on independent legal grounds. Lower federal courts have approved educational enrichment programs even though the desegregation plans in which they appeared contained no racial balancing measure. Some lower federal courts have even approved such programs over the objection of school authorities.[98] Desegregation plans composed only of educational enrichment components may be the only feasible form of school "desegregation" for school districts in which one race is overwhelmingly predominant.[99]

Educational enrichment programs and racial balancing may be useful remedies, but they are hard to come by. The intent test is no less an obstacle to African Americans in school desegregation cases than it is in housing cases. Proving a legislative body's state of mind is extremely difficult; school officials can easily hide their motives from public scrutiny. Discriminatory motivations may be even easier to conceal in the North than in the South, because the former's history of *de jure* segregation is not as extensive as the latter's.

The intent test, in short, is no friend of the African American working class. By making the task of proving segregative intent in school cases very difficult, the intent test subordinates the interest of this class in equal educational opportunity. This subordination both frustrates attempts to culturally diversify racially isolated schools and impedes efforts to acquire sufficient resources to support good basic schooling in institutions that cannot be culturally diversified. If the Supreme Court provided more effective equipment to deal with an educational problem that is in large part the legacy of prior racial subordination, much of that problem would come to an end—an end that is long overdue.

Higher Education.   Low enrollment in colleges and graduate schools has several causes. There is, of course, the undeniable fact that African Americans score an average one to two standard deviations below the mean on standard tests of all kinds, although this fact must be seen in light of the continuing discussion of how these tests may be biased against African Americans.[100] Another important factor may be the upsurge of racism on college campuses during the 1980s. Such racism, as Joseph Duffey, chancellor of the University of Massachusetts at Amherst, has recognized, creates "a perception that blacks and other minorities are no longer welcome on college campuses."[101] Most unsettling, campus racism may adversely affect the academic progress of African Americans already in college, an obstacle that must seem formidable to a high school student contemplating the future. Color can affect the character or candor of the advice one receives from white professors and academic advisors. Also, as one observer notes, "subtle racism may be creating a sort of self-fulfilling prophecy, denying to many black and other minority-group students, no matter how bright and well-prepared they are, full participation in higher education at its best."[102] Such slights and insults as being the last person picked as a lab partner, the recipient of requests to feel your hair or the extra muscles the coaches claim you have in your legs, or within hearing distance of the white student in the dormitory who proclaims that he "didn't want niggers living on the floor" cut deeper than wounded pride and hurt feelings.[103] Many educators believe that "the way minority students are perceived and treated at a school has a direct bearing on their ability to perform well academically. 'Success and the feeling of belonging are intimately connected.' "[104]

The dearth of African American faculty members must also have an effect on a young African American's decision to go to college. African American teachers and professors not only serve as important role models but also can help students deal with racism and its pernicious effects. The absence of this essential resource from campus may be seen as a strong indication of the college's true feelings toward African Americans—that they are unwelcome.[105]

The fact that so many college-educated African Americans must still contend with employment discrimination may also be very discouraging for high school students who are considering college. Vulnerability to employment discrimination dramatically discounts the market value of an African American's college degree. Why incur the added expense and years of study needed to acquire a college education when, as 62 percent of African Americans believe, their chances of advancing to managerial or supervisory positions are not as good as those for whites?[106] Along with campus racism and the paucity of minority college professors, racial discrimination in the nation's top jobs may help to explain why African American high school students have not responded well to expanded recruitment programs instituted by many colleges and universities in response to the college enrollment problem.[107]

Cutbacks in federal financial aid contribute significantly to the low number of African Americans enrolled in college. According to a report by the United Negro College Fund and the National Institute of Independent Colleges and Universities, the shift in federal financial aid from direct grants to loans since 1980 has hit African Americans especially hard.

Some 42 percent of UNCF students come from families whose income is at the poverty level or below, and 30 percent are from families earning less than $6,000 a year. . . . These same students have fewer alternative resources to fall back on. Their families are poorer, they earn less at their summer jobs, they are more likely to live in states that offer relatively small amounts of grant assistance and they receive little institutional assistance.[108]

Samuel DuBois Cook, president of Dillard University, an African American university in New Orleans, offers this insight about the effects of declining federal grants:

What we are seeing is the undercutting of hope, the erosion of ambition and expectation. The availability of loans doesn't necessarily solve the problem. In a lot of cases, you're talking about loans that amount to an entire family income. A lot of young people are simply afraid to undertake that kind of obligation, even for the worthy cause of education.[109]

Significant reductions in federally and privately funded recruitment programs for gifted African American high school students also worsen the college enrollment problem. Upward Bound, for example, which is run through federal grants to colleges, served some 33,000 students in 1985, compared to a peak of 51,000 students in 1973. On the whole, Upward Bound and three major private programs "served about 85,000 fewer students [in 1986] than five years [earlier].[110]

The racial omission tenet is certainly among the most important reasons there are fewer African Americans attending college today than there were ten years ago. Enforcement of this tenet by colleges and universities, as well as by federal officials, has had a direct impact on the number of African American college students. Since 1978, colleges and universities have placed less emphasis on race in the admissions process. This shift in emphasis did not come out of the blue; rather, it came as a response to a Supreme Court decision, *Regents of the University of California v. Bakke*, that at least in part embraces the racial omission tenet.[111]

In *Bakke*, a divided Supreme Court ruled five to four that state educational institutions could not set aside a specific number of slots for which only racial minorities could compete. Of the majority, only Justice Powell rested his decision on the Constitution (the equal protection clause). Justice Stevens and the other three justices who joined in his opinion (Burger, Stewart, and Rehnquist) felt that there was no need to reach the constitutional issue, because the quota could be invalidated on statutory grounds. They specifically held that the quota violated Title VI of the 1964 Civil Rights Act, which prohibits federal funds from going to programs that discriminate on the basis of race, color, or national origin.[112]

Going the opposite direction, the Court also ruled five to four that the equal protection clause does allow state educational institutions to use race in "a properly devised admissions program." For Justice Powell, race could be used only as one factor in the admissions process and only to achieve a diverse student body. But for Justices Brennan, White, Marshall, and Blackmun, race could be used to counteract the lingering effects of prior racial subordination (including societal discrimination) as well as present-day racial subordination.[113] Unlike Justice Powell, the other four justices would not apply the strict scrutiny test to race-conscious remedies designed to assist minorities. Rather, they favored applying an intermediate level of scrutiny—somewhere between the strict scrutiny test and the rational basis test—mainly to ensure that the remedy in question did not stigmatize, stereotype, or especially burden any other minorities. Finally, Justice Brennan's group also upheld the use of the quota under Title VI, on the grounds that "Title VI prohibits only those uses of racial criteria that would violate the fourteenth amendment if employed by a State or its agencies; it does not bar the preferential treatment of racial minorities as a means of remedying past societal discrimination to the extent that such action is consistent with the fourteenth amendment."[114]

Bakke is a poor case from which to draw conclusions about the effect of the equal protection clause in general, and the strict scrutiny test in particular, on college admissions. Only Justice Powell invalidated the quota on equal protection grounds. He was also the only justice to use the strict scrutiny test. True, Justice White joined in that part of Justice Powell's opinion relying on the strict scrutiny test. But Justice White also joined Justice Brennan's opinion in full, which caused Justice Powell to view him as an advocate of intermediate scrutiny.[115] Significantly, the four justices who would not scrutinize benign quotas strictly— Brennan, Marshall, Blackmun, and (possibly) White—have not won the day in subsequent benign quota cases. Since *Bakke,* a majority of Supreme Court justices, including Justice White, have taken the position that all explicit racial classifications, whether racially exclusive or inclusive, are subject to strict scrutiny and that only national security or the defendant's past or current intentional discrimination—not societal discrimination—will justify the use of such a classification.[116]

To the extent that the strict scrutiny test effectively prohibits the use of explicit, racially inclusive classifications in college admissions, it could be argued that this test subordinates the civil rights interest of African Americans in higher education. But it can also be argued that *Bakke* itself, even viewed without reference to the strict scrutiny test, does the same thing. *Bakke* set in motion a tone of inflexibility, and even racial insensitivity, in the admissions process that has had a direct impact on African American college enrollment in the past decade. Post-*Bakke* admissions at the University of California at Davis Medical School, the defendant in the case, illustrate this point.

In 1978, this medical school, like other state educational institutions throughout the country, restructured its admissions process to comply with *Bakke*. The redrawn affirmative action plan did not, however, yield more or even the same number of new African American students as the pre-*Bakke* plan did; in fact, it produced far fewer. The medical school at Davis has experienced a "sharp decline in black enrollment since 1978."[117] The school hired an affirmative action specialist, Margie Beltran-Atencio, who had experience in affirmative action programs at other medical schools, to deal with its enrollment problem. Her assessment of Davis's post-*Bakke* affirmative action plan is instructive. She asserts that the plan "unfortunately didn't do as much as it could have. . . . It lacked a certain human touch, . . . too much reliance was placed on evaluation of a student's application, rather than [evaluation] of 'a human person.' "[118]

Bakke, in short, subordinates the civil rights interests of African Americans in at least two ways. First, it invalidates the use of benign quotas, except under extremely limited circumstances. Whether on constitutional, statutory, or any other grounds, invalidating the use of admissions quotas to rectify past societal discrimination or to otherwise promote racial inclusion is sure to have a negative effect on equal educational opportunity for African Americans. Second, *Bakke*'s rejection of such racial preferences has been read incorrectly by colleges and universities as providing a mandate to assume an inflexible or insensitive attitude toward minority applicants. *Bakke* allows the subtle use of race in the admissions process, which, of course, is not as effective as a more aggressive race-conscious admissions program. But the programs developed in response to *Bakke* do not take full advantage of even this small bone. Too often, they focus too much on traditional academic indicators and too little on underlying racial dynamics or the "whole person."[119] This approach disproportionately denies admission to the few promising African Americans who dare to apply to college.

Bakke's racial subordination clearly contributes to the college enrollment problem. Without the use of quotas and with colleges relying mainly on traditional admissions criteria, fewer African American students will be admitted to college or graduate school. *Bakke* and the resultant admissions processes clearly do not counteract the enrollment problem; they simply allow it to exist. As a wiser Supreme Court stated on another occasion and in a slightly different context, sometimes "affirmative race-conscious relief may be the only means available 'to assure equality of employment opportunities and to eliminate those discriminatory practices and devices which have [worked] . . . to the disadvantage of minority citizens.' "[120]

Summary

A typical member of the African American working class is a semi-skilled or unskilled blue-collar or service worker, or perhaps a clerical worker, and has an annual household income between $10,000 and $25,000. A working-class family has a lifestyle that is above the subsistence level, although it is likely to use public recreational facilities, to rent its home, and generally to have less control over the events in its life than a middle-class family has.

Like the middle-class, the African American working class shoulders a disproportionate amount of societal hardships in employment, housing, and education, although this chapter has focused primarily on the last two areas. In housing, "smiling discrimination," steering, and other forms of complex racial discrimination, along with segregation, are the major racial disparities facing the African American working class. In primary education, racial disparities consist of second-generation discrimination and resegregation in integrated schools and the lack of cultural diversity and adequate resources in predominantly African American schools. In higher education, low college enrollment is the major problem. These racial disparities within the American working class are linked to a system of racial subordination. Legal doctrines, procedures, and processes designed to implement or to vindicate the racial omission and racial integration tenets subordinate the civil rights interests of the African American working class.

Racial subordination in housing can emerge in several specific ways. The intent test makes the task of proving housing discrimination under the equal protection clause extraordinarily difficult. Literally applied, another judicial doctrine, the strict scrutiny test, forbids the use of racial occupancy controls—a powerful desegregation tool and one of the few means of effectively counteracting complex racial discrimination. The Fair Housing Act sanctions certain types of housing discrimination and segregation, makes enforcement by private parties unrealistic, provides for only weak enforcement by public officials, and offers little deterrence against simple or complex racial discrimination and segregation.

Specific patterns of racial subordination can likewise be identified in education. In primary education, the tenet of racial integration affects African Americans attending integrated schools, whereas the tenet of racial omission, through the intent test, also affects those attending separate, or racially isolated, schools. The educational needs of African American children are often slighted in court-ordered integration plans—these children may bear the brunt of integrative techniques or may face various forms of re-segregation and discrimination in "integrated" schools. The intent test places a near-impossible burden on African Americans, who must first prove segregative intent on the part of state or school officials before a federal court will desegregate schools or provide authority for a racially isolated school to use public funds for educational enrichment programs. In higher education, colleges and graduate schools attempting to comply with the *Bakke* decision, either in fulfillment of a perceived legal obligation or as a matter of institutional policy, have abandoned use of admissions quotas for African Americans or have placed too much weight on traditional academic indicators, failing to take the full measure of the person applying.

These racially subordinating features of the legal system contribute to the housing and educational problems faced by the African American working class. Complex racial discrimination and de facto segregation in housing are prolonged and possibly encouraged by antidiscrimination laws that leave African Americans unequipped to fight the necessary battles. Various forms of second-generation discrimination and resegregation in integrated schools—overrepresentation of African American children in EMR placements and lower-level tracks, biased student discipline, one-way busing and other integration techniques that place a heavier burden on minority students—are engendered by mindless integration, reflecting the low priority placed on the educational needs of African American children. The lack of cultural diversity and adequate educational resources has persisted long after *Brown I* in part because proof of segregative intent is an extremely heavy burden to meet.

Finally, African American college enrollment is sure to stagnate at post-*Bakke* low levels when colleges and universities jettison the most effective means of admitting promising African American students—racial quotas—or when the admissions process otherwise fails to take the full measure of the person applying. Given the difficulty of proving discriminatory intent and the unlikely possibility that a rejected African American high school student could sue a college for discrimination, admissions quotas for African Americans may be the only effective way to counteract residual discrimination and racism in the admissions process.

Chapter Four

The African American
Poverty Class

Defining Characteristics

We will use the terms *African American poverty class* and *poor African Americans* to refer to those individuals and families who have no legitimate source of income, who rely in whole or in part on meager amounts of public assistance, or who earn wages below the poverty line, which has been set at approximately $11,000 annually for a family of four during the late 1980s.[1] If we use the income level of $10,000 and below as the measuring rod for class size, we find that approximately one-third of all African Americans belong to this socioeconomic class. (See the table and the chart on pp. 37 and 38.) Again, however, I am less concerned with an income bracket itself than with the socioeconomic characteristics, conditions, and problems a household normally buys into at that particular income level.

This statistical profile of poor African American households may help to bring the picture into focus:

- Fourteen percent of these households are made up of family units headed by a husband and a wife. Roughly equal groups of the men are semi-skilled or unskilled blue-collar or service workers (assembly-line workers, laborers, food handlers, domestic workers, for example), retired, not in the labor force (not working and not actively looking for work), or unemployed (but actively looking for work). Roughly equal groups of the women are semi-skilled or unskilled blue-collar or service workers, retired, primarily homemakers, or unemployed.

- Forty-one percent of the households are families headed by women. Among these heads of household, 58 percent are not in the labor force, 8 percent are unemployed, 25 percent are semi-skilled or unskilled blue-collar or service workers, and 8 percent are clerical or sales workers (secretaries, sales clerks, telephone operators, postal workers).

- Three percent of the households are families headed by men in which the head of household is not in the labor force.

- Twenty-one percent of the households consist of unmarried women with no dependents. Approximately 33 percent of these women are not in the labor force, 17 percent are unemployed, 17 percent are semi-skilled or unskilled blue-collar or service workers, and 33 percent are retired.

- Twenty-one percent of the households consist of single men, of whom approximately 33 percent are not in the labor force, 17 percent are unemployed, 33 percent are semi-skilled or unskilled blue-collar or service workers, and 17 percent are retired.[2]

These statistics clearly indicate that poor African Americans live at the low end of the American dream. But they can only hint at the life of a discernible subculture, or subclass: the African American underclass. This subclass, a relatively new segment of society, adds a special dimension to poverty in America.

The term *underclass* was not part of civil rights discourse during the 1960s. Journalist Ken Auletta popularized the term in a 1982 book entitled *The Underclass*.[3] Auletta wrote about the hard-core unemployed, concentrating on what he perceived as values and behaviors quite different from those of mainstream society. A CBS Reports documentary by Bill Moyers, "The Vanishing Black Family: Crisis in Black America," is perhaps most responsible for making the term *underclass* a household word.[4] This 1986 television documentary dramatized for the entire nation some of the attitudes, values, and behavior patterns of African American teenagers, both male and female, from broken families.

Today, the term *underclass* has come to mean more than the hard-core unemployed or individuals from broken families. There is, however, no generally accepted definition of the underclass.

Rather, there are several competing definitions, most of which were debated at a conference convened by the Joint Center for Political Studies on March 5, 1987, in Washington D.C. Without revisiting that debate, we can nevertheless summarize three alternative definitions of the underclass that were presented at the conference: the long-term poor (individuals living below the poverty line for eight of the past ten years); the inner-city poor (which necessarily excludes the rural poor); and individuals residing in areas in which a high percentage of the residents are unemployed, are dependent on welfare, have dropped out of high school, or live in female-headed families. This last description, slightly modified, emerged as what might be called a consensus definition: "poor people who live in a neighborhood or census tract with high rates of unemployment, crime, and welfare dependency."[5]

Estimates of the size of the underclass range from a high of 60 percent of the poor to a low of 16 percent.[6] These figures, of course, depend on the definitions employed. Also, because such measurements rely chiefly on government-conducted surveys, they can provide at best only rough approximations. Government census takers are often reluctant to enter minority neighborhoods, and many minorities are reluctant to talk with government officials who ask personal questions; "the result is a substantial (20 percent, perhaps) undercounting of the nonwhite population."[7]

Amid the uncertainty surrounding our understanding of the underclass, one thing seems clear: most scholars believe that the existence of the African American underclass in the inner city—where individuals are trapped in an intergenerational cycle of dysfunction and self-destruction—presents "a special agony for America" and that this agony is a particular phenomenon of the post–Jim Crow, post-1960s period. Indeed, some scholars would limit the definition of the underclass to include only the African American or Hispanic underclass as it has developed during this period. Others would apply the term only to the inner-city African American underclass.[8]

Two additional observations should be noted. First, inner-city areas, in which most underclass African Americans reside, "are not only ecologically and economically very different from areas in which poor urban whites tend to reside, they are also very different from their own ecological and economic makeup of several decades ago"[9]—a difference that will be examined in the pages to follow.

Second, although the size of the American underclass varies with the definition chosen to describe it, most scholars who have studied the matter agree that the African American underclass represents a greater percentage of the African American poverty class than the white underclass does of the white poverty class.[10] It is important to understand that the underclass—particularly its urban segment—is characterized by socioeconomic conditions that are not manifested evenly throughout the American poverty class. Instead, these conditions are experienced disproportionately by poor African Americans and have thus become part of today's version of the American race problem.

The Subordination Question
Intra-Class Racial Disparity

What constitutes intra-class racial disparity within the American poverty class? What unique or distinguishing features are inherent in the lives of underclass African Americans—the long-term poor and unemployed isolated in ghettoes? Welfare dependency, broken families, unemployment, unusual vulnerability to the "low-wage explosion" (the poverty-level wages paid by many newly created jobs),[11] crime, drugs, gangs, or malnutrition? The answer, I believe, is none of the above. Instead, these conditions are evidence of a deeper, more fundamental phenomenon.

When one pulls this evidence together, it becomes clear that it is the force underlying these conditions—*a proclivity toward a pattern of dysfunction and self-destruction, manifested in particular behaviors, value systems, and attitudes*—that fundamentally distinguishes underclass African American communities from other poor communities in America. This current is more organic and widespread within this segment of African American society than the high rate of welfare dependency, single-parent families, joblessness, or other identifying characteristics. It also helps to explain the profusion of often confusing socioeconomic conditions, including the damaging effects of the low-wage explosion—

the lives of underclass African Americans are moving in a direction that leaves them totally unprepared for skilled employment.

The dysfunctional and self-destructive lifestyle of the African American underclass is also sustained in part by racial sensibility, which itself is a legacy of earlier systems of racial subordination. Racial sensibility is a most insidious "cultural disease." Its symptoms include an inability to manage mixed or negative feelings regarding one's racial identity—low self-esteem, self-hate, anger, and defiance; an inability to draw strength, pride, determination, or energy from African American culture; and a general inability to successfully adapt to the white-dominated world. The problems African Americans often experience with racial sensibility may partly explain why white ethnic groups, Southeast Asian and other recent immigrants, and even black West Indians have made greater economic and social progress than African Americans as a whole.[12]

Most important, my characterization of the African American underclass is not intended to subscribe to the Banfield-Lewis "culture of poverty" school of thought.[13] I readily acknowledge that most members of this underclass have imbibed behaviors, values, and attitudes that differ from those of the mainstream and that are dysfunctional in the context of a service-oriented, highly complex society. I also argue that the underclass shares in the responsibility for solving its own problems.

I do not, however, concede that the African American underclass is in large part to blame for its economic privation or its wrongheadedness. Many of the problems of the underclass (as distinguished from the problems of the working poor or the short-term welfare poor) are related to structural changes in the economy, such as the loss of manufacturing jobs in the cities and the increase in service jobs,[14] as well as to our civil rights policies. Thus, although they may sometimes be couched in "culture of poverty" language, my views about the underclass really tend toward those of William Ryan, who criticized Banfield for blaming the victim and ignoring the ways in which society, through class ordering, causes poverty.[15] It is equally wrong today to blame the victim and ignore the extent to which external forces—history, civil rights policy, the economy, and even the very fact of living outside the mainstream—can affect a group's culture. Underclass status need not be permanent. It is neither culturally de-termined nor a matter of fate. It can be changed; underclass African Americans want it changed; and it must be changed.

Young People and the Urban Underclass. A close examination of the lives of African American teenagers in the urban underclass serves to bring many of the negative behavior patterns, attitudes, and value systems into sharp focus. Together, female and male teenagers are involved in most of the serious problems within the underclass: teenage pregnancy, dropping out of school, and a large share of welfare dependency, crime, drugs, malnourished babies, and single-parent households.[16]

The pattern of dysfunction and self-destruction often begins with teenage pregnancy. Clearly, the lack of sex education, in-cluding access to and knowledge about the proper use of contra-ceptives, is a factor in some teenage pregnancies.[17] But in many cases adolescent girls get pregnant in spite of sex education, for-mal or informal. Why? One reason is the desire for a sense of identity and achievement. When educational, occupational, and other avenues to status and success are closed off, motherhood may appear to be a rational choice. (Conversely, a middle-class girl who has college and career in sight is likely to be more mo-tivated to use contraception to avoid pregnancy.) Teenagers also bear children in an attempt to compensate for a lack of nurturing and emotional support from family, school, and community. The desire to love and to be loved is the reason that comes through most strongly in numerous responses to the question, "Why did you get pregnant?"

The response of an African American teenager from Atlanta is typical: "I didn't think my mother noticed me." So too is the statement of another teenager from Newark: "Children will smile when no one else will. . . . They will always be there."[18] Janet Schultz, a nurse-practitioner in Chester, Pennsylvania, who has treated scores of pregnant teenagers, sums up her experience:

Children get pregnant—teenagers get pregnant—because they want to get pregnant; they want to have babies. It's not for lack of birth control. Every child knows where to get birth control. They could even tell us where to get birth control. It's available; it's not expensive—in fact, a teenage girl who would like to get the birth control pill does not need . . . permission from her parent to be treated at a medical facility for gynecologic care in order to get birth control pills. She's what we call an "emancipated minor" when it comes to sexual matters, and she can sign for her own care and therefore get birth control pills. The girls want to have babies.[19]

Children bearing children represents only the first of many self-defeating acts to come. Teenage mothers ignite a series of interrelated, intergenerational problems. The first, which begins with the pregnancy itself, is failing to complete high school. In New York City, for example, pregnancy is the single most common reason teenage girls drop out of school.[20] The pregnancy of a very young girl can also have an adverse effect on the baby's health and consequently on the social cost of infant care. Pregnant teenagers are "far less likely than other expectant mothers to receive prenatal care, thus increasing the risk of bearing low-birth-weight babies requiring extensive medical care at public expense."[21] Babies with a low birth weight can experience both physical and mental developmental problems, called the "failure to thrive" syndrome.[22]

Unlike their counterparts of thirty or forty years ago, teenagers who become pregnant today are less likely to marry right away and less likely to give up their babies for adoption. Thus, many young (often extremely young) girls enter the world of single parenthood. Having dropped out of high school and lacking her own means of transportation, access to child care services, or marketable skills to obtain a job, the teenage mother is usually compelled to go on welfare. In New York City, 70 percent of new teenage mothers are likely to be receiving public assistance within eighteen months.[23]

Going on welfare does not solve the problem of malnourished children, another condition within the underclass that is especially acute among the children of teenage parents. One official explained: "We have multiple kids who are malnourished and . . . some of them are malnourished because the families don't have enough money for food. Sometimes it's because they don't budget money well, but they don't have a whole lot to budget."[24] In addition, African Americans in the underclass, like most other poor people, are not nutritional experts, nor do they

have access to the best food bargains.[25] And many of these individuals do not have "the kind of sophistication or education that
allows them to work very well with . . . [local nutritional
agencies]."[26]

African American teenagers may be ill prepared to care for
their children's nutritional and other physical needs, but they are
equally ill prepared to teach their children a very important
psychosocial survival skill: how to deal with racial sensibility.
Having to cope with racial sensibility is a central distinction between poor African Americans and poor whites; this racial phenomenon simply does not figure into the life chances of white
people.

The importance of teaching African American children how to
handle the psychological problems of being a racial minority in a
racist society is made clear by two leading African American psy-
chiatrists, James P. Comer of Yale University and Alvin Poussaint
of Harvard University (who is also an advisor for television's "The
Cosby Show"). In their book *Black Child Care*, Comer and
Poussaint maintain that, although good child-rearing principles "are fundamentally the same for all," African American parents "will occasionally need to act in special ways." Because our
society "so profoundly threatens" the self-esteem of African
American children, Comer and Poussaint argue that parenting requires special efforts to provide for the child's psychological well-
being. The African American child, who is "still made to feel inferior to whites," must be "trained to cope with white
oppression." Parents must, among other things, pass on "to a
growing child both the strengths of the old culture and the rules
and techniques essential for successful adaptation in the modern
world." These techniques include the art of being "practical as
well as cunning," learning "how to win some sort of acceptance
from belligerent whites," and even acquiring the habit of containing one's "aggression around whites while freely expressing it
among blacks."[27]

It is very unlikely that teenage parents, who are forced into a
kind of premature adulthood, can themselves master or effectively communicate these sophisticated rules and techniques to
their children, especially given the complexity of post-1960s

racial dynamics. Even older and wealthier African Americans find this parental burden to be particularly difficult in today's racial climate.[28]

Thus, as an African American infant suffering from "failure to thrive" syndrome grows into a malnourished child, on the way to becoming a racially unschooled teenager, the future looks bleak. The possibility of educational achievement seems remote, given the problems with intellectual, cultural, and emotional growth that may occur over the years and the problems such a child may encounter in the public school system (discussed in Chapter 3). Many teenagers drop out of school simply to escape the frustrations and humiliations that come with educational failure, seemingly unaware or unafraid of what dropping out will do to their chances of finding a good job. Other than a strong sense that money is a commodity one should not do without, there may be little guidance or nurturing from the home. Indeed, home life can become quite unpleasant, with tensions mounting as the family struggles through days of poverty and despair. Virtually on their own at an early age, teenagers look for ways to survive and to embellish life in an environment of scarcity. Females often turn to pregnancy and motherhood as a way of arriving at a productive life. Males frequently look elsewhere—the streets.

Coping in the streets is a cruel way for teenagers to try to develop personal growth and fulfillment. They succeed only in becoming children of the streets, playing host to a multitude of social and cultural evils: crime, drugs, vandalism, street hustle, resentment and bitterness against society, and teenage pregnancy and all its attendant problems. Claude Brown, whose highly acclaimed autobiography *Manchild in the Promised Land* made America aware of the problems of an African American youngster growing up on the streets of Harlem in the 1940s and 1950s,[29] describes the environment and some of the motivations and coping techniques of today's prematurely adult male:

Today's manchild is a teen-ager between the ages of 13 and 18, probably a second-generation ghetto dweller living with his unskilled, laboring mother and three or four sisters and brothers, maybe one or two cousins, all sharing a tiny three-, four- or five-room apartment in a dilapidated tenement of low-income, city-owned housing developments, commonly called "the projects." . . .

The motivations, dreams and aspirations of today's young men are essentially the same as those of the teen-agers of their parents' generation—with a few dramatic differences. They are persistently violent. They appear driven by, or almost obsessed with, a desperate need for pocket money that they cannot possibly obtain legally. . . .

Like his progenitor, [today's manchild] seeks the answers to life's "unknowable whys" through informal mysticism and mind-altering media collectively called getting "high." . . .

Yet, the unimaginably difficult struggle to arrive at a productive manhood in urban America is more devastatingly monstrous than ever before. All street kids are at least semi-abandoned, out on those mean streets for the major portion of the day and night. They are at the mercy of a coldblooded and ruthless environment; survival is a matter of fortuity, instinct, ingenuity and unavoidable conditioning. Consequently, the manchild who survives is usually more cunning, more devious and often more vicious than his middle-class counterpart. These traits are the essential contents of his survival kit.[30]

The African American underclass is not the only group in our society that suffers from a pattern of dysfunction and self-destruction. Male teenagers between the ages of fifteen and eighteen, regardless of race or socioeconomic level, have the highest incidence of involvement in crime.[31] And, of course, the white underclass, with all its similar problems of poverty, alienation, broken homes, welfare dependency, and criminal behavior, is also prone to self-defeating mores.[32] None of these groups, however, behave in response to attitudes and value systems quite like those found in the African American inner-city ghetto.

The ghetto is a constant reminder to all African Americans of earlier subordinating systems. To members of the underclass, it is also a symbol of society's indifference and frequent hostility toward them in particular. Skirmishes with the police—angry white men in screaming cars—pervasive economic privation, and the many failed attempts to "make it" in a perplexing white world (in school, on the job, and so on) all help to create a deeply ingrained aversion, especially in African American males, to the values of the larger, alien white world. Life in the ghetto can engender a very real sense that whites have purposefully limited opportunities for African Americans, that society has closed off every avenue of stardom, except "stardom in crime." John Edgar Wildeman captures many of these complex attitudes and values in his book *Brothers and Keepers:*

You remember what we were saying about young black men in the street-world life. And trying to understand why the "square world" becomes completely unattractive to them. It has to do with the fact that their world is the GHETTO and in that world all the glamour, all the praise and attention is given to the slick guy, the gangster especially, the ones that get over in the "life." And it's because we can't help but feel some satisfaction seeing a brother, a black man, get over on these people, on their system without playing by their rules. No matter how much we have incorporated these rules as our own, we know that they were forced on us by people who did not have our best interest at heart. . . .

In the real world, the world left for me, it was unacceptable to be "good," it was square to be smart in school, it was jive to show respect to people outside the street world, it was cool to be cold to your woman and the people that loved you. The things we liked we called "bad." "Man, that was a bad girl." The world of the angry black kid . . . was a world in which to be in was to be out—out of touch with the square world and all of its rules on what's right and wrong. The thing was to make sure it's contrary to what society says or is. . . .

. . . The world's a stone bitch. Nothing true if that's not true. The man had you coming and going. He owned everything worth owning and all you'd ever get was what he didn't want anymore, what he'd chewed and spit out and left in the gutter for niggers to fight over. Garth had pointed to the street and said, If we ever make it, it got to come from there, from the curb.[33]

These attitudes and values give content to the pattern of dysfunction and self-destruction within the African American underclass and distinguish this segment of society from other groups that engage in similar behavior. However, although these negative attitudes and values are part of the fabric of this group's lifestyle, it would be wrong to conclude that members of the underclass are solely to blame. Both structural changes in the economy and racial subordination have played significant roles in the creation and enhancement of this pattern. The issue of racial subordination is considered next.

Racial Subordination

Slavery and Jim Crow.   It is not the case that a sizable segment
of African American society joined the ranks of the underclass on
its own volition during the decades since the 1960s. Many of
these individuals had no choice; they emerged from the Jim
Crow system heavily encumbered by poverty and despair and
thus were already on the road to underclass status. Given the
duration and intensity of slavery and Jim Crow, it would not have
been difficult to anticipate in the late 1960s that these historical
subordinating systems would have a residual effect on African
Americans and society as a whole for many years to come.[34]

Indeed, in its 1968 report on the causes of America's race
riots, the National Advisory Commission on Civil Disorders,
better known as the Kerner Commission, cited some of the lingering effects of slavery and Jim Crow: acute unemployment,
high underemployment, shabby housing, second-rate education,
poor municipal services, inadequate welfare assistance, and, of
course, racism. Significantly, the commission said that "segregation and poverty converge on the young to destroy opportunity
and enforce failure. Crime, drug addiction, dependency on welfare, and bitterness and resentment against society in general and
white society in particular are the result."[35]

These findings are dramatically illustrated by statistics from the
late 1960s and early 1970s. African Americans came out of the
Jim Crow era with an unemployment rate roughly twice as high
as the rate for whites; a poverty rate for individuals and intact
families more than three times that of whites; and income levels
for males and intact families that were only 58.1 percent and 61.4
percent, respectively, of the income levels recorded for their
white counterparts.[36] The percentage of African American men
and women concentrated in the lowest-paying, least-skilled jobs
(primarily private domestic service and farming) was nearly three
times as great as the percentage of white men and women holding such jobs.[37] African American men earned only 57.5 percent
as much as comparably experienced white men; when both experience and education were taken into account, African American
men earned between 60 and 70 percent of the wages paid to
white males of similar backgrounds.[38]

African Americans were almost twice as likely as whites to live in rental housing, and their homes were less likely to contain all essential plumbing facilities. African Americans endured more than twice as much overcrowding in urban housing and more than three times as much in rural housing as did whites, regardless of whether the housing was owner-occupied or rented. In education, the percentage of high school graduates among whites was more than double and the percentage of college graduates was almost triple the percentages for African Americans.[39]

The continuing effects of earlier racial subordination cannot be dismissed by pointing to the fact that some African Americans, even some from the poverty class, have been able to excel in spite of these conditions. Simply put, not all African Americans are the same. "Sure," observes Carl Rowan, an African American who is a syndicated newspaper columnist, "a common bond of genes, of suffering, of grievances and yearnings does tie together all blacks in this country."[40] But some are stronger or luckier than others. "Blacks have always distinguished between the person who is in the ghetto and the one with the ghetto in himself. The former is a striver, the latter a defeatist."[41] Rowan notes that "when a thousand are bound in chains, only a few Houdinis will emerge. Those who have done so simply turned out to be stronger than their shackles were."[42]

Nor can the current effects of past subordinating systems be discounted by pointing to other ethnic groups, who can also lay claim to a legacy of suffering but who have surmounted barriers to gain entrance into mainstream American society. The African American experience in the United States is wholly different from that of other ethnic groups in this country, including the recent Asian immigrants who have done so well in record time. No other ethnic group was brought here against its wishes and then enslaved and humiliated so thoroughly by society and government.

Too many Americans seem to have forgotten—or perhaps have never read—the Kerner Commission's findings on this subject. In addressing the question of why so many African Americans, in contrast to European immigrants, have been unable to escape from the ghetto and poverty, the commission cited, among other things, certain racial and cultural factors:

The Disability of Race. The structure of discrimination has stringently narrowed opportunities for the Negro and restricted his prospects. European immigrants suffered from discrimination, but never so pervasively. . . .

Cultural Factors. Coming from societies with a low standard of living and at a time when job aspirations were low, the immigrants sensed little deprivation in being forced to take the less desirable and poorer-paying jobs. Their large and cohesive families contributed to total income. Their vision of the future—one that led to a life outside of the ghetto—provided the incentive necessary to endure the present.

Although Negro men worked as hard as the immigrants, they were unable to support their families. The entrepreneurial opportunities had vanished. As a result of slavery and long periods of unemployment, the Negro family structure had become matriarchal; the males played a secondary and marginal family role—one which offered little compensation for their hard and unrewarding labor. Above all, segregation denied Negroes access to good jobs and the opportunity to leave the ghetto. For them, the future seemed to lead only to a dead end.

Today, whites tend to exaggerate how well and quickly they escaped from poverty. The fact is that immigrants who came from rural backgrounds, as many Negroes do, are only now, after three generations, finally beginning to move into the middle class.

By contrast, Negroes began concentrating in the city less than two generations ago, and under much less favorable conditions.[43]

Myriad other consequences flow from the unique historical experiences of African Americans. In addition to the socioeconomic problems discussed above, there is also the lack of a legacy of opportunities from which today's African Americans can benefit. Government-imposed racial exclusion permitted earlier generations of African Americans to amass very few opportunities for themselves—in education, business, the professions, and so on— leaving even less to bequeath to future generations.

Psychosocial problems are also among the consequences of this historical subordination. What has been dubbed "sorriness," for example, might be seen as a "cultural disease" afflicting some in the African American community. A sort of arrested adolescence, it helps to explain some of the dysfunctional behavior of underclass African American men, such as the intra-racial violence that sometimes results from the failure to vent anger and frustration in a mature manner.[44] "Sorriness" is similar to the "Peter Pan

syndrome" in that both terms describe young men who refuse to grow up or accept responsibility. There is, however, an
important difference between the two terms: one who suffers
from "sorriness" faces the prospects of long-term poverty, prison,
physical injury, or even death, especially without family resources to cushion the blows or pick up the pieces. James Baldwin describes this cultural disease in his book *The Evidence of
Things Not Seen:*

It is a disease that attacks Black males. It is transmitted by Mama,
whose instinct—and it is not hard to see why—is to protect the Black
male from the devastation that threatens him the moment he declares
himself a man. All of our mothers, and all of our women, live with this
small, doom-laden bell in the skull, silent, waiting, or resounding, every hour of every day. Mama lays this burden on Sister, from whom she
expects (or indicates she expects) far more than she expects from
Brother; but one of the results of this all too comprehensible dynamic is
that Brother may never grow up—in which case, the community has
become an accomplice to the Republic.[45]

Racial sensibility, discussed earlier in this chapter, must also
be seen as a psychological consequence of African Americans' history. Failure to deal with this "inheritable" problem can cause
motivational disabilities—especially in young men, who, for example, may be "less willing to compete aggressively for the opportunities that are open or less willing to submit to industrial
discipline." Moreover, parents who themselves have not been
able to handle racial sensibility may affect the entire family structure—their mishandling of their own problems may have an impact on "a child's aspirations and on the guidance available."[46]
    Given the enormous disadvantages African Americans carried
into post-1960s America, it should surprise no one that such serious conditions remain with us today. What may surprise some,
however, is the role that formal equal opportunity plays in sustaining the residue of prior racial subordination and in creating
new forms of subordination.

Formal Equal Opportunity.   If slavery and Jim Crow have sown
the seeds of the African American underclass, formal equal opportunity has done its share to nurture their growth. Formal
equal opportunity—through its policy of racial integration, in

particular—has contributed to the formation of the underclass, and continues to do so, by failing to give any priority at all to the concerns of those in the African American poverty class who stand to benefit from racial separation. Racial integration is intrinsically at odds with racial separation; they are wholly incompatible. The push toward integration has been dominant in African American inner-city communities since the 1960s, and it has helped to promote the development of dysfunctional and self-destructive behaviors, attitudes, and values among those who now populate the underclass.

Despite this assertion, there is no denying that most poor African Americans have been helped by racial integration in the past several decades. In 1964, for example, 49.6 percent of the African American population was classified as part of the poverty class; this figure had declined to 35.7 percent by 1983. Racial integration was not the sole reason for this decline, of course; during the same period the percentage of the white population in the poverty class also decreased (from 14.9 percent to 12.1 percent), and the size of the poverty class overall, as a percentage of the total population, decreased from 19 percent to 15.2 percent. But the size of the African American poverty class decreased at a greater rate, suggesting that a significant part of that decline resulted from an expansion of opportunities brought about at least in part by racial integration.[47] There is also little doubt that most poor African Americans, particularly the working poor, actually desire residential integration and integrated public schools, although support for the latter has declined somewhat since the 1960s.[48]

But there is also reason to believe that at least one subclass of poor African Americans, the underclass, is better served by a policy of racial separation. We can understand this by looking at how a policy of integration subordinates the most pressing civil rights interest of the African American underclass and by considering how racial separation can be a legitimate civil rights policy alternative.

In discussing the subordination question, we must first identify a relevant civil rights interest. The subordination question presupposes the presence of such an interest—that is, a claim against the government for equal access to an extant opportunity.

Does the African American underclass have a civil rights interest at stake? Indeed it does.

The nature of this civil rights interest, heard in the many voices raised earlier in this chapter, finds expression in George Bernard Shaw's astute observation about poverty: "Poverty does not produce unhappiness; it produces degradation"—degradation, humiliation, the absence of human dignity or respect. These issues reduce themselves to a claim for an equal opportunity to achieve a decent standard of living, which is a claim more immediate, more basic than any of the other equality claims discussed in previous chapters (equal employment, housing, and educational opportunities).

There is no doubt that the civil rights interest of the African American underclass—a claim for an equal opportunity to achieve a decent standard of living—is legitimate. This opportunity is made available to Americans in general. It comes with membership in American society, a privilege of citizenship made available even to (or perhaps especially to) the poor. The land of opportunity promises the poor a chance to reinvent themselves, for it would be unthinkable (un-American) to banish anyone to eternal poverty. And, indeed, most poor households do escape poverty. The American poverty class is not static; it is fluid. Its composition changes continually, with most households moving out of the ranks of the poor within one or two years, having slipped into poverty through the loss of a job, the death or disability of a spouse, or some other catastrophic event.[49] Clearly, the claim for an equal opportunity to attain a reasonable standard of living is even more than a legitimate claim in American society; it strikes at the essence of the American experience.

It is also clear that the chance to escape from poverty may not be as available to poor African Americans as it is to poor whites. With long-term and even intergenerational poverty gripping a much larger percentage of poor African Americans, it is at least arguable that these individuals (especially members of the underclass) do not enjoy an opportunity to better their living standards that is roughly equal to the opportunity enjoyed by poor whites. And I would argue that one important reason for this intra-class racial disparity involves the application of our fundamental civil rights policy since the end of Jim Crow—in other words, it involves racial, rather than class, subordination.

The tenet of racial integration subordinates the civil rights interest of the underclass by depleting African American communities of vital resources—resources that are necessary for sustaining a vibrant culture and stable families. Racial integration, in other words, has been something of a boon for those African Americans least handicapped by the emotional and physical hardships of slavery and Jim Crow. It has given these individuals, mainly from the middle class and the working class, the opportunity to move out of previously segregated communities. But the departure of so many stable families and talented leaders from African American communities has resulted in a concomitant loss of valuable community resources. There has been not only a steady depletion of economic resources, such as money that could be recycled within the community, but also—and more important—a drain of individuals capable of supplying wisdom and guidance to young African Americans in the ghetto.

William Julius Wilson also notes the negative effect that the exodus of stable families and individuals has had on today's African American ghettoes. But he tends to discount the connection to civil rights policy, because he sees less discrimination today than, say, in the 1940s.[50] The problem with this analysis is that it fails to look closely enough at the transformation of previously segregated communities. Clearly, the exodus on which both Wilson and I focus was made possible by the radical change in our fundamental civil rights policy, from separate-but-equal to formal equal opportunity. Racial integration provided a *first-time* opportunity for talented African American individuals and stable families to move out of racially isolated communities.

It is impossible to overstate the importance of the middle class to African American communities. Middle-class African Americans were leaders and role models in segregated communities. By words and, more important, by lifestyle, they helped to shape and direct the attitudes, behavior, and value systems of others living there. They interjected crucial "mainstreaming" (American middle-class) elements into the community, not occasionally but continuously. As one observer explains: "A generation ago, racist law and custom confined both [the strivers and the defeatists] to the same neighborhoods. Strivers set the tone—in commerce, religion, social life, politics. They were role models. They provided the leavening that made Harlem, instead of the archetypal slum, into a varied, textured community that was black America's cultural capital."[51]

Middle-class African Americans were perhaps most important as role models for the children of poverty. Children become only what they can imagine themselves to be. And their visions are clearly affected by what they see in their environment. If all the adults around them are chronically unemployed or work in poorly paid jobs with little security, children may simply accept this as their own fate. But if African American children see African American adults going to a job every morning and bringing home a paycheck to pay the bills and support a reasonably comfortable lifestyle, and if they see African American adults become successful professionals and leaders, then their understanding of their own potential is expanded.

In their book *Black Child Care*, Comer and Poussaint make this essential point by referring to "significant others." This concept is another way of stressing the importance of community support in the emotional and psychological development of children, especially in teaching African American children how to deal with racial sensibility. Even children raised in the poorest of homes, who may have grown up with strong feelings that their parents were unable to provide for their economic and social well-being, can learn how to successfully adapt to today's world as an African American, developing a work ethic and an "attitude of black pride, self-confidence, and assertiveness" from others in their communities.[52]

Wilson makes a similar observation. Framing it in terms of the "social isolation" of the underclass, he notes that "the residents of highly concentrated poverty neighborhoods in the inner city today not only infrequently interact with those individuals or families who have had a stable work history and have had little involvement with welfare or public assistance, they also seldom have had sustained contact with friends or relatives in the more stable areas of the city or in the suburbs." One result of such isolation is that even suburban whites often learn of job vacancies in the inner city before underclass African Americans do.[53]

During the Jim Crow era, these significant others (stable families and striving individuals) were in abundant supply in African American communities. Housing segregation, to the unintended benefit of scores of African American children, trapped these human resources within the communities. African American men and women of achievement—lawyers, doctors, dentists, businesspersons, schoolteachers, and other skilled workers—were admired and imitated in segregated communities. They spoke and acted with considerable authority on matters of survival and success in "the white world." They were symbols of achievement and offered young African Americans visible alternatives to a life of illiteracy, crime, drug addiction, welfare dependency, and abject poverty. Clearly, but for racial integration, middle-class culture would still be a significant force in African American communities today—there simply would be nowhere else for the African American middle class to live. Comer strikes a similar note: "After World War II, . . . successful blacks began moving out of the inner-city, taking their money, leadership and role models, leaving the poor isolated and alienated. Whites began moving to the suburbs, taking quality education and jobs with them. These trends left certain parents—black and white—less able to transmit desirable values to their children."[54]

The argument that racial integration has to some extent been harmful to underclass African Americans suggests not only that racial separation can be helpful to this segment of African American society but also that it is a legitimate (though, for the most part, not legally enforceable) civil rights policy in the United States today. The legitimacy of racial separation can be seen in two ways. First, some argue that emphasizing racial mixing (whether it is emphasized by African Americans, whites, government, or social institutions) can cause African Americans to be preoccupied with gaining acceptance from whites or entrance to white institutions at the expense of building alternative African American institutions, forging a strong racial identity, and creating support mechanisms for African American society as a whole as well as for the underclass. This argument seems theoretically correct in that any group can benefit from paying undivided attention to itself; one cannot serve two masters at the same time. The extent of the empirical support for this argument is unclear, however. African American institutions in general have not been as strong as white institutions, although it is true that they have not enjoyed an equal level of financial support from society.[55] Many African Americans believe their institutions can perform at least as well as white institutions, given the same level of financial resources.

Second, racial separation by white ethnic groups has a long and accepted history in American society. Although society has never looked askance at Jews, Italians, Poles, and other ethnic groups who maintained their own enclaves and engaged in various forms of separatism for self-improvement, it has looked with suspicion and even disdain on African American collectivism. During the "Black Power" stage of the civil rights movement, white society placed tremendous pressure on talented young African Americans, many of whom are now members of the middle class, to avoid expressions of separatism or nationalism. Of course, many young African Americans were self-motivated to pursue integration over separation. But white liberals in particular, many of whom were close allies of and sometimes mentors to young African Americans, argued that structures such as the all-black community center, college dormitory, or dining table were radical, reverse racism, or a subversion of the civil rights movement. And today that line of argument continues in Allan Bloom's best-seller, *The Closing of the American Mind*.[56] The argument against separatism, however, was and continues to be based on an erroneous understanding of the civil rights movement. Most African Americans saw the civil rights movement, in essence, not as a struggle to "capture a white person" (i.e., to integrate), but as a struggle to free themselves from government-sponsored racial oppression. It was about freedom—hence, the "freedom songs," "freedom marches," and "freedom trains." Having won desegregation, which most would not give up, African American individuals and classes must now decide whether separation or integration is best for them.

The answer to that dilemma seems clear: African Americans, regardless of class, must pursue integration over separation as a general matter of strategy. But one must keep in mind the distinction between diagnosis and prescription. In diagnosing the American race problem, it cannot be denied that racial integration, whatever its effects on the middle class and the working class, has had seriously negative consequences for socioeconomic conditions within poor African American communities. In prescribing solutions for the American race problem, however it is equally clear that de facto resegregation or a widespread practice of racial separation, however legitimate a policy it may be, would be a poisonous brew; it would have dangerous ramifications on society as a whole, and it would prevent African Americans and whites from learning to respect and live with one another. Not all legitimate or widely supported public policies (community expectations) in a democracy are deserving of further extension by individuals, groups, or government.

My prescription for the American race problem attempts to avoid the extreme of resegregation or rampant separatism by calling for a limited expression of separatism—African American self-help. Unlike some who would use racial separatism for racial exclusion, I would advocate using it for self-improvement and racial inclusion. This will be the focus of the next part of the book.

Summary

African Americans with annual incomes below the poverty line are typically single or are part of single-parent households. Most are unemployed, semi-skilled or unskilled blue-collar or service workers, or retired. The long-term poor isolated in rural or inner-city ghettoes and unemployed for extended periods of time can be seen as an underclass, a subgroup of the poverty class. These individuals exhibit behavior patterns, sets of attitudes, and value systems that offer few springboards from which to launch a successful life. Underclass African Americans live lives of despair, lives that move toward social and economic dysfunction and self-destruction. It is an existence far removed from mainstream society.

The role of the American political and economic system in creating such social and cultural pathology cannot be denied. Ending only in the 1960s, government-sanctioned racism left African Americans with tremendous social and economic disadvantage. Since the 1960s, many more poor African Americans than poor whites have fallen deeper into poverty and have become even more removed from mainstream society, as a result of structural changes in the economy, the sheer weight of the lingering effects of slavery and Jim Crow, and the implementation of our basic civil rights policy.

This policy, formal equal opportunity, contains a racially subordinating feature that has contributed to the rise of the African American underclass. Racial integration, one of the tenets of formal equal opportunity, subordinates the primary civil rights interest of underclass African Americans—an equal opportunity to achieve a decent standard of living—by draining valuable resources from previously segregated African American communities. Those who are left behind, especially the children, are deprived of stable families and individuals who act as community leaders and role models. Without these human resources, there are few left within the neighborhood to continuously expose children to the behaviors, attitudes, and values of mainstream society; to regularly help them deal with racial sensibility, "sorriness," and other problems stemming from historical and modern racism; to act as a force opposing dysfunctional and self-destructive behaviors; and to teach them survival skills that could help to guide them out of a life of poverty and despair. Formal equal opportunity, in short, gives no priority to the special needs of the African American underclass.

Part Two

Resolving the American Race Problem

Chapter Five

African American Self-Help

The Concept

If the argument advanced in Part I—that the conventional application of our civil rights laws and policies contributes to the American race problem—is substantially correct, then it seems clear that this problem cannot be resolved without government intervention. Only the Supreme Court, Congress, and the president have the power to modify the way our civil rights laws and policies are implemented or to redeploy our economic resources. Realistically, however, I do not envision the federal government charging to the rescue of African Americans, at least not in this day and age. Even in a more favorable political climate, the government is unlikely to provide full support for the civil rights interests of African Americans.

This is not to say that one should jettison genuine efforts to redirect our civil rights laws and policies. These endeavors must continue; there is no other choice. But while they continue, African Americans cannot wait to be rescued by the government. Even if the government surprises us by coming through, the African American community must take matters into its own hands as much as possible. The question is, What is possible?

I believe that what is both necessary and possible is a well-focused, intensive, long-term program of self-help, something that has never been attempted by African Americans in this country. Such a program would at a minimum help African Americans, especially those from the working and poverty classes, to overcome some of the effects of both class and racial subordination and thus to attain greater social and economic stability, even if governmental remedies never materialize. Necessarily, the details of the program must be tailored to the socioeconomic conditions that exist in each class within African American society.

The concept of self-help discussed here deals with a special kind of African American economic development and draws on African American heritage. It is a voluntary, nonprofit program of self-support in which the African American middle class in part helps itself but mostly helps working-class and poor (especially underclass) households help themselves. The ultimate goal of this self-help program is to move the maximum number of poor African Americans into the ranks of the working class and the maximum number of working-class African Americans into the middle class. Such an improvement in the lives of members of the lower classes would necessarily resolve some aspects of intra-class racial disparity.

This self-help program also envisions institutional support, such as African American professional organizations or corporate executives, through their companies, working to provide a writing or math teacher, a science program, a computer lab, an after-school or weekend employment program for students attending a predominantly African American inner-city school, or assistance in working with local school boards or city halls.[1] These badly needed educational resources can significantly contribute to upgrading the level of education in racially isolated public schools. In addition, the intangible contribution can often be as important as the tangible, for an infusion of outside attention from the African American "establishment" helps to provide students with what they need most: "a clear, unified message that [*their*] school is important, and that people care about them."[2] These institutional support programs are extremely important. But because they are not particularly new and because they have received much attention in recent years, especially in the popular media, this chapter focuses primarily on the question of household support, which is the most important feature of the program.

The concept of household support calls on members of the African American middle class to work one-on-one, on a long-term basis, with working-class and poor individuals and families, in a sort of "adopt a family" program that focuses on changes in the lifestyles of working-class and poor African Americans. It is a program in which no economic assistance is required, except perhaps in a true family "adoption" scenario, discussed later. With that exception, the only assistance required from the African American middle class comes in the form of information sharing and coaching.

There are three varieties of information sharing, each of which will be discussed in more detail later in the chapter. The first asks middle-class African Americans who participate in the program to share their understanding of the behaviors, values, and attitudes that are necessary for successful living in American society. Some of this information might include the fundamentals of household budgeting, long-term planning, and smart consumer spending. A second type of information concerns the availability of resources within the community—employment opportunities, adult training and educational programs, child care, medical programs, and housing. Once gathered and disseminated, this information can enable poor and working-class African Americans to take advantage of governmental or community resources.

The final type of information sharing has less to do with class condition than with racial identity; it involves the teaching of racial "survival skills." Middle-class African Americans can share the benefit of their experience in surviving racism at many levels—the racist supervisor, co-worker, salesperson, teacher, "friend," or institution—and in deriving pride and strength from the African American ethos. These survival skills are extremely important and worthy of being passed on to other African Americans coming through the system. Helping others deal with racial sensibility and with what has been termed "sorriness" (discussed in Chapter 4) are other survival skills that the middle class can offer. These two psychosocial problems are prominent supports for the pattern of dysfunction and self-destruction found within the African American underclass. Most African Americans have had some experience in dealing with these problems at some time during their lives, and many members of the middle class have found successful ways to overcome or handle them.

Simply exposing working-class and poor individuals to information regarding middle-class behaviors, values, and attitudes, community resources, and African American survival skills is not enough, however. To be effective, a program of self-help must

provide them with an opportunity to incorporate the new information into their daily lives. This process of internalizing new
information is crucial if these individuals are to change their lifestyles. Coaching allows this internalization to occur, not only
through instructing, demonstrating, and directing, but also
through pushing, prompting, and motivating—"cheerleading," if
you will. As individuals and families develop and change, there
will be mistakes regression, embarrassment, and reluctance to
change old habits. The coach needs to be sensitive to this part of
human nature and to be ready to offer all the moral support the
situation requires.

"Teachers" and "pupils" can come together in this self-help
program in essentially two ways: one is formal and relies on traditional institutions within the community; the other is informal
and perhaps more natural. Formally, churches, barber shops
(some African American ministers also work as barbers), community centers, social organizations (such as the Elks and Masons),
local branches of the NAACP and the Urban League, and professional and business associations can act as conduits for bringing
program participants together. These institutions could set up criteria for screening participants. They might want to check on
anything from prior criminal record to compatibility with the program, although participants in such a program are likely to be a
self-selected group—only men and women of the highest integrity are likely to be attracted to a program that offers no opportunities for exploitation, pecuniary or otherwise. Also, there is
nothing in the program to prevent individuals from offering assistance to another person on their own.

Advertisements throughout the community (store windows,
announcements at churches and at professional and business
association meetings, public service radio spots, community news-
papers, flyers dropped door-to-door, and so forth), perhaps aug-
mented by some personal contacts, could bring the program to
the attention of African Americans in all classes. There is very
little cost involved in this type of advertisement, and what little
there is could be donated or absorbed by the institution.

The participants could use one of the community institutions
as a meeting place, or meetings could take place somewhere else;

the pupil's home is probably the best place. A Saturday morning or a weekday evening once or twice a week for an hour or so could be enough to impart information, identify community or governmental resources that might be available, suggest and evaluate activity, and work out problems with the head of the household. There should be no expectation that money will be exchanged during the course of these meetings or at any other time. Meetings with a single household could last up to a year or more, depending on how long it takes to solve the most pressing problems.

A less formal way of matching teacher with pupil is through the family unit. The African American middle class is often tied to other classes through family—a sister, brother, niece, nephew, cousin, or other family member within the working class or the poverty class. This connection provides an opportunity for a teacher-pupil match that may be especially meaningful. In addition to meetings in the home, even closer and more continual contacts might be possible among relatives. A teenaged nephew, for example, might benefit from a year of living with his middle-class aunt or uncle, where he could finish high school with some coaching in his academic work and where he could be away from the negative influences of the ghetto streets. Having an extra person to care for requires an outlay of cash, of course, and could even become quite expensive. But there may be ways to recover some of the expense, such as claiming the child as a dependent on one's tax return.

As with most things in life, flexibility is the key to the success of a self-help program. It is difficult, at best, for individuals to work together one-on-one for an extended period of time. Thus, the structuring and operation of such an intensive program must allow the participants to make whatever changes they deem appropriate. As long as the main objective of the program remains in sight—helping others help themselves by improving their socioeconomic condition and tackling the societal obstacles that lie in their path—just about any configuration is possible.

There is no doubt that this proposal places demands on members of the middle class. But there is no alternative, because middle-class African Americans are in the best (if not the only) position to provide the full range of help that other African Americans need to help themselves. They have experience with living successfully in a society that many rightfully perceive as racially hostile. They have the knowledge to impart, and, as I argue in the last section of this chapter, they have pressing reasons to disseminate and to coach that knowledge.

But this proposal also places demands on members of the working class and the poverty class, who are being asked to examine and alter certain habits and aspects of their lifestyle and to implement what could be difficult changes in family relations, financial matters, social contact, and so forth. Why should they listen to or share this with a person who may be a total stranger?

When I worked as a corporate lawyer in New York City in the 1970s, I had an opportunity to volunteer my services to small businesses, typically family-owned, that had been looted during a citywide power outage. The owners were people who were trying to scratch out a living on the Lower East Side, in an area that was so infested with crime that few businesses were able to obtain insurance. Many had been wiped out—their inventory stolen, their property extensively damaged, themselves physically injured in some instances—and some had even incurred liability to others, such as the proprietor of a dry cleaning business who had no insurance and who lost all his customers' clothing. They were all strangers to me. Yet from the moment I arrived, they were grateful for whatever help I could provide, always pleasant with me (although they were going through what may have been the worst time of their lives), very open about their businesses and personal affairs, and extremely cooperative. They were willing to implement my suggestions, because I was willing to help them help themselves without asking for anything in return.

Working-class and poor African Americans, like their white counterparts, are generally interested in building a better life. To attain that goal, most people are usually willing to listen to a more knowledgeable person, to one who has "made it," if that person is willing to give up some free time to help out in a way that is not demeaning or condescending. People are often willing to open up their lives if they know that you have their best interests at heart and that you share common concerns.

Applications

A self-help program for the African American middle class itself would focus on some of the problems particular to this group, discussed in Chapter 2—loneliness, disaffection, stress and hypertension, John Henryism, complex racial discrimination, and de facto segregation in high-level jobs. Obviously, no program of self-help can resolve all of these problems. Only the government, for example, can provide a remedy for complex racial discrimination and de facto segregation in employment. If these key problems are settled, other employment-related problems can eventually be resolved also.

Self-help can, however, ameliorate concerns such as loneliness, disaffection, and John Henryism indirectly, through networking. By establishing contacts—professional and social—with one another, middle-class African Americans can open new channels of communication, understanding, and information sharing. Through local and national professional and business organizations, they can come together to find wisdom or at least a sympathetic ear for their employment problems. Some of these organizations already exist, such as the National Bar Association, the oldest minority lawyers' group in the nation. Others may have to be created. Local branches of organizations such as the NAACP and the Urban League also offer opportunities for networking, as well as opportunities to help other African Americans. The Links, Jack and Jill, and other traditional organizations designed for middle-class children could be expanded to act as sources of adult networking.

At the working-class level, self-help takes on a different character. The only way to fully resolve the intra-class racial disparities faced by members of the African American working class (as discussed in Chapter 3) is through a combination of governmental remedies and self-help, including the type of institutional support described at the beginning of this chapter. Yet it is possible to relieve some of the pressures caused by the class-based problems this group faces through a self-help program consisting only of household support, with middle-class African Americans "adopting" working-class individuals or families, as outlined earlier.

To understand how this can be done, one must begin with the factual premise that many working-class African Americans are but one step removed from poverty. Any serious financial crisis—loss of a job, a divorce, a long-term illness—can throw a family or individual into poverty for the first time, or perhaps once again. With less income than members of the middle class, working-class African Americans have less control over the events in their lives and less margin for error in running their personal affairs.

The logical place for a middle-class African American to begin helping a working-class family is therefore with the latter's financial situation. A budget may need to be created, or an existing one may need to be reexamined. The household budget must include a line item for compulsory savings, however small and however difficult, because the habit of saving or investing is an essential step in upward mobility in American society. Spending categories and limits need to be reviewed often and faithfully observed, with an eye toward sacrificing short-term pleasures in favor of long-term family goals—a down payment on a house in a nicer part of town, a better-paying job, college for the children. Discussion should focus on making wise consumer choices. The benefits of saving enough money to pay cash for an item rather than buying it "on time" and thereby incurring a 15 or 18 percent finance charge should be clear. Likewise, it must be emphasized that the overuse of credit cards can trap a family in a mountain of debt that can take years to clear away.

Working-class African Americans should be encouraged to investigate and use available services for both adults and children within their communities. Churches, community centers, YMCAs, and YWCAs often provide a variety of educational, recreational, social, and cultural programs, many of which are free. Through exposure to new ideas and people, these programs can enrich one's personal life and increase employment opportunities.

Education must become an even greater priority within the family, especially when children are involved. The home environment must be conducive to learning, with a quiet period and space allotted for studying. As many books and magazines as possible should be provided, and reading for pleasure strongly encouraged. Trips to the library and museums must become routine, and PBS substituted for MTV more frequently. The family must, in short, develop the attitude that education is fun, challenging, and an integral part of one's life.

Locating remedial education, job appraisal, and job training programs for adults is also an important part of self-help. These programs offer adults an opportunity to improve their marketable skills and hence their ability to acquire a better job, better housing, and better education for their children if they are parents. Although it is often difficult for a parent, especially a single parent, to successfully complete these programs, it is possible with the support of the entire family.

Although most of the concerns described above are more related to problems of class subordination, there is one aspect of racial subordination that household support can deal with effectively—racial sensibility. Long hours of frank conversations between middle-class and working-class African Americans on the problems of living in a racist society can be enormously beneficial. How to deal with racism on the job and with racial sensibility inside oneself are topics that need to be explored as thoroughly as possible. Perhaps no African American ever completely resolves all his or her race-related anxieties. But there are ways of managing both the external and the internal conditions that can bend a minority person out of shape. Much of becoming a member of the African American middle class is learning how to deal with the harsh realities of life as a person of color in a white society.

Realistically, despite efforts on both sides, some working-class African Americans will not achieve greater social or economic stability. Some will slip into the poverty class or even the underclass, perhaps encountering such overwhelming socioeconomic problems that no change of lifestyle will help, problems that only governmental remedies can solve. Others will be content to stay where they are. Some will lack the internal strength to alter their lifestyles or the good fortune to be able to put all the pieces together—household organization, job training, and so forth. The possibility that some will fail, however, is no reason not to try.

Among the poverty class, some African Americans, such as those working steadily in low-paying jobs, could benefit from the level of self-help (institutional and household support) applied to the working class. Most, however, especially those in the underclass, need more assistance. The availability of governmental remedies (mainly the creation or development of employment training and opportunities) would increase the effectiveness of any self-help program directed toward the African American poor. But even without these much-needed remedies, there are ways in which a program centered on household support can help.

A self-help program designed for underclass African Americans must deal directly and frankly with the subculture of this group. To be effective, any such program has to delegitimize and reverse the dysfunctional and self-defeating behavior patterns, values, and attitudes that afflict many in the underclass. The mores of underclass African Americans must be brought closer to those of other African Americans and of mainstream society. Adopting mainstream norms does not mean that poor African Americans must become invisible, docile, or a "model minority." Nor does it mean that they must mimic whites, accepting racial stereotypes. Rather, it means an emphasis on excellence and achievement by African Americans in American society. It is a process by which poor African Americans can become stronger and more secure, by which they can achieve some measure of the social and economic success consistent with human dignity.

This process should begin with the two largest and most troubling segments of the underclass—female-headed families (especially those headed by teenage mothers) and alienated young men. Single females with families must learn how to redirect their lives and, by extension, the lives of their children. The teacher must help the pupil to locate educational or job training programs and child care for the children, perhaps with a friend or neighbor of the pupil if other child care services are unavailable or too expensive. Because of the dearth of family income or assets, special emphasis needs to be given to values such as frugality and perseverance and to behaviors such as family budgeting and long-term planning. In this bony environment, living without establishing spending priorities is irrational, and living beyond one's means is suicidal.

If there are teenage members of the adopted family, they need special attention. They must feel loved. A close watch on their activities—whom they see and where they go—must be the rule rather than the exception for the parent. Only with such caring can one even hope to avoid teenage pregnancy, drug abuse, crime, and other problems that plague adolescents.

In the course of aiding female-headed families, middle-class African Americans will inevitably come face-to-face with alienated young males, for these individuals wear several hats. Some are unwed teenage fathers, some are repeat criminal offenders, and some are high school or grade school dropouts. All lack steady employment. Given the variety of social pathology surrounding these young men, a unique self-help strategy, possibly including additional community resources, is called for.

If the young man is responsive to one-on-one talks with a parent or middle-class African American, close monitoring of his activities by the parent and continual communication with the teacher or role model could be important. The communication should attempt to help him redirect his life and deal effectively with the internal battles, perhaps involving "sorriness" or racial sensibility, that may be raging within him and contributing to self-destructive behavior. Teaching racial survival skills could be a key contribution in this case.

Some young African American men, however, are so alienated or rebellious that they are beyond the reach of frank talks with a parent or middle-class teacher. Drug addicts, repeat criminal offenders, and similar individuals may need a more structured, totally controlled environment in which to live. An environment similar to the one offered by Delancey Street may be the best hope for helping these young men.

Delancey Street was established in 1971 by John Maher, then thirty years old, and three other ex-convicts. Delancey Street is essentially a rehabilitation facility for hard-core, down-and-out former drug addicts and ex-convicts. It continues to be run by experienced "insiders" and other persons who have special knowledge about this segment of society. Delancey Street attempts to teach a new way of life to its "family" members, men and women who languish far outside mainstream society. The lessons it teaches are, on balance, good: the work ethic, respect for authority, reliance on local community resources, disdain for welfare, self-help, private enterprise, and personal integrity.

The Delancey Street Foundation, which runs Delancey Street is privately funded. It owns and operates several private businesses, which appear to be profitable. More important, Delancey Street seems to have a good rehabilitation record and therefore could be a model for mainstreaming the alienated African American youth.[3] A project like Delancey Street could give such a young man what he needs most: time and the right environment in which to mature.

Defense of the Concept
The African American Middle Class

The "adopt a family" proposal, as a strategy designed to provide household support, places a heavy burden on the African American middle class. Is it realistic to think that a significant number of middle-class African Americans are willing to shoulder this burden? The question is crucial, because the alternatives seem limited and because, in the absence of substantial involvement from the middle class, the socioeconomic problems of the African American working and poverty classes are rapidly worsening.

Self-interest may be the most persuasive argument that can be used to induce middle-class African Americans to participate in this self-help program. Simply put, people respond when their own interests are on the line. Two kinds of self-interest could motivate the middle class to participate, the first based on class, the second rooted in racial kinship.

The class motivation concerns the defense of the middle-class lifestyle that many have struggled so hard to attain. As crime, drugs, and other problems of the underclass become more acute, they will inevitably find their way into the neighborhoods of middle-class African Americans, even those who live in suburban communities. In fact, this has already begun to happen. The middle class cannot afford to stay on the sidelines.

Racial kinship, the second motivation, concerns the social image of African Americans as a group. All African Americans will benefit when the racial group is no longer associated with the negative images of poverty, unemployment, unskilled labor, broken families, and crime. As the late Judge William Hastie, the first African American federal judge, observed years ago: "Say what you will, a man does not choose as his boon companion an individual whom he never sees in dress clothes except when [that individual is] carrying a tray at his banquets."[4] Benefits that could accrue to middle-class African Americans from a more positive social image of the race in general may be as significant as better job or housing opportunities or as mundane as better service in restaurants and department stores, less hostile encounters with the police, an easier time hailing a taxicab in New York City. But, cumulatively, these benefits could diminish an array of annoying adventures that often make life miserable for all African Americans.

The phenomenon of racial kinship reflects the fact that racial minorities and females are inclined to be group-focused, whereas white males tend to be focused on the individual.[5] In a sense, racial and sexual oppression in this society have always been deployed at the group rather than at the individual level. If an African American is hired as dean of a law school and then fails at the job, the law faculty will be very wary of hiring an African American as its next dean. But if the dean is a white male who falls flat on his face, the law faculty is unlikely to be particularly circumspect about hiring a white male as its next dean. Clare Boothe Luce once remarked: "Because I am a woman, I must make unusual efforts to succeed. If I fail, no one will say, 'She doesn't have what it takes.' They will say, 'Women don't have what it takes.'"[6]

The final argument that might induce the African American middle class to participate in a self-help program is based on simple necessity (and perhaps a little altruism). Middle-class African Americans are in the best—and the only—position to help redirect the behavior patterns, values, and attitudes of the underclass and to offer advice to other African Americans. Because of racial kinship, working-class and poor African Americans may be willing to allow a "brother" or "sister" into their lives to teach them, in words and by example, how to survive comfortably and how to excel, psychologically as well as materially, in a society still struggling with discriminatory traditions and racism.

Helping individuals help themselves in this context is a chore with an important psychological component. One must be able to assert, from one's own experience, what I call the African American survival maxim: *You have the right to be angry about centuries of racial exploitation as well as present-day racism and racial discrimination. But you do not have the right to dwell on that anger, to feel guilty about these matters, to suffer low self-esteem, or to react in other self-destructive ways."* It would be difficult for most middle-class whites, however well intentioned, to be close enough to an African American individual or family to offer this type of tough advice. The element of race mitigates against most white people being able to win the trust and respect necessary to function as teachers in the program I have proposed. Moreover, few middle-class whites are informed or sophisticated enough to grasp the psychological ramifications of the African American experience in this country. Attempts by whites to deal with questions such as racial sensibility or "sorriness" risk being not only maladroit but even harmful. If these observations are even partly correct, then it becomes imperative for middle-class African Americans to make this intensive self-help program succeed.

African American Working and Poverty Classes

The concept of household support calls on working-class and poor African Americans to learn and practice the survival techniques necessary in a racist society; to jettison values and behaviors that are dysfunctional and self-defeating; and to adopt certain features of white middle-class culture while drawing from the strengths of African American culture—becoming, in a sense, bicultural in order to succeed in mainstream society. Some working-class and poor African Americans may look askance at both these general tasks and the particulars discussed earlier in the chapter. Some may find it extremely difficult to sacrifice for an uncertain future, especially in a society that emphasizes instant gratification. Others may reject the idea of adapting to mainstream America, seeing this as a form of Booker T. Washington accommodationism or, worse, a contemporary version of Uncle Tomming.[7]

These are difficult and important issues. Clearly, it is not easy to advise anyone to forego an immediate and certain pleasure in favor of a promise of better times ahead, especially if the good times are likely to go to someone else. Particularly in underclass households, where families simply try to survive one day at a time, conditions do not lend themselves to this type of logic or custom.

But the ability to sacrifice and persevere toward long-term goals is not entirely chimerical in underclass communities. For example, African American teenage mothers, like all mothers, desire a better future for their loved ones, and most are prepared to do what they can to attain that end. Moreover, matriarchal sacrifice and struggle for children and family are deeply rooted in African American culture. For more than three centuries, African American mothers have scrubbed floors, washed clothes, and raised children for white people from dawn to dusk just to feed, clothe, and shelter their own families. In so doing, they have taken nothing for themselves except the hope for a better life for their children.

Indeed, it is precisely because African American women have been willing to "pay off the mortgage" so that their children might live a less encumbered life that the concept of "mother" is so revered in African American culture. Blood has been spilled and lives even lost in the African American community in defense of a mother's honor. Teenage mothers must tap into the tradition of the African American matriarch to find strength to "pay off the mortgage." Middle-class African Americans need to help them discover this tradition through information sharing and coaching.

Knowledge of African American history and culture may also help motivate underclass males to participate in a self-help program on a long-term basis. African American men, too, have made tremendous sacrifices for their families—long hours of backbreaking menial labor amid a constant barrage of racial insults that rip away at one's dignity. Better-known African American men of achievement can also serve as models and inspiration—Prince Hall, Frederick Douglass, E. E. Just, W. E. B. DuBois, Charles Houston, A. Philip Randolph, Paul Robeson, Martin Luther King, Jr., Thurgood Marshall, A. Leon Higginbotham, Jr., Jesse Jackson, and others. It is only by understanding that African American men have been the "marines" in the struggle against racial bigotry and discrimination—the first to go and the first to die—that an African American youth can begin to draw strength from his heritage. Middle-class African Americans must help the underclass youth discover the best of African American culture, for society will surely remind him of the worst.

Sacrifice and perseverance are framed by two other important elements of African American culture. One is the role of the church as both a community leader and a spiritual force in African American society. African Americans have traditionally relied on the church for wisdom and direction in the secular world; it has never been simply a weekend spiritual retreat. The church has had an important and diurnal presence in the lives of African Americans, supplying a steady stream of well-educated, middle-class intellectuals and activists who were just as interested in re-forming society as in reforming the soul. Adam Clayton Powell, Jr., Vernon Johns, Martin Luther King, Jr., Jesse Jackson, and countless other ministers operating on a smaller scale are known more for their social engineering than for their religious crusades, although some would not separate the two.

The belief that American society is hostile is another major element of the African American heritage. One need only peruse the writing of African American intellectuals to see this negative, suspicious view of society ("the system" or "the Man"). Society as more foe than friend is a strong theme in African American literature from Langston Hughes to Arna Bontemps to Gwendolyn Brooks, from Richard Wright to Ralph Ellison to James Baldwin, from Maya Angelou to Toni Morrison to Alice Walker.

To motivate their participation in a serious program of self-help, African Americans from the working class and the poverty class must come to see that sacrifice, perseverance, the church, and an understanding of "the system" connect in a way that informs a unique worldview—a distinct African American perspective—that is difficult, if not impossible, for white Americans to access intellectually and emotionally. This perspective acknowledges that life is especially hard and unfair for African Americans, but it also asserts that they always find the strength to pull through. African American culture thus becomes a point of racial pride and a rallying cry all in one.

Does household support constitute accommodationism or Uncle Tomming? Is it a form of what might be called "neo-Negroism" for middle-class African Americans to ask others to duplicate their successes? Is the price of success cultural suicide—and thus too high? The answer to each of these questions is a definite no.

One must begin with the traditional definition of culture: the sum of the behaviors, values, and attitudes that differentiate one group of people from another. Culture is transmitted intergenerationally through stories, poems, songs, and other forms of written and spoken language; through family structure, religious practices, and similar institutions; through art, sculpture, architecture, and other physical objects; and through rituals such as dance, holidays, and celebrations. Groups usually choose, inherit, and shape their own culture; but some aspects of culture are often thrust upon a group by external conditions, such as poverty or physical isolation from the dominant culture. Culture has both "good" and "bad" elements. The work ethic is a positive cultural trait in the dominant American culture; racism and sexism are not.[8]

Based on this definition of culture, one must conclude that there are several cultures among African Americans, each manifested roughly along class lines. The underclass subculture, for example, is distinct from those of the middle class, the working class, and even other groups of poor African Americans. In addition, some of the elements of the underclass subculture—such as crime, drugs, and welfare dependency—are clearly "bad," in the sense that they are harmful to individuals in the group, to other African Americans, and to society as a whole. Many of these norms and behaviors are influenced by the isolation of the underclass from mainstream society and its opportunities. The group thus has no choice but to make its own opportunities in order to survive. With the help of governmental resources, these "bad" cultural elements can and must be cut away from the underclass subculture, changing its character altogether. I do not see this as accommodationism or Uncle Tomming. I see it as common sense.

African American culture is by no means a balkanized culture, however. There are certain customs and values among African Americans that transcend socioeconomic boundaries. African American culture also has elements that are both similar to and different from the mainstream, white American culture.

Commitment to excellence and an emphasis on education and work are among the behaviors, values, and attitudes that African Americans as a group hold in common not only with mainstream society but also with various other racial or ethnic groups in the United States. Both African Americans and whites must understand that these cultural traits are not owned by white Americans alone. And African Americans must realize that striving for the highest grade in class and performing one's job to the best of one's abilities do not constitute "selling out" or becoming an Uncle Tom. These are things African Americans have traditionally and unabashedly believed in and practiced, things that any racial or ethnic group must do to succeed in American society.

Cultural differences between African Americans and whites may be more significant than their cultural similarities, however. Although some of these differences are undoubtedly the product of the African American's African roots, most probably result from centuries of racial exclusion and forced adaptation or resistance to racial subordination. Many of these differences are real sources of strength, as discussed earlier, and can help African Americans excel. But others can be liabilities in the dominant culture and should be recognized as such.

One of these cultural liabilities may involve the language style of African American children who are isolated in the inner city or in rural communities.[9] These children sometimes speak a cultural dialect known as "Black English," a dialect that is not well understood in mainstream society. This language is not a bastardization of standard English, as some have supposed. Rather, it is a language with its own grammar, meaning, and linguistic integrity. It is to standard English what the Mexican or Cuban dialect is to standard Spanish.[10] It is also a cultural liability in the sense that one cannot advance very far in the dominant culture using only "Black English," for standard English is the principal language used in education, employment, and all other major fields of endeavor in our society.

As most minorities who have attained a measure of socioeconomic success well know, the dominant American culture does not accommodate unique languages, customs, or other minority cultural traits. If a minority expects to succeed in the white world, these legitimate cultural phenomena must be "suspended," as it were. Like other groups in American society who retain their cultural identities, African Americans must master the dominant culture, bring it with them to work or to school, and leave their own culture at home or use it at appropriate times. To state that African Americans must become bilingual and bicultural is a statement of fact about life in modern American society. It is not an assertion about racial ideology, be it accommodationism or otherwise. This is the message that middle-class African Americans must get across to their African American brothers and sisters.

As there is with any proposal, there is an element of uncertainty that attaches to this program of self-help. I am betting, however, on the recognition of self-interest, on the recognition of necessity coupled with altruism, and on the strengths of African American culture to bring this program to fruition. But I will be satisfied (for the moment) if I have succeeded in devising a logical matrix that points African Americans in the right direction.

Chapter Six

Governmental Remedies

If Charles Murray is correct, then this book should have ended with Chapter 5. Expressing the traditional conservative view of the disadvantaged, which contains elements of the "blame the victim" school of thought, Murray proposes a program that, in his own words, "consists of scrapping the entire federal welfare and income-support structure for working-aged persons, including AFDC, Medicaid, Food Stamps, Unemployment Insurance, Worker's Compensation, subsidized housing, disability insurance and the rest. It would leave the working-aged person with no recourse whatsoever except the job market, family members, friends and public or private locally funded services."[1]

Applied to the American race problem, this prescription would rely entirely on African American self-help. What the government and the public must come to accept, however, is that *no* amount of self-help alone can solve this problem. Governmental remedies—resources beyond the means or control of any group of private citizens, African American or white—are needed, in addition to self-help, to address the problems of intra-class racial disparity described earlier in this book. Discrimination and segregation in employment and housing, institutional discrimination, poor primary education, and low African American college enrollment cannot be ended without government assistance. Governmental remedies, working concurrently with an intensive program of African American self-help, offer the only realistic way to resolve America's oldest social and moral dilemma.

The federal government needs to provide both legal and economic remedies. Legal remedies are necessary primarily to correct intra-class racial disparities facing the African American middle and working classes. To be effective, these remedies must end the underlying problem of racial subordination. This means that the racial omission and racial integration tenets must be reimplemented to give greater priority to the civil rights interests of middle-class and working-class African Americans in employment, housing, and education. Some poor African Americans (the working poor, for example) could also benefit from these remedies.

Economic remedies deal with the most pressing intra-class racial disparity encountered by the African American poor—which is the existence of a comparatively large underclass—and with the problem of poverty in general. An employment opportunities program is the only way the government can give adequate weight to the primary civil rights interest of the African American poor, an opportunity to achieve a decent standard of living. This employment program must include job training and creation, income transfers, and child care services, tailored to fit the American context.

By that, I mean that such a program must recognize and accept the limited role of government in the American liberal democratic state. The compact between government and the individual in American society provides for limited social services, unlike socialistic societies. American society does not seek to *guarantee* the basic necessities or "achievements" of life—adequate employment, food, shelter, clothing, and so on—from cradle to grave. Nor does it seek to guarantee an individual's personal happiness or psychological well-being. It seeks only to create *opportunities* that will enable individuals to take care of themselves, to maximize their personal happiness. It is the responsibility of the individual, not the government, to satisfy personal needs, be they material or emotional.

The limited role of government is a major reason why self-help on the part of African Americans is a necessary component of any strategy for solving the American race problem. A self-help program must enable poor and working-class African Americans to take advantage of government-created opportunities for personal success. It must be able to move struggling African Americans into position to take advantage of decent housing and good education, to compete effectively for better jobs, and to excel in these jobs once they get them.

Thus, the only realistic strategy involves both a role for government and a role for African Americans themselves. The responsibilities of African Americans were discussed in Chapter 5; the responsibilities of the government are the subject of this chapter.

Legal Remedies

In several respects, racial omission and racial integration are poor proxies for formal equal opportunity. They are sometimes at odds with each other, as in the case of racial occupancy controls, in which racial omission suggests that we should tolerate resegregation, whereas racial integration commands just the opposite. Moreover, neither operational premise is sufficiently faithful to racial inclusion, which is the spirit, the social goal, the sine qua non of formal equal opportunity, as discussed in Chapter 1. Instead of opening opportunities for African Americans in employment, color blindness has too often led to the rejection or discharge of competent African American applicants or employees or to the denial of other employment opportunities. Instead of creating opportunities for African Americans in education, racial mixing has often resulted in the firing of competent African American administrators and teachers and in the use of African American children as cannon fodder in the war to capture white pupils. None of this is what the lawyers who argued *Brown I* before the Supreme Court had in mind.

I do not, however, advocate that federal judges or Congress abandon racial omission and racial integration as guideposts in implementing formal equal opportunity. On balance, they have been useful to African Americans, wise guides for making this a better society. But I do advocate that federal decision makers and policy makers give greater attention and weight to the societal objective of formal equal opportunity—racial inclusion. We should not allow the tail to wag the dog. Racial omission and racial integration (formal equal opportunity) are simply different paths to racial inclusion; they are not the be-all and end-all of civil rights.

The legal reforms proposed here attempt to address the problem of racial subordination in ways that for the most part are consistent with racial omission and racial integration but ultimately are supportive of racial inclusion. At the same time, these proposals do not unnecessarily trammel the interests of white Americans.[2] They are based, then, on the premise that civil rights policy is fundamentally a mechanism by which the historically *excluded* are *included* in mainstream society and its power centers, a process by which they are given access to America's bounties as first-class, not second-class, citizens.

The African American Middle Class

Legal remedies must be devised to redress the racial subordination of this class's civil rights interests in equal employment opportunity, equal housing opportunity, and equal educational opportunity in college and graduate schools, which result in intra-class disparities between middle-class African Americans and whites. This section describes legal remedies designed to deal with the employment problem; discussion of problems in housing and higher education is deferred to the next section, which focuses on the African American working class.

The legal reforms needed to promote the equal employment opportunity interest of the African American middle class are not terribly complicated. The government must simply cure certain defects in Title VII antidiscrimination law and in racial preference, or affirmative action, law. Once these legal reforms are in place, middle-class African Americans will have the resources to deal with employment problems such as complex racial discrimination, conspicuous racial stratification in high-level employment, stress and hypertension, loneliness, and disaffection.

Title VII antidiscrimination law should be reformed in five specific areas.[3] First, the burden of persuasion concerning the defendant's justification for the appearance of discrimination in individual disparate-treatment cases should be placed on the defendant rather than on the plaintiff. The defendant would then have the burden of persuading the trier of fact as to the veracity of its own "legitimate, nondiscriminatory reason" for the apparent discrimination. This modification in statutory gloss regarding the allocation of the burden of persuasion seems fair and rational, because the defendant is in the best, if not the only, position to know its own true motivations. Since the time of James Thayer, Judge Charles Clark, and other pioneers in evidence and civil litigation, it has always been deemed fair and reasonable to place the burden of persuasion, as well as the burden of allegation, as to a particular item of evidence on the party in control of such evidence.[4] Also, shifting the burden of persuasion to the defendant, and thereby easing the plaintiff's burden, would further the congressional design behind Title VII—which is to open employment opportunities for African Americans in occupations that have been traditionally closed to them—because plaintiffs would be in a better position to win more Title VII cases. Placing the burden of persuasion on the defendant could also help deter perjured evidence, which frequently occurs in civil cases.[5]

Second, the taint standard should replace the substantial-factor standard as the standard of causation in disparate-treatment cases. A Title VII plaintiff should be able to prove a case of disparate-treatment discrimination merely by showing that the unfavorable treatment in question was motivated in some part, however small, by an impermissible criterion, rather than having to prove that the unfavorable treatment was substantially motivated by an impermissible criterion. This particular reform not only would further the congressional intent behind Title VII but also would be clearly in line with the Supreme Court's own view that Title VII tolerates no racial discrimination, subtle or otherwise, in the implementation of employment decisions.[6]

Third, the bifurcated litigation model should be adopted over the unitary litigation model in mixed-motive cases. Under the bifurcated litigation model, adopted by Judge Gesell but later overturned by the Supreme Court in *Price Waterhouse v. Hopkins*, a distinction is drawn between liability and remedy. The plaintiff's burden of proof goes to the issue of liability, and the defendant's goes to the issue of remedy. If the plaintiff proves that the action of the defendant (the employer) was motivated by an impermissible criterion, either slightly or substantially, the plaintiff is able to prove disparate-treatment discrimination and, unless there is an affirmative defense, a violation of Title VII. The employer can then escape the imposition of certain Title VII remedies by proving that it would have taken the same action without the impermissible motive.

Although this model does not provide relief in the form of back pay or reinstatement for the plaintiff if the employer meets its burden, it does make it easier for the plaintiff to prove employment discrimination. Not only is this in line with Title VII's ultimate aim of promoting racial inclusion, but it also enhances Title VII's deterrence value, because when a finding of liability is made, an injunction may be issued against future acts of discrimination by the employer, who can be cited for contempt of court if the injunction is violated. The plaintiff's attorneys' fees—often a substantial amount—may also be shifted to the employer.

Some might argue that the bifurcated litigation model, by making it easier for the plaintiff to prove discrimination, would encourage the filing of frivolous employment discrimination cases under Title VII. This seems unlikely, however, because the plaintiff must still pass through the EEOC and its administrative apparatus before getting to court,[7] and there is no reason to believe that a plaintiff, having been advised by counsel that personal relief may not be forthcoming even if liability is established, would proceed to court or even proceed to file a charge with the EEOC without a serious case.

Fourth, the employer's evidentiary burden in mixed-motive cases should be governed by the clear and convincing evidence standard rather than by the preponderance of evidence standard. Given the fact that the employer, as Justice O'Connor recognizes in her concurring opinion, "has created the uncertainty as to causation by knowingly giving substantial weight to an impermissible criterion,"[8] it seems fair that the employer should bear the responsibility of clarifying the issue of causation convincingly.

Fifth, judicial hostility to applying Title VII's antidiscrimination provisions to high-level employment is simply an abdication of judicial responsibility. There is nothing in Title VII's legislative history to support the denial of Title VII relief to minorities who are corporate managers and professionals. Federal judges must faithfully apply Title VII to all jobs, at whatever level.

It is important to note that none of these proposed changes in Title VII law is incompatible with the racial omission tenet; each one also promotes racial inclusion. Placing the burden of persuasion on the defendant, switching to the taint standard of causation, adoption of the bifurcated litigation model and clear and convincing evidentiary standard in mixed-motive cases, and judicial fidelity to Title VII via-à-vis high-level employment are in fact *more* consistent with the racial omission tenet and *more* supportive of racial inclusion than is current Title VII law. Jointly and individually, these changes would augment Title VII's effectiveness and would result in the successful prosecution or deterrence of more employers bent on using race in an exclusionary manner or to otherwise discriminate against African Americans.

Even if Title VII were improved along the lines suggested above, the problems of complex racial discrimination and segregation in employment would not be solved, however, for litigating an employment discrimination case would still be unthinkable in the minds of many astute African American professionals. Title VII litigation at this level can be protracted—it has taken as long as eleven years in some cases—and whether one wins or loses, the plaintiff carries the stigma of being a troublemaker, which can hound him or her for years. For this reason, even some successful litigants have discouraged other individuals from suing employers, and some civil rights lawyers refuse outright to represent plaintiffs in employment discrimination suits against high-level employers.[9]

Other than better public enforcement of Title VII antidiscrimination law (in which the government, rather than an applicant or an employee, becomes the plaintiff), this de facto loophole can be closed only through improvements in racial preference law. If African Americans were hired or promoted in greater numbers, there would be fewer reasons for individuals to bring employment discrimination lawsuits and thus place themselves in jeopardy. This, of course, is not the major reason for improving racial preference law—primarily, such improvements would end discrimination that escapes detection under current Title VII law and promote racial inclusion, thereby making our pluralistic society a better place for all to live.

One way to improve racial preference law is to collapse constitutional racial preference law into statutory racial preference law—that is, the Constitution's strict scrutiny test could be abolished for all racial classifications in favor of Title VII's test. The latter requires a twofold inquiry: does the racial classification in question (whether or not it favors minorities) promote racial inclusion; and, if so, does it unnecessarily trammel the interests of the group it disadvantages (usually white males)? Application of this test would give public-sector employers the same ability that private-sector employers now have to create racial preference programs for the purpose of correcting racially imbalanced workforces. This proposal is presented in greater detail in the following section.

The African American Working Class

Legal remedies for this class must address the problem of racial subordination in three areas: employment, housing, and both primary and higher education. One of the most important remedies in the area of employment involves Title VII.

The African American working class encounters many of the same obstacles with Title VII that the middle class confronts, and the reforms proposed in the preceding section would also benefit the working class. But working-class African Americans face the additional problem of not having the financial resources or the time to become involved in drawn-out civil rights litigation. Thus the Title VII reforms offered for the middle class will not be sufficient for the working class or the working poor; a much more radical change in Title VII is required.

Specifically, Title VII needs to be restructured. The EEOC, the government agency charged with enforcing Title VII, should be reconstituted into the Equal Employment Administration (EEA) and given the power to sue on behalf of individuals on its own initiative (as well as the power to bring pattern or practice cases, a power the EEOC currently possesses). Plaintiffs in low-income brackets would thus be given free legal representation. Equally important, a new federal agency, the Equal Employment Commission (EEC), should be established and, unlike the EEOC, given quasi-judicial powers. This means the EEC (like the FHC, discussed in conjunction with housing law reforms) would have the power to issue precedent-setting rulings in employment cases, which could be reviewed by either the federal district courts or the federal appellate courts. Title VII cases would be adjudicated more quickly in a forum set aside to hear only those cases. The remedial powers under Title VII would basically remain unchanged, with the exception that compensatory damages (including damages for emotional distress), punitive damages, and cease-and-desist orders would be added. These modifications would give working-class and poor African Americans incentive to sue and a fighting chance of success, thereby augmenting the deterrence value of Title VII.

This restructuring of Title VII is compatible with the racial omission tenet and would promote racial inclusion. The proposed changes could aid in the prosecution of employment discrimination and, to that extent, deter future discrimination. Low-income African Americans would thus have greater and more equal access to America's employment markets.

Antidiscrimination law in housing must also be reformed. Three specific areas require the most serious attention. First, the effects test must be restored as a standard of liability in housing litigation under the equal protection clause. The effects test should be treated *pari passu* (on an equal footing) with the intent test, because if a zoning law or referendum effectively excludes African Americans from a residential area, the defendant's state of mind is, at that moment, immaterial. What is most important to African Americans is the fact that they are discriminated against and denied housing. From that perspective, which some lower federal courts have accepted but which the Supreme Court has not, the pain is the same regardless of the defendant's intent. In short, placing the effects test on an equal footing with the intent test would allow minorities to challenge a state, city, or municipal land-use barrier on the grounds of its exclusionary effects as well as on the basis of any invidious motivation behind it.

It is true that the intent test can be circumvented by using federal laws other than the equal protection clause to attack land-use restrictions. But these laws—the Fair Housing Act and Section 1982—contain other features that severely limit their usefulness as an alternative to the equal protection clause. Matters are not appreciably improved at the state level, for the states offer an uneven scheme of civil rights protection and procedural laws that on the whole are not as advanced as federal law.

Damage awards (monetary relief) in housing litigation is a second area where reform is needed. Judges and juries must begin to award more generous damages in housing cases. Larger awards not only would make litigation under the Fair Housing Act and Section 1982 cost-efficient but also would deter would-be discriminators.

Finally, and perhaps most important, the Fair Housing Act must be completely overhauled. A Fair Housing Administration (FHA) should be created and given enforcement powers. Specifically, the FHA would have the power to investigate and settle charges of housing discrimination under the Fair Housing Act, the power to represent an aggrieved individual in a lawsuit, and the power to sue on its own behalf to challenge a pattern or practice of unlawful behavior. In addition, the FHA would have similar authority to bring individual and systemic cases under Section 1982.

A Fair Housing Commission (FHC) should also be created and given quasi-judicial powers, perhaps modeled after the California Fair Employment and Housing Commission (FEHC), created under the California Fair Employment and Housing Act.[10] The FHC, whose decisions could be appealed to either the federal district courts or federal appellate courts, would have the power to render precedent-setting decisions in housing disputes arising under the Fair Housing Act and Section 1982, whether these cases were brought by the FHA or by private parties. The FHC would also have statutory authority to grant both attorneys' fees and a wide variety of relief: administrative cease-and-desist orders, civil penalties, and compensatory and punitive damages.

A revised Fair Housing Act would also abolish both the "Mrs. Murphy's boardinghouse" and the single-family house exemptions. These exemptions currently place a significant section of the housing market outside the reach of federal antidiscrimination law. Such exemptions should be unacceptable, because they certainly do not promote racial inclusion.

Some of these housing reforms have already been enacted in the 1988 amendments to the Fair Housing Act.[11] Rather than creating a separate enforcement agency similar to my FHA, the amendments provide the Secretary of Housing and Urban Development with powers to investigate and conciliate charges of housing discrimination. Although HUD is given no prosecutorial powers, it is authorized to forward individual or class action cases to the Justice Department for prosecution. The Justice Department can also litigate class actions on its own initiative. Most meritorious complaints filed by aggrieved individuals are not likely to be prosecuted, however, because the Justice Department, operating on limited resources, will undoubtedly continue to commit most of its lawyers to criminal prosecutions, civil class actions, and glamorous, high-profile civil actions involving individuals and corporations, such as antitrust and securities violations. For this reason, a separate enforcement agency like the proposed FHA, devoted to the "smaller" case is a better alternative.

Instead of creating a separate quasi-judicial agency similar to my FHC, the amendments allow cases to be heard before administrative law judges, whose decisions are enforceable in federal court. An aggrieved party, however, can bypass the administrative process and sue directly in federal court. A federal judge can award attorneys' fees and can even appoint an attorney at the public's expense. A rich array of administrative and judicial remedies also come with the amendments: preliminary injunctions; actual and punitive damages; and civil penalties ranging from $10,000 to $50,000, which an administrative law judge can impose, and from $50,000 to $100,000, which a federal judge can assess in class actions.

The amendments do not, however, end any of the important exemptions. Owners of boardinghouses and single-family houses can still legally discriminate. There is little doubt that the amendments are a great improvement over the preexisting law, which was on the books for twenty years before being amended. It is equally clear, however, that the amendments do not go far enough and that more should have been done along the lines suggested here.

Each of my proposed changes in housing law is compatible with the racial omission tenet and promotes racial inclusion without unnecessarily hurting white Americans. Indeed, restoring the effects test as an alternative standard of liability under the equal protection clause, providing more liberal monetary relief in all successful housing litigation (promised in the 1988 amendments), and further restructuring of the Fair Housing Act would allow better implementation of the racial omission tenet and give a stronger boost to racial inclusion than existing housing law does. These modifications not only would end existing forms of legalized racial exclusion in housing but also would expand the prosecution of illegal housing discrimination and segregation and, to that extent, would effectively deter future discriminators.

In the area of primary education, two kinds of reforms are needed, one for integrated schools and the other for racially isolated schools. In integrated schools, African American administrators and teachers must be given greater control over matters concerning the curriculum, student placement, and discipline, as a safeguard against the racial disparities discussed in Chapter 3, including second-generation discrimination and resegregation.

For racially isolated schools, modification of the standard of liability in single-district and multidistrict school desegregation cases is a badly needed reform. As in the housing context, the effects test must be brought in as an additional standard of liability. Plaintiffs must be able to use either standard of liability to invoke a federal court's remedial power under the equal protection clause. If the existence of a one-race school or district cannot be justified on nonracial grounds, its very existence should be sufficient to open the door to a plethora of remedies by the federal courts. Once the door is open, the plaintiffs can then select educational remedies tailored to their particular needs and paid for by public funds—remedial or intensive education in the fundamentals, an African American awareness program, racial mixing, or other plans. In the absence of a racial antecedent to the creation of a racially isolated school, a self-help program like the one discussed in Chapter 5 offers the best chance for improving the quality of education in African American schools, although, of course, it cannot adequately address the issues of racial mixing or cultural diversity.[12]

Recognition of the effects test in equal protection litigation is not a radical or unrealistic legal reform. Neither the single-intent nor the multiple-intent standard of liability is to be found anywhere in the Fourteenth Amendment or in its legislative history. The intent test is a legal standard fashioned by judges, and the same judicial creativity that produced the intent test could establish the effects test as an alternative standard of liability under the equal protection clause.

In higher education, the racially inhospitable admissions process created by *Bakke* must be altered. One desirable change seems fairly uncomplicated: it would simply entail evaluating an applicant's "whole person." Given that *Bakke* allows for the subtle use of race in the admissions process, it seems logical to conclude that an admission decision based in part on an African American applicant's unique experience would not be legally inappropriate. An admissions officer can look at traditional academic indicators but can also give substantial weight to other factors that may be more predictive of academic success— motivation (which is an extremely important predictor for African American students),[13] recommendations, personal interviews, family history, and a general evaluation of the obstacles the applicant has overcome.

Bakke's treatment of racial quotas is a more difficult form of racial subordination to remedy. Although the *Bakke* decision cannot be viewed as a clear statement of equal protection law, subsequent Supreme Court decisions have adopted in principle Justice Powell's understanding of the equal protection clause. It now appears that an explicit racial classification, such as an admissions quota, will be struck down under the equal protection clause unless prior intentional racial discrimination can be proved. In other words, the strict scrutiny test, along with its incorporation of the intent test, applies even though the racial classification may be intended to benefit minorities.

One way to deal with the strict scrutiny test in this context is to, again, allow plaintiffs to use the effects test to prove past racial discrimination. An admissions process that has a disproportionate impact on African American applicants and that cannot be justified on nonracial grounds should be deemed to be just as violative of the equal protection clause as an admissions process tainted by discriminatory intent. In either case, the court should be allowed to use its remedial powers to impose an admissions quota on the institution in question. This quota would require the institution to set aside several slots in each class for which African American applicants would compete among themselves.

It would also permit the institution to create special academic support programs for African American enrollees.

The effects test is not an efficient way to invoke an African American admissions quota, however. Litigation, which is needed to bring the effects test into play, is too time-consuming, costly, and ad hoc. A more systemic approach is needed, one that would allow *voluntary* adoption of an admissions quota. This would necessitate a change in constitutional racial preference law, a frontal assault on the strict scrutiny test.

Several reforms in constitutional racial preference law have been proposed to deal with the strict scrutiny test. For example, while recognizing that some elevated level of judicial scrutiny is required when a public entity uses a racial classification, some members of the Supreme Court have proposed alternative levels of judicial scrutiny more flexible than the strict scrutiny test. Justices Marshall, Brennan, and Blackmun would sanction racial classifications that serve important governmental objectives and that are substantially related to the achievement of those objectives.[14] Justice Stevens would permit the use of a racial preference if the public interest vindicated by that use and the means employed to implement that interest justify the resulting adverse effects on the disadvantaged groups.[15] Any of these alternative tests seem acceptable, but I also believe that one can devise an easier and more efficient test as an alternative to the strict scrutiny test.

I would advocate abolishing the strict scrutiny test for all racial classifications and merging constitutional racial preference analysis with statutory racial preference analysis. Statutory racial preference law has advanced the greatest distance in the employment field, in which institutions covered by Title VII are allowed to establish voluntary racial preference programs as long as the programs are designed to promote racial inclusion and do not "unnecessarily trammel the interests" of the group disadvantaged by the racial classification. The racial inclusion element essentially means that the purpose of the racial preference must be to break down historical patterns of racial segregation and hierarchy or to otherwise open opportunities for minorities that have been traditionally closed to them. Thus, a racial preference designed to

promote racial inclusion is one that attempts "to change the outward and visible signs of yesterday's racial distinctions and, thus,
to provide an impetus to the process of dismantling the barriers,
psychological or otherwise, erected by past practices."[16]

There is no single way to define the Supreme Court's formulation concerning "unnecessarily trammeling the interests" of the
disadvantaged group. Basically, it means that the disadvantaged
group, often white males, must be treated fairly under the totality of the circumstances, which includes the purpose of the racial
preference program. Usually, this requirement is satisfied if
white males, for example, are not denied access to the opportunity or resource governed by the program and if the program is
"temporary" in the sense that it will expire when the racial imbalance is eradicated.[17]

Using this formula, the Supreme Court could uphold a college's use of an admissions quota for African Americans. By increasing the presence of African American students on college
campuses, such an admissions quota would operate to break
down old patterns of racial hierarchy and to provide an impetus
for dismantling existing educational barriers erected by past and
present racial subordination. These barriers include standardized
admissions tests such as the SAT, as well as the skepticism with
which many admissions officers and college professors view African American applicants. The educational interests of rejected
white applicants would be no more trammeled than the interests
of those who are rejected for other reasons (such as a student's
relatively poor academic record, the need for geographic diversity among the student body, a student's lack of legacy status, or
the need for substantial financial aid). Also a rejected white applicant would have access to other schools much more readily
than would a rejected African American applicant. Finally, the
racial preference program would expire when it was no longer
needed; it would not be intended to continue in perpetuity regardless of need.

Should the Supreme Court adopt this suggestion for replacing
the strict scrutiny test, the Court would also be in a position to
sustain the use of racial occupancy controls. Racial occupancy
controls operate to change the outward and visible signs of prior
racial subordination—namely, housing segregation—by maintain-

ing integrated neighborhoods. In addition, racial occupancy controls do not unnecessarily trammel the interests of whites, because whites and minorities would have at least an equal chance
of acceptance or rejection by the housing authority or municipality (in some cases, in fact, whites would have a *better* chance of
acceptance) and because the controls would expire once integration could be ensured. Racial occupancy controls, in short, could
do an excellent job of promoting the racial integration tenet and
racial inclusion.

Collapsing constitutional racial preference law into statutory racial preference law would greatly simplify all racial preference
law. By abolishing the strict scrutiny test for racial classifications,
this proposal would establish a single legal formula for determin-
ing the permissibility of all voluntary racial preference programs,
whether the programs favor minorities or whites. Courts would,
of course, retain their inherent equitable powers to impose a racial preference program on an institution as a remedy for a
proven violation of constitutional or statutory law. (In this case, it
would be necessary to have the effects test as an alternative standard of liability, in order to give African Americans a fighting
chance to prove a violation of constitutional law.)

Does the suggestion for replacing the strict scrutiny test frus-
trate the racial omission tenet? At first glance, it would appear
that it does, because it calls for the explicit use, rather than the
omission, of race. But matters are not that simple, especially not
in a society as complex as ours.

There is nothing intrinsically wrong with using race in lawmak-
ing or policy formulation. The Supreme Court uses race frequently in construing statutes and the Constitution. My proposal
is exactly patterned after the Supreme Court's use of race in the
Title VII context. I argue that constitutional and statutory racial
preference law should be merged. Hence, my proposal no more
frustrates the racial omission tenet than do the Supreme Courts'
affirmative action rulings under Title VII.

Some might argue that the Constitution calls for a more limited use of race than any statute does. Yet, there is nothing in the
Constitution itself that implies such a view of existing or future
acts of Congress relative to the Constitution. Clearly, Congress
could pass a statute on some matter that explicitly requires a

more limited use of race than is dictated under current constitutional law. Perhaps the only fair and logical thing to say is that some elevated level of judicial scrutiny is required when race is a factor in institutional decision making, because over the years institutions have established a terrible record in making decisions based on race.

Furthermore, my proposal uses race in a manner that is far different from its traditional use by institutions in our society. Here, race would be used to open opportunities for those groups traditionally excluded from mainstream society. This proposal is conscious of race for the purpose of promoting racial inclusion, which is the direction in which the racial omission tenet seeks to take society, not for the purpose of bolstering racial exclusion. This use of race, in short, is not invidious; it opens doors that would otherwise remain shut, forces institutions to consider individuals they otherwise would ignore, and makes for a better society.

Some would argue that any use of race is immoral, even if not illegal, because it sets up the individual as a sacrificial lamb. But morality cannot be determined solely by reference to the individual. As Plato understood, questions of morality and justice must be decided by considering the individual in relation to the design of society. And it is clear that the morality of society is enhanced when race is used to give traditionally excluded persons greater access to a better life.[18]

Economic Remedies

The economic remedies proposed here are designed to respond to racial subordination within the poverty class. The most striking intra-class racial disparity among poor Americans can be seen in existence of a relatively large African American underclass, particularly in the inner cities. These remedies attempt to compensate for the depletion of valuable community resources from African American urban communities, caused in part by the nation's drive toward racial integration. They give high priority to the primary civil rights interest of poor African Americans, the opportunity to achieve a decent standard of living. Once these economic remedies are in place, a program of African American self-help could be much more effective in overcoming the dysfunctional and self-destructive patterns of behaviors, values, and attitudes that plague the underclass subculture.

Taken as a whole, these economic remedies constitute an employment opportunities program. This program does not seek to guarantee a job to all African Americans; rather, it stresses employment opportunities. The program has three primary features: income transfers, employment and training, and child care. Some of these elements have already been incorporated into federal and state welfare or workfare plans, but not everyone in need of assistance (young African American men, for example) can qualify for these programs. Also, income maintenance, rather than employment opportunities, remains the mainstay of most welfare and workfare programs. The employment opportunities project described here could easily run concurrently with these traditional programs.

Any citizen over the age of thirteen whose family income is at or below the poverty line would be eligible for this program— female or male, married or single, regardless of race. Theoretically, and in terms of our focus here, the program should be race-specific, applying only to African Americans because of the uniquely invidious legacy of racial oppression and exclusion they face. Realistically, however, such a program would neither get through Congress nor garner the support of most white Americans. Political reality therefore necessitates extending it to all Americans on a needs-only basis. This effort would still have an appreciable effect on the employment problems of poor African Americans, particularly those from the underclass.

Income transfers, a subsistence allowance, would be provided only during transition periods, that is, when a participant is engaged in either job training or remedial education. This subsistence allowance could be increased to help cover transportation and child care expenses if needed. Following the philosophy of the earliest social welfare legislation, the amount of the subsistence allowance should be set below the lowest regional wage scale. To avoid undermining the work incentive, no one receiving public assistance would collect more than a worker earns. A housing subsidy and Medicaid would also be provided during transition periods. Both would continue for a time after the participant finds a job, unless the employer provides its own health insurance, in which case Medicaid would cease immediately.

Private-sector employment would be preferred over public-sector jobs. Federal, state, and local tax incentives could nurture private-sector employment within inner-city communities or the suburbs. Companies could own and operate their own bus services, creating jobs for drivers and mechanics, to transport workers from their inner-city homes to suburban job sites.

This program would not disturb the long standing American practice of having the government provide remedial education for the public (a practice that may, in any event, be changing).[19] It would, however, shift job training, traditionally performed at this level by the government, to the private sector. Moreover, this strategy is consistent with a recent trend in corporate educational gift-giving that favors primary schools over colleges and universities.[20] Rather than giving 20 percent of its charitable contributions to public schools, an employer would invest one-half or more of those funds in job training programs conducted at the workplace or at a recreational center, church, or YMCA located in the inner city. Whether the employer gives to public schools or to job training, the money serves the same purpose: it helps to create a well-trained work force.

The creation of job training programs should be more attractive to corporations than blind gift-giving to public schools, however, because job training provides employers with more control over the development of their work force. An employer-managed job training program is designed to teach skills that are most useful to the employer, that will eventually integrate the new workers into core product lines, that can lead to positions of growth in the company. Who is in a better position than the employer to assess its own developing job needs and to teach the requisite skills?

Some job training would necessarily be directed to low-skill employment, both because low-skill jobs are sometimes the only ones available and because some program participants will lack sufficient education for more highly skilled jobs. These individuals should be encouraged to establish a good track record in the positions they hold and to attend night school or community college to acquire the skills needed to compete for better opportunities within or outside the company. Many working persons, even those in workfare programs, have taken such classes to improve their level of education and, as a result, their employment outlook.

Child care could be handled in one of several ways. Under one approach, local school districts could provide care at taxpayer expense in the same way that public education is now provided to local communities. Full-time preschool programs could be set up, and after-school activities expanded to care for pupils in elementary grades. Jobless individuals from the poverty class could be trained and certified to staff these programs, providing employment opportunities for them at the same time. Although this approach would be expensive (child care workers *should* be paid a decent salary), for the parents it could offer convenience, relative safety, and affordability.

Another approach is for the government to provide an allowance for child care to program participants. This approach would give parents freedom to select from a wide range of services, from nationwide franchised operations to church-run centers to a neighbor who cares for three children in her own home. One major problem with this approach is that the allowances would have to be large enough to give parents a full range of choices; an annual allowance of as much as $3,000 to $5,000 would be needed. Another problem with this approach is that it does not address the critical shortage of quality child care. Unlike the first approach, this one deals only with the demand side of the child care problem, not with the supply side.

It might also be possible to have employers provide child care facilities on the job. As in the first approach, these facilities could be staffed by trained persons from the poverty class. The employer, the government, and the user would share in the cost of these facilities. This approach would, of course, add to the employer's cost of doing business (liability insurance would increase, for example), but it offers convenience and peace of mind for the parents, which results in happier and more productive employees.

Child care is expensive, no matter which approach is chosen. Massachusetts, for example, through its ET welfare program, paid about $3,500 a year for each child in 1986. But child care is also a vital service. We should not forget that government has in the past provided vital services deemed too risky or too expensive for individuals or the private sector to shoulder alone.[21]

Epilogue

One wishes it would disappear, like a bad dream at night's end. But the American race problem will not go away without creative energy and moral effort. We as a nation may find the strength on which to act if we hold in our hearts the vision articulated by John Donne: "Any man's death diminishes me, because I am involved in mankind; and therefore never send to know for whom the bell tolls; it tolls for thee."

In large part, the challenge of this book has been to bring some creative energy to the problem. I might summarize and round out the design of that endeavor by emphasizing three of the several themes advanced here.

The first is a general theme that ties the various parts and chapters of the book together. It states simply that no understanding or resolution of the American race problem in this day and age can be complete without giving serious attention to civil rights laws and policies and to the class divisions in African American society. Historically, the federal government has played the dominant role in creating and perpetuating social and economic disparities between the races; and it has done so largely through its enactment, interpretation, and application of civil rights laws and policies. That is reason enough to give close scrutiny to the impact of federal civil rights policies on African Americans today. Any complete analysis must also recognize the class stratification within African American society. To ignore the deep socioeconomic divisions carved out in that society is to miss an important element of reality in any discussion of the American race problem or civil rights.

The second and third themes are less sweeping than the first. The second argues that our fundamental civil rights policy—what

I have called "formal equal opportunity"—is conceptually sound but operationally flawed. I am not, in other words, prepared to conclude that our basic civil rights policy is conceptually flawed in the sense that it has only a philosophical attachment to equal opportunity and, as a result, does not go far enough to compensate for the socioeconomic position African Americans inherited from slavery and Jim Crow. Instead, I argue that the problem with formal equal opportunity is the way in which it has been applied since *Brown v. Board of Education*. This theme can help to forge a realistic understanding of the American race problem, one that is sensitive to both civil rights and class strata.

The final theme carries two qualifications. It argues that the American race problem can be resolved only by an intensive program of African American self-help *and* governmental assistance (legal and economic remedies) functioning concurrently. Government must open opportunities, as only government can, and African Americans must move themselves into position to take advantage of these new opportunities.

The qualifications to this theme are made in deference to reality. The first concerns governmental assistance—legal remedies in particular. Although it is always difficult to effect significant changes in civil rights laws and policies, it may be possible for civil rights advocates to win small victories, which can accumulate into large gains over time, by developing legal remedies designed to reimplement rather than destroy formal equal opportunity. If civil rights advocates can demonstrate that their proposals promote formal equal opportunity, if they can convince the government that they are not attempting to bring down the edifice of formal equal opportunity—that their proposals will not convert equality of opportunity into equality of results—then perhaps there is some hope for success, even in today's political climate. Such success is not guaranteed, however.

The second qualification states that although *joint* governmental and private action is crucial, certain socioeconomic conditions faced by African Americans can be appreciably improved with self-help alone. African Americans therefore should not put their lives on hold waiting for a governmental rescue, which I seriously doubt will come in this or the next generation. My skepticism is based neither on an assessment that the federal government is powerless to help African Americans (which it certainly is not) nor on the belief that the current political climate discourages effective governmental action (which it certainly does). Rather, it is predicated on a study of our civil rights legacy—including congressional and judicial application of formal equal opportunity— that has taught me several things. From slavery to today, the federal government has consistently demonstrated an unwillingness to share in or give any weight to an African American perspective on how racial problems should be solved. In addition, there are in fact legitimate (although not equally compelling) interests on both sides of the American race problem, and there is racism, the old enemy of African Americans. Consequently, an intensive program of self-help on the part of African Americans becomes imperative.

It is not outside the realm of possibility, of course, that the federal government will come through. But after three centuries of unsuccessful runs at the problem, one would have to be like Pollyanna to count on this. Nevertheless, the door remains open.

There is also the possibility that African Americans may not come through on their end of the deal, either. Perhaps they will not want to make the sacrifices necessary for a successful attempt at self-help.

Thus, the question posed at the beginning of this book—how can African Americans be accorded genuine equal opportunity in American society?—yields two large dilemmas, one involving all Americans, the other a private matter among African Americans. Only time can provide the answers. But our heads and hearts will be troubled until these dilemmas are resolved.

Notes

Preface

1. Gunnar Myrdal, *An American Dilemma: The Negro Problem and Modern Democracy* (New York: Harper and Brothers, 1944; New York: Pantheon, 1964). For a recent attempt to update Myrdal's study, describing the progress of African Americans from 1939 to the present as a glass half empty, see Gerald D. Jaynes and Robin M. Williams, Jr., eds., *A Common Destiny: Blacks and American Society* (Washington, D.C.: National Academy Press, 1989).

2. Charles Murray, *Losing Ground: American Social Policy, 1950–1980* (New York: Basic Books, 1984); Daniel P. Moynihan, *Family and Nation* (San Diego: Harcourt Brace Jovanovich, 1986); William Julius Wilson, *The Truly Disadvantaged: The Inner City, the Underclass, and Public Policy* (Chicago: University of Chicago Press, 1987).

3. Thomas Sowell, *The Economics and Politics of Race: An International Perspective* (New York: William Morrow, 1983). Sowell intensified his attack on civil rights one year later in his book *Civil Rights: Rhetoric or Reality?* (New York: William Morrow, 1984).

4. Glenn Loury, "The Better Path to Black Progress: Beyond Civil Rights," *New Republic*, October 7, 1985, pp. 22–25.

5. Reynolds Farley and Walter R. Allen, *The Color Line and the Quality of Life in America* (New York: Russell Sage Foundation, 1987), p. 261.

6. Derrick A. Bell, Jr., *And We Are Not Saved: The Elusive Quest for Racial Justice* (New York: Basic Books, 1987).

7. Jaynes and Williams, *A Common Destiny;* Kristin Bumiller, *The Civil Rights Society: The Social Construction of Victims* (Baltimore: Johns Hopkins University Press, 1988); Harold Crust, *Plural But Equal:*

Blacks and Minorities in America's Plural Society (New York: William Morrow, 1987).

Introduction

1. See, respectively, *City of Richmond v. J. A. Croson Co.*, 109 S. Ct. 706 (1989); *Martin v. Wilks*, 109 S. Ct. 2180 (1989); *Wards Cove Packing Co. v. Atonio*, 109 S. Ct. 2115 (1989); *Patterson v. McLean Credit Union*, 109 S. Ct. 2363 (1989).

2. *Wards Cove Packing Co. v. Atonio*, 109 S. Ct. 2115, 2136 (1989), Justice Blackmun dissenting with Justices Brennan and Marshall.

3. In analyzing what might come to be known as the Civil Rights Massacre of 1989, many have failed to notice that even the liberal justices on the Court (Brennan, Marshall, Blackmun, and Stevens) participated in some of the carnage. In a sex discrimination case that applies equally to race discrimination and is widely viewed as pro-plaintiff (*Price Waterhouse v. Hopkins*, 109 S. Ct. 1775 [1989]), the Supreme Court expressly declined to follow the lead of District Court Judge Gerhard Gesell and others in rulings that would have increased the deterrent value of Title VII of the 1964 Civil Rights Act, the nation's principal employment discrimination law, by making it easier for Title VII plaintiffs to establish liability where evidence of discrimination exists. See discussion of this decision in Chapter 2.

4. White Americans had their civil rights protected for many years, at least vis-à-vis African Americans, by the institution of slavery and Jim Crow laws. And with the end of slavery and Jim Crow, whites have found less use than African Americans for the protection offered by civil rights laws and policies, given the socioeconomic advantages they were bequeathed from history and given that racial discrimination is not randomly distributed in this society even today. For a good discussion of the distribution of socioeconomic advantage during the decade after Jim Crow, see Lester Thurow, *The Zero-Sum Society: Distribution and the Possibilities for Economic Change* (New York: Basic Books, 1980), pp. 184–187. For an excellent discussion of the uneven distribution of racial discrimination in society after Jim Crow, see George Schatzki, "United Steelworkers of America v. Weber: An Exercise in Understandable Indecision," *Washington Law Review* 56 (1980): 56–57.

5. See, e.g., John Hope Franklin, *From Slavery to Freedom: A History of Negro Americans*, 3d ed. (New York: Vintage Books, 1969); A. Leon Higginbotham, Jr., *In the Matter of Color: Race and the American Legal Process—The Colonial Period* (New York: Oxford University Press, 1978); Juan Williams, *Eyes on the Prize: America's Civil Rights Years, 1954–1965* (New York: Viking, 1987).

6. Pub. L. No. 89–110, 79 Stat. 445 (1965) (codified as amended at 42 U.S.C. § 1971 [1982]).

Before we can assess the remaining political inequality, African Americans will have to register and vote in greater numbers. African Americans do not register and vote as often as they can and should. No doubt, in some areas, they continue to face restrictive barriers such as at-large elections, gerrymandering, and annexation of voting districts, all covered in the Voting Rights Act. But, as some African American leaders expressed at a 1988 conference on policy issues convened by the Joint Center for Political Studies, voter registration and mobilization are the primary tools for increasing African American political power. See "Black Leaders Gather at the Fifth National Policy Institute to Discuss Critical Policy Issues," Conference Report, *Focus*, May 1988, pp. 7–8.

7. In 1964, for example, 49.6 percent of all African Americans lived in poverty, compared to 14.9 percent of all whites (William Kornblum and Joseph Julian, *Social Problems*, 6th ed. [Englewood Cliffs, N.J.: Prentice-Hall, 1989], p. 232). And in 1940, the first year a question concerning occupation was included in the census, 37 percent of African American males worked as domestic servants or laborers, compared to 9 percent of white males; and 6 percent of African American males held white-collar jobs, compared to 36 percent of white males (U.S. Bureau of the Census, *Sixteenth Census of the United States: 1940, Population* [Washington, D.C.: U.S. Government Printing Office, 1940], vol. 3, pt. 1, table 61). See also Farley and Allen, *Color Line*, pp. 256–270.

See Chapter 2 for a discussion of the recent growth of the African American middle class.

8. See, e.g., John J. Macionis, *Sociology* (Englewood Cliffs, N.J.: Prentice-Hall, 1987), pp. 218, 236–239.

9. See, e.g., *Hazelwood School District v. United States*, 433 U.S. 299, 308n.14 (1977) (relying on statistical methods employing this theory); Melvin Humphrey, *Black Experience Versus Black Expectations*, Research Report no. 53 (Washington, D.C.: Equal Employment Opportunity Commission, 1977), p. 27.

10. Farley and Allen, *Color Line*, p. 6.

11. Wilson, *The Truly Disadvantaged*.

12. See, e.g., National Opinion Research Center, *General Surveys* (Chicago: National Opinion Research Center, 1983), p. 234.

13. See, e.g., Higginbotham, *In the Matter of Color*, p. 61 (quoting Lorenzo G. Green, *The Negro in Colonial New England, 1620–1776* [New York: Columbia University Press, 1942], p. 17); Franklin, *From Slavery to Freedom*, pp. 101–102.

14. Maybe the government has been leveling with us in a way. The Reagan administration and now the Supreme Court have been demonstrably opposed to civil rights, although neither would say so. Speaking for the Bush administration, Vice-President Dan Quayle announced at the NAACP's 1989 annual convention that "all Americans," including government, must help resolve the problems African Americans face (*San Diego Tribune*, July 12, 1989), but such pronouncements are often made simply as a matter of politics.

15. See Chapter 4 for a discussion of the changing composition of the poverty class.

16. Martin Luther King, Jr., *Stride Toward Freedom: The Montgomery Story*, Perennial Library ed. (New York: Harper and Row, 1964), p. 199.

17. 42 U.S.C. §§ 2000e–2000e-17 (1982).

18. 42 U.S.C. §§ 3601–3617 (1982); 42 U.S.C. § 1982 (1982). The Fair Housing Act was recently amended (Fair Housing Amendments Act of 1988, P.L. 100–430, 102 Stat. 1619, September 13, 1988). Those amendments, which do not correct all the deficiencies in the act, are discussed in Chapter 6.

19. *Regents of the University of California v. Bakke*, 438 U.S. 265 (1978).

20. See Wilson, *The Truly Disadvantaged*.

21. Wilson cites the exodus of middle-class and working-class African Americans from previously segregated communities as a possible explanation for the rise of the underclass. He does not, however, link this racial dynamic to civil rights policy (id., pp. 7, 30–62, 143–144, 160–161).

22. See, e.g., Samuel Spencer, Jr., *Booker T. Washington and the Negro's Place in American Life* (Boston: Little, Brown, 1955); W. E. B. DuBois, *The Autobiography of W. E. B. DuBois* (New York: International Publishers, New World Paperbacks, 1970). Washington believed that African Americans should try to win the respect of whites "by proving their usefulness to society through the acquisition of wealth and morality" (August Meier, Elliott Rudwick, and Francis Broderick, eds., *Black Protest Thought in the Twentieth Century*, 2d ed. [Indianapolis: Bobbs-Merrill, 1971], p. xxv), which essentially meant that they should not focus on social or political protest against racism and discrimination, should accept segregation and Jim Crow's separate-but-equal policy, and should favor vocational training and manual labor at the expense of higher education. DuBois and other African American intellectuals of his day (such as Monroe Trotter, publisher of the *Guardian*, the first

African American paper to openly attack Washington) disagreed with this philosophy of accommodation. But there was substantial agreement among Washington, DuBois, and other African American leaders concerning the necessity for self-help, which for them entailed an emphasis on racial pride and solidarity and support for African American businesses. Spencer, *Booker T. Washington*, pp. 148–158, 160; DuBois, *Autobiography*, pp. 138, 209; Meier, Rudwick, and Broderick, *Black Protest Thought*, pp. xxii–xxix, 3–74; Elliott Rudwick, *W. E. B. DuBois: Propagandist of the Negro Protest* (New York: Atheneum, 1969). Washington and his philosophy of accommodation came to prominence in September 1895 in a speech he gave, as head of Tuskegee Institute, at the Atlanta Cotton Exposition (DuBois, *Autobiography*, p. 428). But Washington achieved greater notoriety with the publication of his autobiography, *Up from Slavery*, first published in 1901. For further discussion of various schools of African American thought, see, e.g., Roy L. Brooks, "Twentieth Century Black Thought: Ideology and Methodology," *Phi Kappa Phi Journal* 53 (1973): 46–57.

23. King, *Stride Toward Freedom*, pp. 21–22.

24. The idea that middle-class African Americans have unique skills and knowledge may raise the issue of whether I am claiming that African Americans possess, either innately or through experience, an Afrocentric vision—a racially distinct voice, in contrast to a Eurocentric or a feminist voice, for example—and, if so, whether I am also asserting that such a worldview is intellectually or emotionally inaccessible to whites. I explore this issue further in Chapter 5. For now, I simply assert that people learn from their experiences and that middle-class African Americans, having already experienced what other African Americans will encounter as they move up the socioeconomic ladder (racism, discrimination, the weight of slavery and Jim Crow, and so on), are in a better position to give guidance than are middle-class whites, whose life experiences are different in significant respects from African Americans of any class. Middle-class African Americans, in short, know the terrain well, whether or not they are able to articulate a racially distinct metaphysics or worldview based on their experiences.

Perhaps I should also note here that many African American scholars argue for the existence of a distinct black perspective (or "blackness") consisting of African and American (Western) elements; see, e.g., Henry Gates, Jr., *The Signifying Monkey: A Theory of Afro-American Literary Criticism* (New York: Oxford University Press, 1988); Molefi Kete Asante, *The Afrocentric Idea* (Philadelphia: Temple University Press, 1987). One controversial element of the argument—that whites cannot access this frame of mind—goes back a long way. For example, in a 1927 correspondence between the African American historians Carter G. Woodson and Charles Wesley, Wesley argued that white historians could not report the history of African Americans as "successfully" as African American historians, because "the one who feels the pinch can tell the story of the joy or pain more convincingly and truthfully than another" (August Meier and Elliott Rudwick, *Black History and the Historical Profession, 1915–1980* [Urbana: University of Illinois Press, 1986], p. 289). Woodson himself agreed with this view, believing that "men of other races cannot function efficiently because they do not think black" (id.). African American literary figure William Pickens wrote in 1922 that "it is not simply that the white story teller will not do full justice to the humanity of the black race; he *cannot*" (Addison Gayle, Jr., ed., *The Black Aesthetic* [Garden City, N.Y.: Doubleday, 1972], p. xvii; emphasis in original).

If a residual racial perspective that cuts across class lines and other intra-racial differences does inhere in African Americans, surely it consists of at least two ingredients. One is the expectation of struggle, that is, the belief that whether an African American wants to simply get through the day or to tackle more complex endeavors (obtaining a quality education, finding and holding a good job, successfully raising a family), he or she should expect to encounter no dearth of artificial, racial barriers and must be prepared to recognize and then deal with them effectively. I doubt that this vision of existence is fundamental to the way white Americans approach their lives or, if it is, that it is as pervasive among whites as it is among African Americans. This tendency to be in a constant state of "overcoming" may be related to the high incidence of hypertension among African Americans. The second ingredient is the belief that society ("the system" or "the Man") is more foe than friend, a theme echoed by African American writers and social activists from the days of slavery to recent times. See Chapter 5 for further discussion of a racial perspective.

Perhaps the danger of acknowledging a distinct racial perspective is that it may stereotype African Americans. See, e.g., Randall Kennedy, "Racial Critiques of Legal Academia," *Harvard Law Review* 101 (1989): 1786–1787 (sources cited therein). Even a positive stereotype may be negative in that it prevents one from thinking beyond pre-set racial categories and, as a result, denies an individual the opportunity to be judged on his or her own merits.

25. Sheila Kamerman and Alfred Kahn, "Europe's Innovative Family Policies," *Transatlantic Perspectives*, March 1980, p. 12; Wilson, *The Truly Disadvantaged*, pp. 140–164.

Chapter 1

1. The origin of the term *Jim Crow* is lost in obscurity, as C. Vann Woodward points out in his book *The Strange Career of Jim Crow* (2d rev. ed. [New York: Oxford University Press, 1966], p. 7n). The words were first used in a song-and-dance score written in 1832. The term, however, is most often used to refer to the segregation statutes that began to appear in the South before the turn of the twentieth century. The large number, great detail, and effective enforcement of these statutes distinguish them from the black codes that followed the withdrawal of federal troops from the South in 1877, ending the Reconstruction era, and from the ubiquitous slave codes that regulated not only race relations inside the peculiar institution but also relations between whites and free or quasi-free African Americans in the North and South from the inception of American slavery. In the generic sense, Jim Crow refers to the system of discrimination and segregation laws born in the North, developed contemporaneously with slavery, and passed down in a variety of forms intergenerationally through the 1960s.

In this book, the term *Jim Crow* is used in a somewhat more specific sense. Most important, it does not encompass the separate-and-unequal policy that governed interracial relations prior to the "equality" amendments to the Constitution (the Thirteenth, Fourteenth, and Fifteenth amendments) and the "equality" laws enacted by Congress during Reconstruction. Rather, I use the term as coextensive with the separate-but-equal policy brought alive by the Supreme Court's interpretation of the Reconstruction amendments and statutes in the final decades of the nineteenth century. For this reason, *Plessy v. Ferguson* (163 U.S. 537 [1896]), which, more than any other Supreme Court case, institutionalized the separate-but-equal policy, is an appropriate historical "starting date" for Jim Crow.

See Woodward, *Strange Career of Jim Crow*, chaps. 1–3; Franklin, *From Slavery to Freedom*, chaps. 6–19; Derrick A. Bell, Jr., *Race, Racism, and American Law*, 2d ed. (Boston: Little, Brown, 1980), pp. 364–379; Roy L. Brooks, "Use of the Civil Rights Acts of 1866 and 1871 to Redress Employment Discrimination," *Cornell Law Review* 62 (1977): 258, 261–266. On the subject of Reconstruction, see, e.g., Eric Foner, *Reconstruction: America's Unfinished Revolution, 1863–1877* (New York: Harper and Row, 1988).

2. For extensive discussions of the transition from a separate-but-equal public policy to one of formal equal opportunity, see Williams, *Eyes on the Prize*; Richard Kluger, *Simple Justice* (New York: Alfred A. Knopf, 1976); Woodward, *Strange Career of Jim Crow*.

As used in this chapter, the term *community* means more than just a neighborhood or a physical locality; it refers to a society or body of people. For further discussion of this concept, see, e.g., *In re Huss*, 126 N.Y. 537, 27 N.E. 784 (1891).

3. *Plessy v. Ferguson*, 163 U.S. 537 (1896).

4. For further discussion of Washington's philosophy, see the Introduction, above, note 22.

5. See, e.g., Williams, *Eyes on the Prize*, pp. 237–257; Kluger, *Simple Justice*, pp. 1–256; Woodward, *Strange Career of Jim Crow*, pp. 67–110.

6. See *Brown v. Board of Education*, 347 U.S. 483 (1954).

7. Thomas S. Kuhn, *The Structure of Scientific Revolutions*, 2d ed. (Chicago: University of Chicago Press, 1970).

8. Exec. Order No. 8802, 3 C.F.R. 957 (1941).

9. See, e.g., Charles C. Moskos, "Blacks in the Army: Success Story," *Current*, September 1986, pp. 10–17; Philip McGuire, "Desegregation of the Armed Forces: Black Leadership, Protest, and World War II," *Journal of Negro History* 63 (Spring 1983): 147–158; Daniel L. Schaefer, "Freedom Was as Close as the River: The Blacks of Northeast Florida and the Civil War," *Escribano* 23 (1986): 91–116; Saralee R. Howard-Filler, "Two Different Battles," *Michigan History* 71 (January/February 1987): 30–33; Gregory Evans Dowd, "Declarations of Dependence: War and Inequality in Revolutionary New Jersey, 1776–1815," *New Jersey History* 103 (1985): 47–67. One of the best books on African Americans in the military is Richard O. Hope, *Racial Strife in the U.S. Military: Toward the Elimination of Discrimination* (New York: Praeger, 1979).

10. Exec. Order No. 9981, 3 C.F.R. 722 (1948); Exec. Order No. 9980, 3 C.F.R. 720 (1948).

11. See Franklin, *From Slavery to Freedom*, pp. 523–545.

12. See, e.g., Edwin Dorn, "Truman and the Desegregation of the Military," *Focus*, May 1988, pp. 3–4, 12.

13. See, e.g., Franklin, *From Slavery to Freedom*, pp. 546–611.

14. *Brown v. Board of Education* [*Brown I*], 347 U.S. 483 (1954). Lawyers often refer to this decision as *Brown I* to distinguish it from the second Supreme Court decision in the case, rendered in 1955. The second decision, called *Brown II* (cited as 349 U.S. 294 [1955]), deferred implementation of constitutional rights granted in *Brown I* by allowing school desegregation to proceed with "all deliberate speed" rather than immediately.

15. See, e.g., *Shelley v. Kraemer*, 334 U.S. 1 (1948) (Fourteenth Amendment's equal protection clause prohibits state enforcement of ra-

cially restrictive covenants in housing); *Sweatt v. Painter*, 339 U.S. 629 (1950) (African American law students ordered admitted to the all-white University of Texas Law School on the ground that the state law school established for African Americans failed to offer equal educational opportunity); *McLaurin v. Oklahoma State Regents for Higher Education*, 339 U.S. 637 (1950) (state-imposed restrictions placed on African American graduate students attending an otherwise all-white university produced such inequalities as to offend the equal protection clause); *Henderson v. United States*, 339 U.S. 816 (1950) (Southern Railway's discriminatory dining-car regulations violated the equal protection clause). For the best account of the legal history leading up to *Brown I*, see Kluger, *Simple Justice*.

16. *Brown v. Board of Education [Brown II]*, 349 U.S. 294, 297 (1955).

17. Robert Carter, "The Warren Court and Desegregation," *Michigan Law Review* 67 (1968): 247.

18. See, e.g., Thomas R. Frazier, ed., *Afro-American History: Primary Sources* (New York: Harcourt Brace and World, 1970), p. 368 (quoting from the NAACP Legal Defense and Education Fund's summary argument in *Brown I*).

19. Civil Rights Act of 1964, Pub. L. No. 88–352, 78 Stat. 241 (1964) (codified as amended at 42 U.S.C. §§ 1971–2000h-6 [1982]); Voting Rights Act of 1965, Pub. L. No. 89–110, 79 Stat. 445 (1965) (codified as amended at 42 U.S.C. § 1971 [1982]); Fair Housing Act of 1968 (Title VIII), Pub. L. No. 90–284, 82 Stat. 81 (1968) (codified as amended at 42 U.S.C. §§ 3601–3619 [1982 and Supp. 1987]).

20. Skelly Wright, "Professor Bickel, the Scholarly Tradition, and the Supreme Court," *Harvard Law Review* 84 (1971): 769–805.

21. Holmes's maxim is quoted from Oliver Wendell Holmes, Jr., *The Common Law*, ed. Mark Howe (Cambridge, Mass.: Harvard University Press, Belknap Press, 1963), p. 5. This expression appears in a somewhat different form in an unsigned review of Langdell's Contracts book; see Book Note, *American Law Review* 14 (1880): 233–236.

The Langdellian syllogism refers to the legal formalism promoted by the famous Harvard Law School dean, Christopher C. Langdell; see Langdell, *A Selection of Cases on the Law of Contracts* (Boston: Little, Brown, 1871). Not surprisingly, this book received a negative review from Holmes, who was an instrumentalist.

Legal realism, a form of instrumentalism, purports to be a realistic and scientific view of the law, meaning that it: (a) focuses on what judges do rather than on what judges say; (b) is cognizant of the consequences judicial decisions have on the community; and (c) believes all legal institutions operate pursuant to a pleasure-pain calculus in which they attempt to maximize the welfare of the greatest number of individuals within the community. See, e.g., Jerome Frank, *Law and the Modern Mind* (New York: Tudor, 1930); Karl N. Llewellyn, *Jurisprudence: Realism in Theory and Practice* (Chicago: University of Chicago Press, 1962). In contrast, legal formalism is primarily concerned with the internal order of law, deductive logic, or what Roberto Unger has called "a restrained, relatively apolitical method of analysis" ("The Critical Legal Studies Movement," *Harvard Law Review* 96 [1983]: 565).

Various scholars have provided a detailed analysis of legal realism and legal formalism. See Oliver Wendell Holmes, "The Path of the Law," *Harvard Law Review* 10 (1897): 457–478; this is a restatement and refinement of conclusions worked out by Holmes in *The Common Law* (originally published in 1881). See also Benjamin N. Cardozo, *The Nature of the Judicial Process* (New Haven, Conn.: Yale University Press, 1921). Two other books by Cardozo may provide a more definitive statement of his views on legal process and the social end of law: *The Growth of the Law* (New Haven, Conn.: Yale University Press, 1924); and *The Paradoxes of Legal Science* (New York: Columbia University Press, 1928). Holmes was a utilitarian; see H. L. Pholman, *Justice Oliver Wendell Holmes and Utilitarian Jurisprudence* (Cambridge, Mass.: Harvard University Press, 1984). To the extent that Cardozo appeals to considerations of what he calls "social welfare" for guidance in deciding cases, he too can be classified as a utilitarian. In his later books, however, Cardozo seems more metaphysical, perhaps a neonatural law jurisprudent, undertaking a search for generalized principles of law. On utilitarianism, see, e.g., Jeremy Bentham, *An Introduction to the Principles of Morals and Legislation* (New York: Hafner, 1948); Gerald J. Postema, *Bentham and the Common Law Tradition* (Oxford: Clarendon Press, 1986). For a recent defense of legal formalism, see Ernest J. Weinrib, "Legal Formalism: On the Immanent Rationality of Law," *Yale Law Journal* 97 (1988): 949–1016.

22. *Regents of the University of California v. Bakke*, 438 U.S. 265 (1978).

23. For further discussion of this argument, see, e.g., Owen Fiss, "A Theory of Fair Employment Laws," *University of Chicago Law Review* 38 (1971): 235–341.

24. See, e.g., Joel J. Kupperman, "Relations Between the Sexes: Timely vs. Timeliness Principles," *University of San Diego Law Review* 25 (1988): 1027–1041; Roy L. Brooks, "The Affirmative Action Issue: Law, Policy, and Morality," *University of Connecticut Law Review* 22 (1990): 323–372.

Chapter 2

1. Stephen Rose, *The American Profile Poster* (New York: Pantheon, 1986), p. 9. For a general discussion of class stratification in American society, see, e.g., Richard T. Schaefer, *Sociology,* 3d ed. (New York: McGraw-Hill, 1989), pp. 204–243; Macionis, *Sociology,* pp. 217–260.

2. Bart Landry, *The New Black Middle Class* (Berkeley and Los Angeles: University of California Press, 1987), pp. 5–11.

3. See Rose, *American Profile,* p. 8.

4. See Robert B. Hill, "The Black Middle Class Defined," *Ebony* (special issue), August 1987, pp. 30–32; Andrew F. Brimmer, "Income and Wealth," *Ebony* (special issue), August 1987, pp. 42–48; Andrew Hacker, "American Apartheid," *New York Review of Books,* December 3, 1987, pp. 26–33.

5. For a more detailed discussion, see U.S. Bureau of the Census, *Current Population Reports: Money Income and Poverty Status in the United States: 1988,* Series P-60, no. 166, advance data from the March 1989 Current Population Survey (Washington, D.C.: U.S. Government Printing Office, 1989). Compare that document with U.S. Bureau of the Census, *Current Population Reports: Money Income of Households, Families, and Persons in the United States: 1987,* Series P-60, no. 162 (Washington, D.C.: U.S. Government Printing Office, 1989).

6. The statistics presented here are drawn from data originally assembled by the Bureau of Labor Statistics and compiled and refined in Rose, *American Profile,* pp. 12–13, 21–22. For more detailed discussion of the African American middle class, see Bart Landry's *The New Black Middle Class,* as well as a two-part article by Landry: "The New Black Middle Class," pts. 1 and 2, *Focus,* September 1987, pp. 5–7; October 1987, pp. 6–7.

7. On housing segregation, see Farley and Allen, *Color Line,* p. 150; Sean-Shong Hwang et al., "The Effects of Race and Socioeconomic Status on Residential Segregation in Texas, 1970–1980," *Social Forces* 63 (March 1985): 732–747. On geographic separation, see Wilson, *The Truly Disadvantaged,* pp. 7, 30, 49, 56, 143–144.

8. Farley and Allen, *Color Line,* p. 205.

9. For further discussion, see Regina Austin, "Resistance Tactics for Tokens," *Harvard Blackletter Journal* 3 (1986): 52–53.

10. In a fairly recent national survey, only 6 percent of African Americans questioned said they trusted "most white people" (National Opinion Research Center, *General Social Surveys, 1972–1983: Cumulative Codebook* [Chicago: National Opinion Research Center, 1983], p. 118).

11. Leon Lewis, "About Men: In On the Game," *New York Times Magazine*, February 3, 1985, p. 70.

12. Vidiadhar S. Naipaul, *The Enigma of Arrival* (New York: Alfred A. Knopf, 1987).

13. See Roy L. Brooks, "Anti-Minority Mindset in the Law School Personnel Process: Toward an Understanding of Racial Mindsets," *Law and Inequality: A Journal of Theory and Practice* 5 (1987): 6; Roy L. Brooks, "Life After Tenure: Can Minority Law Professors Avoid the Clyde Ferguson Syndrome?" *University of San Francisco Law Review* 20 (1986): 421.

14. Linda Williams, "Stress of Adapting to White Society Cited as Major Cause of Hypertension in Blacks," *Wall Street Journal*, May 28, 1986. Williams's article describes several recent studies. For more information on health problems among African Americans, see, e.g., U.S. Bureau of the Census, *Statistical Abstract of the United States, 1985*, 106th ed. (Washington, D.C.: U.S. Government Printing Office, 1986), p. 72, table 112.

15. Williams, "Stress of Adapting."

16. Roger Wilkins, *A Man's Life: An Autobiography* (New York: Simon and Schuster, 1982), pp. 54–55.

17. Williams, "Stress of Adapting."

18. See John P. Fernandez, *Racism and Sexism in Corporate Life: Changing Values in American Business* (Lexington, Mass.: Lexington Books, 1981); Larry Reibstein, "Many Hurdles, Old and New, Keep Black Managers Out of Top Jobs," *Wall Street Journal*, July 10, 1986; Carol Hymowitz, "Many Blacks Jump Off the Corporate Ladder to Be Entrepreneurs," *Wall Street Journal*, August 2, 1984; Gary Rivlin, "Climbing the Legal Ladder: Some Kinds of Discrimination Die Hard," *American Bar Association Update*, Fall 1981, pp. 28–49. See also Floyd Dickens and Jacqueline Dickens, *The Black Manager: Making It in the Corporate World* (Saranac Lake, N.Y.: American Management Association, 1987).

19. Establishing the existence of disproportionate employment discrimination can be a bit tricky for two reasons. First, the term *discrimination* is a term of art, that is, it has special legal definitions: "disparate treatment" (unfavorable treatment because of one's race or color) and "disparate impact" (racially neutral employment policies, practices, or procedures that have a disproportionately negative effect on a racial group). (These terms are discussed in more detail later in Chapter 2.) Unless otherwise specified, both meanings are incorporated in my use of the term *discrimination* throughout this book.

Second, discrimination does not exist, at least not in a legal sense, until a court (and, really, the Supreme Court) says so. A judicial finding of discrimination, however, has an uncertain quality about it. The finding is empirical (a question of fact), analytical (a question of law applied to the facts), and policy-driven (a question of who bears the burden of proof). In addition, a lower court's finding of discrimination is subject to reversal either on direct appeal or years later when and if the issue comes before the court again in another case. Thus a careful review of judicial determinations (the "best" evidence available) is inconclusive evidence of the existence of even a legally controlled concept of discrimination.

Given the uncertainty inherent in judicial determinations, I rely on *claims* of discrimination as well as *proofs* (judicial determinations) of discrimination to establish intra-class racial disparity. Claims include personal perceptions of discrimination, government agency fillings of discrimination cases in federal courts, and private cases of discrimination filed and reported in the federal case reporters at all three federal levels—trial level (district courts), intermediate appellate level (circuit courts of appeal), and highest appellate level (Supreme Court).

Personal perceptions of discrimination cannot be ignored. Even if they are "wrong" or exaggerated, they are real to the perceiver. More important, these perceptions affect an African American individual's behavior and chances for success and personal happiness. There is also good sociopsychological evidence that these perceptions are mostly accurate; see, e.g., Charles Lawrence, "The Id, the Ego, and Equal Protection: Reckoning with Unconscious Racism," *Stanford Law Review* 39 (1987): 317–388.

20. My research assistant, Lincoln B. Smith, and I conducted what might be called "juri-statistical" research of employment discrimination cases brought before the federal courts in 1987. We used Westlaw, a standard research device in law, accessing its database of primary and secondary legal authorities through the "allfed" library (see Westlaw 1989 version [St. Paul, Minn.: West Publishing]). For a more detailed description and analysis of this research, see Lincoln B. Smith, "Juri-Statistical Methods in Legal Research" (typescript, December 1989). See generally *Westlaw: Introductory Guide to Legal Research* (St. Paul, Minn.: West Publishing, 1988).

21. *Annual Report of the Director of the United States Courts, 1987* (Washington, D.C.: U.S. Government Printing Office, 1987), p. 208, table C4.

22. The United States Courts Administrator does not keep statistics on the percentage of plaintiff victories in civil actions in general.

23. See *West's Federal Practice Digest Edition, 1975 to Date* (St. Paul, Minn.: West Publishing, 1984), Civil Rights Sec. 9.10. This case digest, consisting of several volumes, is updated weekly with advance sheets published by West.

24. For example, in Michael J. Zimmer, Charles A. Sullivan, and Richard Richards, *Cases and Materials on Employment Discrimination*, 2d ed. (Boston: Little, Brown, 1988), the chapters dealing with the concept of discrimination (chaps. 1–4) report only a few major federal cases involving a white plaintiff. Casebooks, of course, provide very limited and purposeful case collections.

25. See, e.g., Equal Employment Opportunity Commission, *Twenty-Third Annual Report—1988* (Washington, D.C.: EEOC, 1989); Equal Employment Opportunity Commission, *Eighteenth Annual Report—1983* (Washington, D.C.: EEOC, 1984).

26. On corporations, see "Special Issues—Progress Report on the Black Executive: The Top Spots Are Still Elusive," *Business Week*, February 20, 1984, pp. 104–105; Derek Dingle, "Will Black Managers Survive Corporate Downsizing?" *Black Enterprise*, March 1987, pp. 49–55. On law firms, see Edward Burke, "3,700 Partners, 12 Are Black," *National Law Journal*, July 2, 1979, p. 1; Ralph Smith, "The Invisible Lawyer," *Barrister*, Fall 1981, pp. 42–49. On law faculties, see Brooks, "Anti-Minority Mindset, " pp. 101, 105–106; Derrick A. Bell, Jr., "The Price and Pain of Racial Perspective," *Stanford Law School Journal*, April 1986, p. 5.

On the news media, see David Hatchett, "Blacks and the Mass Media," *Crisis*, June/July 1989, pp. 18–26, 68; Noah Griffin, "Broadcasting," *Crisis*, June/July 1989, pp. 28–32, 66; "Double Jeopardy in the Newsroom," *Time*, November 29, 1982, p. 90; Richard L. Levine, "The Plight of Black Reporters: Why 'Unconscious Racism' Persists," *TV Guide*, July 25, 1981, pp. 22–28. On the motion picture and television industries, see Erwin Washington, "Racism and the Movie Industry," *Crisis*, June/July 1989, pp. 34–40, 66; Joy Horowitz, "Hollywood's Dirty Little Secret," *American Visions*, August 1989, pp. 16–21; Scott Hays, "Capturing the Black Experience," *TV Guide*, November 29, 1986, pp. 10–14.

27. See, e.g., James P. Smith and Finis R. Welch, *Closing the Gap: Forty Years of Economic Progress for Blacks* (Santa Monica, Calif.: Rand, 1986), pp. xx–xxi, 85–91; Barbara Bergmann, "An Affirmative Look at Hiring Quotas," *New York Times*, January 10, 1982, sec. 3 (Business). See also "Affirmative Word from Washington," *New York Times*, December 13, 1981, sec. 4 (Week in Review). An unpublished study by the U.S. Labor Department clearly documents the effective-

ness of affirmative action; for discussion of the study, see Robert Pear, "Study Says Affirmative Rule Expands Hiring of Minorities," *New York Times*, June 19, 1983, sec. 1 (main); Mary Thorton, "Affirmative Action Found to Diversify Work Force," *Washington Post*, June 20, 1983, sec. 1.

28. Farley and Allen, *Color Line*, p. 317, chap. 11.

29. Smith and Welch, *Closing the Gap*, p. 23; emphasis added. See id. for figures taken from the Rand Corporation study; and see Walter L. Updegrave, "Personal Finance: Race and Money," *Money*, December 1989, p. 152.

30. As one African American lawyer stated in reference to the low percentage of African American partners in large law firms: "We have long felt that the large, established firms discriminate against minority attorneys, but we haven't had the statistics until now" (Burke, "3,700 Partners," p. 1).

31. Glegg Watson and George Davis, *Black Life in Corporate America: Swimming in the Mainstream* (Garden City, N.Y.: Anchor/Doubleday, 1982). Both were quoted in "Special Issues—Progress Report on the Black Executive," p. 105.

32. The views quoted here were taken from "Special Issues—Progress Report on the Black Executive," p. 105.

33. Id.

34. Levine, "Plight of Black Reporters," p. 22.

35. Id. See also Hatchett, "Blacks and the Mass Media"; Griffin, "Broadcasting."

36. "Double Jeopardy in the Newsroom," p. 90. In *EEOC v. New York News, Inc.* (81 Civ. 337 [S.D.N.Y. 1987]), a jury in the Southern District of New York returned a verdict in favor of the plaintiffs, who charged that between 1979 and 1982 the *New York Daily News* denied promotion and desirable assignments to four African American journalists. Testimony described a newsroom where editors tossed around such epithets as "nigger" and "spic." Despite such specific acts of racism, the jury found discrimination in only twelve of the twenty-three incidents on which testimony was taken, again demonstrating how difficult it is to prove intentional discrimination today. See "Jury Finds Bias by Daily News," *New York Times*, April 19, 1987, sec. 4 (Week in Review).

37. Hays, "Capturing the Black Experience," p. 11.

38. Id. See also Horowitz, "Hollywood's Dirty Little Secret"; Washington, "Racism and the Movie Industry."

39. Barbara Becnel, "Minority Lawyers: Some Firms Fear Client Objections," *Los Angeles Daily Journal*, May 11, 1987. Although four hundred questionnaires were mailed out by the Minority Employment Committee, there were only thirty-five responses. One committee

member said there was no way to determine whether the small number of responses accurately reflected the prevailing attitudes of law partners in Los Angeles, because, as far as he knew, this was the first survey of its kind undertaken by the bar. For an excellent discussion of racism in the legal profession, see Mark Diamond, "A Trace Element in the Law," *American Bar Association Journal*, May 15, 1987, pp. 46–49. See also Doreen Weisenhaus, "White Males Dominate Firms: Still a Long Way to Go for Women and Minorities," *National Law Journal*, February 8, 1988, p. 1.

40. See Schaefer, *Sociology*, p. 246. Prejudice refers to a state of mind, and discrimination refers to behavior. Prejudiced and unprejudiced discrimination by individuals should be contrasted with institutional discrimination, which refers to the denial of opportunities or rights to individuals or groups as a result of the normal operations of an institution or a society.

41. See Brooks, "Anti-Minority Mindset," pp. 107–108; "The 1985 Minority Law Teachers' Conference," Symposium Report, *University of San Francisco Law Review* 20 (1986): 576.

42. Richard Chused, "The Hiring and Retention of Minorities and Women on American Law School Faculties," *University of Pennsylvania Law Review* 137 (1988): 556, table 1.

43. Excluding those who retired or died, 16.7 percent of African American tenured professors left law teaching between the 1980–1981 and 1986–1987 academic years, compared to 7.5 percent of white tenured professors (id., p. 544).

44. Sally Goldfarb, "Education Without Representation," *Student Lawyer*, May 1981, pp. 11–13; Rivlin, "Climbing the Legal Ladder," p. 49.

45. See Bell, "Price and Pain of Racial Perspective," p. 5.

46. The psychological effects of segregative occurrences on African Americans are well documented and have played an essential role in the development of race law. See, e.g., *Brown v. Board of Education*, 347 U.S. 483, 493n.11 (1954). See also *Local 28, Sheet Metal Workers v. EEOC*, 478 U.S. 421, 450 (1986) ("Affirmative action 'promptly operates to change the outward and visible signs of yesterday's racial distinctions and, thus, to provide an impetus to the process of dismantling the barriers, psychological or otherwise, erected by past practices' " [quoting *NAACP v. Allen*, 493 F.2d 614, 621 (5th Cir. 1974)]).

47. Lance Morrow, "The Powers of Racial Examples," *Time*, April 16, 1984, p. 84.

48. EEOC statistics are quoted in Dingle, "Will Black Managers Survive Corporate Downsizing?" p. 51.

49. On law partnerships, see Weisenhaus, "White Males Dominate Firms," p. 1. See also Diamond, "Trace Element," p. 46. According to Roderick McLeod, head of the American Bar Association's Committee on Minorities in the Profession, "By and large, minorities are very underrepresented in all segments of the [legal] profession—in all size firms, corporate legal departments and government" (id., p. 47). See also Paul Marcotte, "The Changing of the Guard," *American Bar Association Journal*, May 15, 1987, pp. 56–62. The information cited on teaching positions in law schools was taken from a 1986 memorandum: Executive Director, Association of American Law Schools, to Deans of Member Schools, Memorandum no. 86–57, September 5, 1986.

On investment banking jobs, see "Blacks and the Wall Street Purge," *Newsweek*, February 1, 1988, p. 38. Although investment banking firms refuse to comment on how many African American employees lost their jobs after the October 1987 stock market crash, it is estimated that as many as one-third to one-half of these employees were laid off. One insider at Solomon Brothers reported that roughly two-thirds of the firm's African American bankers were fired after the crash.

On newspaper editorial positions, see "Double Jeopardy in the Newsroom," p. 90. This source reports that 5.5 percent of newspaper editors are minorities. African Americans, therefore, as only one of several minorities, hold an even smaller percentage of these posts.

50. Farley and Allen, *Color Line*, p. 280; also pp. 256–282.

51. On the equal protection clause of the Fourteenth Amendment, see, e.g., *United States v. Paradise*, 480 U.S. 149, 166 (1987) (cases cited therein); see also *Brown v. Board of Education*, 347 U.S. 483 (1954); *City of Richmond v. J. A. Croson Co.*, 109 S. Ct. 706 (1989). On the equal protection component of the Fifth Amendment's due process clause, see, e.g., *Local 28, Sheet Metal Workers v. EEOC*, 478 U.S. 421, 479–480 (1986) (cases cited therein); see also *Bolling v. Sharpe*, 347 U.S. 497 (1954).

52. On suspect classifications, see e.g., *McDonald v. Board of Election Commissioners of Chicago*, 394 U.S. 802, 807 (1969). Also Polyvios G. Polyviou, *The Equal Protection of the Laws* (London: Duckworth, 1980); "Developments in the Law—Equal Protection," Note, *Harvard Law Review* 82 (1969): 1065–1192. On violations of fundamental personal interests, see, e.g., *Reynolds v. Sims*, 377 U.S. 533, 561–562 (1964). Fundamental personal interests include the right to procreate (*Skinner v. Oklahoma*, 316 U.S. 535 [1942]), the right to vote (*Reynolds v. Sims*, 377 U.S. 533 [1964]), and the right to engage in interstate travel (*Shapiro v. Thompson*, 394 U.S. 618 [1969]).

53. See, e.g., *Wygant v. Jackson Board of Education*, 476 U.S. 267, 273–274 (1986) (Powell, J., concurring); *Palmore v. Sidoti*, 466 U.S. 429, 432 (1984); *Loving v. Virginia*, 388 U.S. 1, 11 (1967). See also *McLaughlin v. Florida*, 397 U.S. 184 (1964); *Shelley v. Kraemer*, 334 U.S. 1 (1948). Some Supreme Court justices have proposed alternative levels of judicial scrutiny; see Chapter 2, note 57, below, and accompanying text.

54. On protecting national security as a compelling governmental interest, see *Korematsu v. United States*, 323 U.S. 214 (1944). On remedying past discrimination, see *United States v. Paradise*, 480 U.S. 149, 166 (1987) (cases cited therein).

55. See, e.g., *McDonald v. Board of Election Commissioners of Chicago*, 394 U.S. 802, 809 (1969), which reads in part: "Legislatures are presumed to have acted constitutionally." In this case, the Supreme Court held that a classification based on handicapped status is not suspect and hence is subject to the rational basis test. On the basis of that test, the Court upheld the constitutionality of the classification under the equal protection clause.

56. Explicit gender-based classifications are not suspect classifications and hence are not subject to strict scrutiny. Neither are they reviewed under the rational basis test. Rather, the Supreme Court employs a "middle tier," or an "intermediate level," of scrutiny. Under this standard, the classification in question must serve important governmental objectives and must be substantially related to the achievement of those objectives. See *Craig v. Boren*, 429 U.S. 191 (1976). See also Gerald Gunther, *Constitutional Law*, 11th ed. (Mineola, N.Y.: Foundation Press, 1985), pp. 642–664; Craig C. Ducat and Harold W. Chase, *Constitutional Interpretation*, 3d ed. (St. Paul, Minn.: West Publishing, 1983), pp. 692, 861–871.

57. *United States v. Paradise*, 480 U.S. 149, 166 (1987). See also *City of Richmond v. J. A. Croson Co.*, 109 S. Ct. 706 (1989). While agreeing that "some elevated level of [judicial] scrutiny is required when a racial or ethnic distinction is made for remedial purposes" (*United States v. Paradise*, 480 U.S. 149, 166 [1987]), some members of the Court have proposed alternative levels of judicial scrutiny. Justices Marshall, Brennan, and Blackmun, for example, would allow racial classifications that serve "important governmental objectives" and are "substantially related to the achievement of those objectives" (*Wygant v. Jackson Board of Education*, 476 U.S. 267, 301 [1986] [quoting *Regents of the University of California v. Bakke*, 438 U.S. 265, 359 (1978)]). Justice Stevens would permit the use of race if the public interest vindicated by such use and the means employed to implement that interest justify the resulting adverse effects on the disadvantaged group (*Wygant v. Jackson*

Board of Education, 476 U.S. 267, 313–314 [1986]). None of these alternative levels of judicial scrutiny have replaced the strict scrutiny test as the dominant mode of constitutional analysis for racial classification. The use of a racial classification to remedy a defendant's prior discrimination is permissible under any of the alternative modes of constitutional analysis. See generally *United States v. Paradise*, 480 U.S. 149, 166n.17 (1987).

58. When an employer voluntarily sets up race-conscious employment practices or policies, it is usually willing to admit to conspicuous racial or sexual imbalance in its work force but quite unwilling to admit to its own discrimination, because that in effect would be admitting to a violation of the law. See, e.g., *Johnson v. Transportation Agency, Santa Clara County, California*, 480 U.S. 616, 619–626 (1987); *United Steelworkers of America v. Weber*, 443 U.S. 193, 209 (1979).

59. *Local 28, Sheet Metal Workers v. EEOC*, 478 U.S. 421, 450 (1986) (quoting *McDonnell Douglas Corp. v. Green*, 411 U.S. 792, 800 [1973]). See also *Thompson v. Sawyer*, 678 F.2d 257, 294 (D.C. Cir. 1982); *Chisholm v. U.S. Postal Service*, 665 F.2d 482, 499 (4th Cir. 1981); *United States v. Lee Way Motor Freight, Inc.*, 625 F.2d 918, 943–945 (10th Cir. 1979); *Rios v. Enterprise Association Steamfitters Local 938*, 501 F.2d 622, 631–632 (2d Cir. 1974); Harry T. Edwards and Barry L. Zaretsky, "Preferential Remedies for Employment Discrimination," *Michigan Law Review* 74 (1976): 9.

60. The unpublished Labor Department report is described in two sources: Pear, "Study Says Affirmative Rule Expands Hiring of Minorities"; and Thornton, "Affirmative Action Found to Diversify Work Force." Reports from the U.S. Commission on Civil Rights are described in "Affirmative Word from Washington"; see also Farley and Allen, *Color Line*, p. 261. The Rand Corporation's findings are reported in Smith and Welch, *Closing the Gap*, pp. 85–91. See also Bergmann, "Affirmative Look at Hiring Quotas."

61. 42 U.S.C. § 2000e–2000e-17 (1982).

62. Section 703(a), 42 U.S.C. § 2000e-2(a) (1982).

63. On employment discrimination on the basis of race, see, e.g., *Slack v. Havens*, 7 Fair Empl. Prac. Cas. (BNA) 885 (S.D. Cal. 1973), aff'd as modified, 522 F.2d 1091 (9th Cir. 1975). Although it is an impermissible basis listed in Section 703(a), color is generally treated as indistinguishable from race; see EEOC Decision no. 72–0454 (September 15, 1971) (unpublished EEOC finding of reasonable cause in a case in which a light-skinned, "white-looking" African American was selected over a dark-skinned African American with Negroid features).

On employment discrimination on the basis of sex, see, e.g., *Dothard v. Rawlinson*, 433 U.S. 321 (1977); *Bundy v. Jackson*, 641 F.2d 934 (D.C. Cir. 1981); *Rosenfeld v. Southern Pacific Co.*, 444 F.2d 1219 (9th Cir. 1971); *Weeks v. Southern Bell Telephone and Telegraph Co.*, 408 F.2d 228 (5th Cir. 1969).

In addition to prohibiting discrimination on the basis of religious observances, practices, and beliefs, Title VII requires employers to accommodate work requirements to religious practices; see, e.g., *Trans World Airlines, Inc. v. Hardison*, 432 U.S. 63 (1977).

On employment discrimination on the basis of national origin, see, e.g., *Espinoza v. Farah Manufacturing Co.*, 414 U.S. 86 (1973).

64. On disparate treatment, see, e.g., *McDonnell Douglas Corp. v. Green*, 411 U.S. 792 (1973). On disparate impact, see *Griggs v. Duke Power Co.*, 401 U.S. 424 (1971).

65. *Teamsters v. United States*, 431 U.S. 324, 335n.15 (1977) (citations omitted).

66. See, e.g., *Wards Cove Packing Co. v. Atonio*, 109 S. Ct. 2115 (1989); *Connecticut v. Teal*, 457 U.S. 440 (1982); *New York City Transit Authority v. Beazer*, 440 U.S. 568 (1979); *Hazelwood School District v. United States*, 433 U.S. 299 (1977).

67. Although the Supreme Court has not stated how large a sample must be in order to be statistically significant, it is clear that a Title VII plaintiff must prove that an employer's selection criteria for hiring or promotion create a "significant" racial disparity (*Albermarle Paper Co. v. Moody*, 422 U.S. 405, 425 [1975]). Generally, the plaintiff must isolate the specific employment practice that is allegedly responsible for any observed statistical disparities (*Wards Cove Packing Co. v. Atonio*, 109 S. Ct. 2115, 2124 [1989]).

68. See, e.g., *United States v. Paradise*, 480 U.S. 149 (1987) (state troopers); *Johnson v. Transportation Agency, Santa Clara County, California*, 480 U.S. 616 (1987) (sex discrimination involving a road dispatcher position); *Local 28, Sheet Metal Workers v. EEOC*, 478 U.S. 421 (1986) (sheet metal workers); *Local No. 93, International Association of Firefighters v. City of Cleveland*, 478 U.S. 501 (1986) (firefighters); *Wygant v. Jackson Board of Education*, 476 U.S. 267 (1986) (teachers); *Firefighters v. Stotts*, 467 U.S. 561 (1984) (firefighters). For a detailed discussion of the use of statistics to prove disparate impact, see, e.g., Barbara Schlei and Paul Grossman, *Employment Discrimination Law*, 2d ed. (Washington, D.C.: Bureau of National Affairs, 1983), pp. 80–161; Elaine W. Shoben, "Differential Pass-Fail Rates in Employment Testing: Statistical Proof Under Title VII," *Harvard Law Review* 91 (1978): 793–813; "Beyond the Prima Facie Case in Employment Dis-

crimination: Statistical Proof and Rebuttal," Note, *Harvard Law Review* 89 (1975): 387–422. The Supreme Court's recent disparate-impact decision in *Wards Cove Packing Co. v. Atonio* (109 S. Ct. 2115 [1989]), which, among other things, places the burden on the plaintiff to disprove the business reason given by the defendant for the statistical disparity within the workplace, strikes a devastating blow to Title VII plaintiffs in such cases.

69. For an excellent discussion of Title VII legislative history, see Francis J. Vaas, "Title VII: Legislative History," *Boston College Industrial and Commercial Law Journal* 7 (1966): 431–458.

Transaction costs include payment of attorneys' fees up front, delay in litigation, and protracted litigation; see, e.g., Edward Levi, "The Business of the Courts: A Summary and a Sense of Perspective," *Federal Rules of Decision* 70 (1976): 212–223; Abraham Chayes, "The Role of the Judge in Public Law Litigation," *Harvard Law Review* 89 (1976): 1281–1316.

70. In a disparate-treatment *class* action, the plaintiff must establish that the defendant regularly and purposefully treated the plaintiff's protected class less favorably than the dominant group was treated or, in other words, that disparate treatment was not an isolated act but a systemic practice. Such disparate treatment is normally proven by statistical evidence (*Teamsters v. United States*, 431 U.S. 324 [1977]; *Hazelwood School District v. United States*, 433 U.S. 299 [1977]) but can also be proven by testimony from numerous individuals (*Teamsters v. United States*, 431 U.S. 324 [1977]) or by the adoption of broad employment practices or policies based on explicit impermissible criteria (*Dothard v. Rawlinson*, 433 U.S. 321 [1977]).

71. On the use of direct evidence see, e.g., *Slack v. Havens*, 7 Fair Empl. Prac. Cas. (BNA) 885 (S.D. Cal. 1973), aff'd as modified, 522 F.2d 1091 (9th Cir. 1975); *Gates v. Georgia-Pacific Corp.*, 326 F. Supp. 397, 399 (D. Ore. 1970), aff'd, 492 F.2d 292 (9th Cir. 1974).

Although statistics can provide circumstantial evidence of discrimination in individual disparate-treatment cases (see Stuart H. Bompey and Barry N. Saltman, "The Role of Statistics in Employment Discrimination Litigation—A University Perspective," *Journal of College and University Law* 9 [1982]: 271), most of the time such evidence in these cases is established without the use of statistics. In *McDonnell Douglas Corp. v. Green* (411 U.S. 792, 802 [1973]), the Supreme Court set forth the primary nonstatistical method of establishing a prima facie case based on circumstantial evidence. It must be proven: "(i) that [the plaintiff] belongs to a racial minority; (ii) that he applied and was qualified for a job for which the employer was seeking applicants; (iii) that, despite his qualifications, he was rejected; and (iv) that, after his rejection, the position remained open and the employer continued to seek applicants from persons of complainant's qualifications."

72. *McDonnell Douglas Corp. v. Green*, 411 U.S. 792, 802, 804–805 (1973).

73. *Texas Department of Community Affairs v. Burdine*, 450 U.S. 248 (1981). "The defendant need not persuade the court that it was actually motivated by the proferred reasons. It is sufficient if the defendant's evidence raises a genuine issue of fact as to whether it discriminated against the plaintiff" (id. at 254–255). See also *Board of Trustees v. Sweeney*, 439 U.S. 24 (1978) (the employer's burden to dispel the adverse inference created by the plaintiff's prima facie case is merely to "articulate" some legitimate, nondiscriminatory reason for the action, not to prove the absence of discriminatory motive); *Furnco Construction Corp. v. Waters*, 438 U.S. 567, 577 (1978) (the employer's burden in rebutting a prima facie case is to show that the employment decision was based on a legitimate consideration and not on an illegitimate one such as race). Thus the ultimate burden of persuasion as to the issue of discrimination always remains with the plaintiff. For a discussion of the law on this subject prior to *Burdine*, see Miguel Mendez, "Presumptions of Discriminatory Motive in Title VII Disparate Treatment Cases," *Stanford Law Review* 32 (1980): 1129–1162.

74. See, e.g., *Green v. McDonnell Douglas Corp.*, 528 F.2d 1102 (8th Cir. 1976) (plaintiff fails to prove pretext).

75. See, e.g., *Banerjee v. Board of Trustees of Smith College*, 648 F.2d 61, 66 (1st Cir. 1981), cert. denied, 454 U.S. 1098 (1981) (subjective reasons for tenure denial); *Powell v. Syracuse University* 580 F.2d 1150, 1156 (2d Cir. 1978), cert. denied, 439 U.S. 984 (1978) (reasons given for inadequate teaching ability were arguably subjective).

76. Referring to the use of fairness as a principle on which to allocate the burden of proof, Edward W. Cleary states: "The nature of a particular element may indicate that evidence relating to it lies more within the control of one party, which suggests the fairness of allocating that element to him" ("Presuming and Pleading: An Essay on Juristic Immaturity," *Stanford Law Review* 12 [1959]: 5). Thus, placing the burden of persuasion on the plaintiff regarding the defendant's "legitimate, nondiscriminatory reason" is hardly compelling from a fairness perspective.

77. See, e.g., *Wards Cove Packing Co. v. Atonio*, 109 S. Ct. 2115, 2124 (1989).

78. For example, the Court in *Wards Cove Packing Co. v. Atonio*, a disparate-impact case, relied on *Texas Department of Community Affairs v. Burdine* (450 U.S. 248 [1981]), a disparate-treatment case, for

the proposition that the plaintiff carries the burden of persuasion as to all specific elements of a Title VII case, including the burden of disproving an employer's business justification for a discriminatory employment condition (*Wards Cove Packing Co. v. Atonio*, 109 S. Ct. 2115, 2125–2126 [1989]).

79. See, e.g., *Bibbs v. Block*, 36 Fair Empl. Prac. Cas. (BNA) 713 (8th Cir. 1984).

80. See Mark Brodin, "The Standard of Causation in the Mixed-Motive Title VII Action: A Social Policy Perspective," *Columbia Law Review* 82 (1982): 297. This article provides an excellent analysis of causation prior to *Price Waterhouse v. Hopkins* (109 S. Ct. 1775 [1989]), discussed later in this chapter. The purpose of Title VII is quoted from H. Rept. 914, 88th Cong., 1st sess., p. 26 (1963); reprinted in *United States Congressional and Administrative News* (1964), p. 2401. See also *United Steelworkers of America v. Weber*, 443 U.S. 193, 202 (1979).

81. 29 U.S.C. §§ 151–169 (1982); on the act's remedial provisions, see *Albermarle Paper Co. v. Moody*, 422 U.S. 405, 419n.11 (1975).

82. 42 U.S.C. § 2000e-5(g) (1982 and Supp. I 1983).

83. Member of Congress Emmanual Celler, who introduced the amendment, stated: "Mr. Chairman, the purpose of the amendment is to specify cause. Here the court, for example, cannot find any violation of the act which is based on facts other—and I emphasize 'other'—than discrimination on the grounds of race, color, religion, or national origin. The discharge might be based, for example, on incompetence or a morals charge or theft, but the court can only consider charges based on race, color, religion, or national origin. That is the purpose of this amendment" (110 *Congressional Record* [1964], p. 2567).

84. See Brodin, "Standard of Causation," pp. 297–299.

85. *Price Waterhouse v. Hopkins*, 109 S. Ct. 1775, 1785n.7 (1989) (citing 110 *Congressional Record* [1964], p. 13837.

86. *McDonnell Douglas Corp. v. Green*, 411 U.S. 792, 801 (1973); emphasis added.

87. *McDonald v. Santa Fe Trail Transportation Co.*, 427 U.S. 273, 282n.10 (1976)

88. *Price Waterhouse v. Hopkins*, 109 S. Ct., 1775, 1797, 1806–1807 (1989).

89. Id. at 1785, 1786.

90. Id. at 1795.

91. *Mt. Healthy City School District Board of Education v. Doyle*, 429 U.S. 274 (1977).

92. *Price Waterhouse v. Hopkins*, 109 S. Ct. 1775, 1804 (1989).

93. See *Bibbs v. Block*, 778 F.2d 1318, 1320–1324 (8th Cir. 1985); *Bellissimo v. Westinghouse Electric Corp.*, 764 F.2d 175, 179 (3d Cir. 1985), cert. denied, 475 U.S. 1035 (1986); *Ross v. Communications Satellite Corp.*, 759 F.2d 355, 365–366 (4th Cir. 1985); *Peters v. City of Shreveport*, 818 F.2d 1148, 1161 (5th Cir. 1987); *McQuillen v. Wisconsin Education Association Council*, 830 F.2d 659, 664–665 (7th Cir. 1987); *Fields v. Clark University*, 817 F.2d 931, 936–937 (1st Cir. 1987); *Berl v. Westchester County*, 849 F.2d 712, 714–715 (2d Cir. 1988); *Terbovitz v. Fiscal Court of Adair County, Ky.*, 825 F.2d 111, 115 (6th Cir. 1987); *Fadhl v. City and County of San Francisco*, 741 F.2d 1163, 1165–1166 (9th Cir. 1984); *Bell v. Birmingham Linen Services*, 715 F.2d 1552, 1557 (11th Cir. 1983); *Price Waterhouse v. Hopkins*, 825 F.2d 458, 420–471 (D.C. Cir. 1987), reversed and remanded, 109 S. Ct. 1775 (1989).

94. See *Price Waterhouse v. Hopkins*, 109 S. Ct. 1775, 1795 (1989).

95. Id. at 1784–1788.

96. Id. at 1784, 1784n.2.

97. Id. See also Brodin, "Standard of Causation," p. 323. Title VII remedies are set out in 42 U.S.C. § 2000e-5(g).

98. 42 U.S.C. § 2000e-5(g).

99. 42 U.S.C. § 2000e-5(k).

100. *Price Waterhouse v. Hopkins*, 109 S. Ct. 1775, 1792–1793 (1989).

101. Id. at 1796.

102. See, e.g., Roy L. Brooks, "Civil Rights Scholarship: A Proposed Agenda for the Twenty-First Century," *University of San Francisco Law Review* 20 (1986): 410; Elizabeth Bartholet, "Application of Title VII to Jobs in High Places," *Harvard Law Review* 95 (1982): 959–978.

103. Bartholet, "Application of Title VII," p. 961 (quoting *Powell v. Syracuse University*, 580 F.2d 1150, 1153 [2d Cir. 1978], cert. denied, 439 U.S. 984 [1978]).

104. *Faro v. New York University*, 502 F.2d 1229, 1231–1232 (2d Cir. 1974). See also *Huang v. College of the Holy Cross*, 436 F. Supp. 639, 653 (D. Mass. 1977); *Johnson v. University of Pittsburgh*, 435 F. Supp. 1328, 1353–1354 (W.D. Pa. 1977); *Cussler v. University of Maryland*, 430 F. Supp. 602, 605–606 (D. Md. 1977); *Peters v. Middlebury College*, 409 F. Supp. 857, 868 (D. Vt. 1976); *Labat v. Board of Education*, 401 F. Supp. 753, 757 (S.D.N.Y. 1975); *Moore v. Kibbee*, 381 F. Supp. 834, 839 (E.D.N.Y. 1974); *Megill v. Board of Regents of the State of Florida*, 541 F.2d 1073 (5th Cir. 1976); *Stebbins v. Weaver*, 537 F.2d 939, 943 (7th Cir. 1976), cert. denied, 429 U.S. 1041 (1977); *Duke v. North Texas State University*, 469 F. 2d 829, 838 (5th Cir. 1972), cert. denied, 412 U.S. 932 (1973); *EEOC v. Tufts Institution of Learning*, 421 F. Supp.

152, 158 (D. Mass. 1975); *Keddie v. Pennsylvania State University*, 412 F. Supp. 1264, 1270 (M.D. Pa. 1976); *Green v. Board of Regents of Texas Tech University*, 335 F. Supp. 249, 251 (N.D. Texas 1971), aff'd 474 F.2d 594 (5th Cir. 1973); *Lewis v. Chicago State College*, 299 F. Supp. 1357, 1360 (N.D. Ill. 1969).

105. 42 U.S.C. § 2000e-1 (1970).

106. The exemption was proposed in a substitute bill submitted by senators Dirksen and Mansfield and later adopted by both the Senate and the House. See *Powell v. Syracuse University*, 580 F.2d 1150, 1153 (2d Cir. 1978), cert. denied, 439 U.S. 984 (1978).

107. 42 U.S.C. § 2000e (1982).

108. See H. Rept. 92–238 (1971), 92d Congress, 1st sess., p. 17; S. Rept. 92–415 (1971), 92d Congress, 1st sess., p. 10. For discussion of Title VII's legislative history, see Roy L. Brooks, "Beyond Civil Rights Restoration Legislation: Restructuring Title VII," *Saint Louis University Law Journal* 34 (1990): 551–566; Vaas, "Title VII: Legislative History."

109. E. R. Shipp, "The Litigiousness of Academe," *New York Times*, November 8, 1987, sec. 12.

110. *Local 28, Sheet Metal Workers v. EEOC*, 478 U.S. 421, 448–449 (1986). The Court is quoting from *United Steelworkers of America v. Weber*, 443 U.S. 193, 203 (1979) (quoting 110 *Congressional Record* [1964], p. 6548 [remarks of Sen. Humphrey]). The Court also stated that "Title VII was designed 'to achieve equality of employment opportunities and remove barriers that have operated in the past to favor an identifiable group of white employees over other employees' " (*Local 28, Sheet Metal Workers v. EEOC*, 478 U.S. 421, 448 [1986] [quoting *Griggs v. Duke Power Co.*, 401 U.S. 424, 429–430 (1971)]). See also *Teamsters v. United States*, 431 U.S. 324, 364–365 (1977); *Franks v. Bowman Transportation Co.*, 424 U.S. 747, 763 (1976); *Albermarle Paper Co. v. Moody*, 422 U.S. 405, 417–418 (1975).

Chapter 3

1. Rose, *American Profile*, p. 8.

2. Id., p. 21.

3. The statistical information presented in this list is taken from id., pp. 12–13, 21–22.

4. "Social Issues: The Roots of Poverty," *Time*, January 5, 1987, p. 49. For additional information on the rise in poverty during this period, see Kornblum and Julian, *Social Problems*, p. 233, which cites government studies and other sources.

5. Irrational economic habits basically entail living beyond one's financial means and misallocating household funds—for example, piling up consumer debt, foregoing savings and investments in order to purchase expensive consumer goods, or buying late-model cars that require not only high monthly payments but also more costly insurance, taxes, and maintenance. Living life for the moment, from paycheck to paycheck or weekend to weekend, and without direction or the constraints of a life-plan—how to prepare for retirement, for example, or how to afford the expenses of raising children—can result in a lifestyle that depletes one's finances.

Crime, drug abuse, and alcoholism can also threaten to destabilize working-class families both financially and emotionally. Any family can become distracted, enervated, or even torn apart by a teenager's criminal acts, a mother's drug addiction, or a father's alcoholism.

6. U.S. Bureau of the Census, *Statistical Abstract of the United States, 1986*, 107th ed. (Washington, D.C.: U.S. Government Printing Office, 1987), p. 423.

7. See, e.g., Richard Edwards, *Contested Terrain: The Transformation of the Workplace in the Twentieth Century* (New York: Basic Books, 1979); Macionis, *Sociology*, p. 243.

8. On the existence of racial wage gaps, see Farley and Allen, *Color Line*, p. 317; also pp. 316–361. Plants, factories, mills, and other industrial facilities have been "a major source of black employment in the twentieth century" (Wilson, *The Truly Disadvantaged*, p. 45). During the past twenty years, these industries have experienced economic decline, caused by many factors: competition from abroad (especially Japan and Germany), which provided cheaper and superior products; the tendency (often in response to such competition) to export capital and jobs overseas, where labor is less expensive and more plentiful; the failure to modernize existing industrial facilities, resulting in part from the shift of capital abroad (Kornblum and Julian, *Social Problems*, p. 437). Layoffs came, and African American workers were among the first to go; they were usually the last hired and hence were unprotected by seniority or even affirmative action (see, e.g., *Firefighters v. Stotts*, 467 U.S. 561 [1984]). Unions were often prepared to accept these losses without a challenge; indeed, many unions have poor track records when it comes to supporting the interests of African Americans in equal employment opportunity. See, e.g., *United Steelworkers of America v. Weber*, 443 U.S. 193 (1979); *Local 28, Sheet Metal Workers v. EEOC*, 106 S. Ct. 3019 (1986); *Local No. 93, International Association of Firefighters v. City of Cleveland*, 106 S. Ct. 3063 (1986); *Martin v. Wilks*, 109 S. Ct. 2180 (1989).

9. Elizabeth Hann Hastings and Philip K. Hastings, eds., *Index to International Public Opinion, 1987–1988* (New York: Greenwood Press, 1989), p. 467.

10. See, e.g., John R. Logan and Mark Schneider, "Racial Segregation and Racial Change in American Suburbs, 1970–1980," *American Journal of Sociology* 89 (January 1984): 874–888; Annemette Sorensen, Karl E. Taeuber, and Leslie Hollingsworth, Jr., "Indexes of Racial Residential Segregation for 109 Cities in the United States, 1940 to 1970," *Sociological Focus* 8 (April 1975): 125–142; Charles Hirschman, "America's Melting Pot Reconsidered," *Annual Review of Sociology* 9 (1983): 397–423; John O. Calmore, "National Housing Policies and Black America: Trends, Issues, and Implications," in *The State of Black America 1986*, ed. Janet Dewart (New York: National Urban League, 1986), pp. 115–149; Reynolds Farley, "The Residential Segregation of Blacks from Whites: Trends, Courses, and Consequences," in *Issues in Housing Discrimination: A Consultation/Hearing of the United States Commission on Civil Rights, Washington, D.C., November 12–13, 1985* (Washington, D.C.: U.S. Civil Rights Commission, 1986), vol. 1, *Papers Presented*, pp. 14–19.

11. Farley and Allen, *Color Line*, pp. 143 (table 5.7), 145. See also Karl E. Taeuber, "Causes of Residential Segregation," in *The Fair Housing Act After Twenty Years: A Conference at Yale Law School, March 1988*, ed. Robert G. Schwemm (New Haven, Conn.: Yale Law School, 1989), p. 37.

12. Hastings and Hastings, *Index*, p. 468.

13. National Opinion Research Center, *General Social Surveys, 1972–1983*, p. 117.

14. In 1980, for example, 68 percent of whites were homeowners, whereas only 44 percent of African Americans owned a home (Farley and Allen, *Color Line*, p. 155).

15. Id., p. 156.

16. See id., pp. 155–157; Charles M. Haar and Daniel W. Fessler, *The Wrong Side of the Tracks* (New York: Simon and Schuster, 1986); Ralph Ellison, *Invisible Man* (New York: Random House, 1952).

17. *West's Federal Practice Digest Edition, 1975 to Date*, Civil Rights Sec. 11.5.

18. African Americans were plaintiffs in eight of the fifteen available cases (53.33 percent) and won five of these cases (62.5 percent). There were no white-only plaintiffs. For further discussion, see Smith, "Juri-Statistical Methods in Legal Research."

19. The studies reported in the next several paragraphs are collected, along with others, in several sources. One of the best is Department

of Housing and Urban Development, *Fair Housing Enforcement Demonstration* (Washington, D.C.: U.S. Department of Housing and Urban Development, Office of Policy Development and Research, 1983), esp. pp. 23–28, 37–44.

20. Id., pp. 23–28.

21. These incidents were reported in "Eight Whites Shot by Black Man After Harassment," *Los Angeles Times* (San Diego ed.), June 12, 1986, pt. 1; William K. Stevens, "Philadelphia Neighborhood Is Starting to Simmer Down," *New York Times*, December 1, 1985, sec. 1 (main); "The Racism Next Door," *Time*, June 30, 1986, p. 40; William Celis III, "Justice, HUD Oppose Housing Segregation, But Enforcement Lags," *Wall Street Journal*, October 28, 1985.

22. It is less common to encounter overt acts of racism today, although incidents such as those in Howard Beach, New York, and in Forsyth County, Georgia, should not be discounted. In December 1986, three African Americans who walked into a diner in the Howard Beach neighborhood of Queens to use a telephone were chased and beaten by a gang of whites, resulting in the death of one of the African Americans, who was forced into the path of an oncoming car by the attack. In Forsyth County in January 1987, the Ku Klux Klan stoned a predominantly African American group that was marching to commemorate Dr. Martin Luther King's birthday. See "Black vs. White in Howard Beach," *Time*, January 5, 1987, p. 48; "Fear of Blacks, Fear of Crime," *New York Times*, December 28, 1986, sec. 4 (Week in Review). See also Walter Leavy, "What's Behind the Resurgence of Racism in America?" *Ebony*, April 1987, pp. 132–139; Samuel Freedman, "Racial Tension in New York Is on Increase Despite Gains," *New York Times*, March 29, 1987, sec. 1 (main); Janice Simpson, "Black College Students Are Viewed as Victims of a Subtle Racism," *Wall Street Journal*, April 3, 1987; "Wrong Message from Academe," *Time*, April 6, 1987, p. 57; Joe Davidson, "Private Schools for Black Pupils Are Flourishing," *Wall Street Journal*, April 15, 1987. See generally Harry S. Ashmore, *Hearts and Minds: The Anatomy of Racism from Roosevelt to Reagan* (New York: McGraw-Hill, 1982).

23. Al Campanis, a former major-league baseball player, was fired from his position as vice-president for player personnel for the Los Angeles Dodgers, the third-highest position in the organization, for the bush-league bigotry he displayed in a television interview on ABC's "Nightline" on April 6, 1987. When asked by anchor Ted Koppel why there were no black managers, coaches, or owners in baseball, Campanis responded that blacks may lack "some of the necessities" for holding managerial positions. After a "flabbergasted" Koppel gave him a chance

to remove his foot from his mouth, Campanis stuck it in deeper by re-marking—from out of left field—that "blacks are not good swimmers because they don't have the buoyancy" ("Grapevine," *TV Guide* [San Diego ed.], April 18–24, 1987, p. A–2; Sam McManis, "Campanis Fired in Wake of Racial Remarks," *Los Angeles Times* [San Diego ed.], April 9, 1987, pt. 3).

For an exploration of feelings that are more hidden, see, e.g., Brooks, "Anti-Minority Mindset," pp. 101–104, 107.

24. "Racism Next Door," p. 40.

25. Other examples of smiling discrimination include the sales clerk in a suburban shopping mall who waits on a white customer before wait-ing on a minority customer who was there first and the nightclub owner who imposes a dress code designed to keep minorities out or who makes it a policy to play a certain type of music (for example, country and western) when "too many" African Americans are on the dance floor. See, e.g., "Shop Here, But Don't Stop Here," *Time*, March 10, 1986, p. 46; "Come Back When You're White," *San Diego Reader*, July 26, 1984; "Subtle Racism Said to Prevail in East Country Area," *East County Today* (San Diego), November 30, 1983; Christopher Reynolds, "Incidents of Racism Increase," *San Diego Union*, December 31, 1983.

26. "Racism Next Door," p. 40.

27. See Kornblum and Julian, *Social Problems*, p. 272; *Fowler v. Mc-Crory*, 1989 U.S. District Lexis 15479, p. 13. See generally *Mackey v. Nationwide Insurance Companies*, 724 F.2d 419 (4th Cir. 1984).

28. Farley and Allen, *Color Line*, p. 203.

29. See T. Harry Williams, Richard N. Current, and Frank Freidel, *A History of the United States to 1877*, 3d ed. (New York: Alfred A. Knopf, 1969), p. 90; Arthur O. White, "The Black Leadership Class and Education in Antebellum Boston," *Journal of Negro Education* 42 (1973): 505–515; Carter G. Woodson, *The Education of the Negro Prior to 1861* (Washington, D.C.: Associated Publishers, 1919).

30. See Williams, Current, and Freidel, *History of the United States*, p. 439; Bell, *Race, Racism, and American Law*, pp. 365–366. On the education of African Americans in the North and South at the turn of the eighteenth century, see Franklin, *From Slavery to Freedom*, pp. 160–161.

31. Bell, *Race, Racism, and American Law*, p. 366. See also Stanley K. Schultz, *The Culture Factory: Boston Public Schools, 1789–1860* (New York: Oxford University Press, 1973), pp. 159–161.

32. *Roberts v. City of Boston*, 59 Mass. (5 Cush.) 198 (1850).

33. In 1980, 62.9 percent of African American children attended schools that enrolled 50 percent or more minority students, in contrast

to the 76.6 percent who attended such schools in 1968. In 1980, 33.2 percent of African American children were in schools with 90–100 percent minority students, down from the 64.3 percent who attended these schools in 1968. The pace of desegregation has slowed considerably since 1976; for discussion of this trend, see Gary Orfield, *Public School Desegregation in the United States, 1968–1980* (Washington, D.C.: Joint Center for Political Studies, 1983), p. 4. More than 90 percent of the students in some metropolitan area schools are African American or Hispanic (Kornblum and Julian, *Social Problems*, p. 382).

34. Hochschild's excellent analysis, from which I draw in the next several paragraphs, appears in her books *Thirty Years After Brown* (Washington, D.C.: Joint Center for Political Studies, 1985); and *The New American Dilemma: Liberal Democracy and School Desegregation* (New Haven, Conn.: Yale University Press, 1984).

35. Hochschild, *Thirty Years After Brown*, p. 5.

36. Id. In my opinion, the practice of tracking should be abandoned altogether. Educational studies show that although students in the higher tracks may gain slightly from tracking, students in the bottom tracks tend to lose ground (id.; Chen-Lin Kulik and James Kulik, "Effects of Ability Grouping on Secondary School Students: A Meta-Analysis of Evaluation Findings," *American Educational Research Journal* 19 [Fall 1982]: 415–428.

37. Hochschild, *Thirty Years After Brown*, pp. 5–6.

38. Id., p. 12. Most studies have found that the younger the children are when desegregation occurs, the more successful the desegregation process, by any measure (id., pp. 12–13). See also Willis Hawley, "Equity and Quality in Education: Characteristics of Effective Desegregated Schools," in *Effective School Desegregation: Equity, Quality, and Feasibility*, ed. Willis Hawley (Beverly Hills, Calif.: Sage, 1981), pp. 297–307.

39. Hochschild, *Thirty Years After Brown*, pp. 12, 46n.29.

40. Robert L. Carter, "A Reassessment of *Brown v. Board*," in *Shades of Brown: New Perspectives on School Desegregation*, ed. Derrick A. Bell, Jr. (New York: Teachers College Press, 1980), pp. 20–28.

41. Derrick A. Bell, Jr., "Serving Two Masters: Integration Ideals and Client Interest in School Desegregation Litigation," *Yale Law Journal* 85 (1976): 471–472. Bell's volume *Shades of Brown* is cited in full in note 40, above.

42. Philip E. Converse et al., *American Social Attitudes Data Sourcebook: 1947–1978* (Cambridge, Mass.: Harvard University Press, 1980), pp. 61, 91.

43. See, e.g., Hochschild, *Thirty Years After Brown*, p. 27.

44. Id.

45. *Ottawa v. Tinnon*, 26 Kan. 1, 19 (1881).

46. Because of inadequate resources, however, African American suburban schools often provide basic education that is only marginally better than that provided by inner-city schools; see, e.g., Hochschild, *Thirty Years After Brown*, p. 8; William P. O'Hare et. al., *Blacks on the Move: A Decade of Demographic Change* (Washington, D.C.: Joint Center for Political Studies, 1982), pp. 21, 49–66.

47. A study of twenty thousand American men showed that 12 percent of those with a high school education or less experienced intergenerational upward mobility, whereas 76 percent of those with a graduate or professional degree experienced such mobility (Peter M. Blau and Otis Dudley Duncan, *The American Occupational Structure*, 2d ed. [New York: Free Press, 1978], p. 57). See also Smith and Welch, *Closing the Gap*, pp. 21–41.

48. See U.S. Bureau of the Census, *Census of Population and Housing: 1980*, Public Use Microdata Samples (Washington, D.C.: U.S. Government Printing Office, 1981).

49. For further discussion of this and other studies, see James W. Vander Zanden, *The Social Experience* (New York: Random House, 1988), p. 476; Linda M. Watkins, "Losing Ground: Minorities' Enrollment in College Retreats After Surge in '70s," *Wall Street Journal*, May 29, 1985; "Dramatic Drops for Minorities: Black and Hispanic Enrollments Are Down at All College Levels," *Time*, November 11, 1985, p. 84.

50. Reginald Wilson and Deborah J. Carter, *Eighth Annual Status Report on Minorities in Higher Education* (Washington, D.C.: American Council on Education, 1989), pp. 1, 2, 20, table 1. See also Edward Fiske, "Enrollment of Minorities in Colleges Stagnating," *New York Times*, April 19, 1987, sec. 1 (main).

51. Wilson and Carter, *Eighth Annual Status Report*, pp. 10, 25–27, tables 4–6.

52. Farley and Allen, *Color Line*, pp. 145–148.

53. Id., p. 148; see generally pp. 148–150; Donald S. Massey and Nancy A. Denton, "Hypersegregation in U.S. Metropolitan Areas: Black and Hispanic Segregation along Five Dimensions," *Demography* 26 (August 1989): 373–391.

54. The equal protection clause of the Fourteenth Amendment protects individuals against legislative action or private action conducted "under the color of state law." The Fifth Amendment, which protects individuals against federal action, has an equal protection component in its due process clause that is coextensive with that of the Fourteenth Amendment. See, e.g., *United States v. Paradise*, 480 U.S. 149, 166n.16 (1987).

55. See, e.g., *Village of Arlington Heights v. Metropolitan Housing Development Corp.*, 429 U.S. 252 (1977); *City of Eastland v. Forest City*

Enterprises, Inc., 426 U.S. 668 (1976); *James v. Valtierra*, 402 U.S. 137 (1971). Land-use barriers may, of course, discriminate on the basis of economic status, but such discrimination apparently does not merit constitutional protection; see *Dandridge v. Williams*, 397 U.S. 471, 485–486 (1970); in accord, *Jefferson v. Hackney*, 406 U.S. 535, 547 (1972). See also *Boddie v. Connecticut*, 401 U.S. 371 (1971), in which the claims of indigents who were unable to pay divorce filing fees were treated as due process rather than as equal protection claims.

56. *Washington v. Davis*, 426 U.S. 229, 244–245 (1976).

57. See, e.g., *Rogers v. Lodge*, 458 U.S. 613 (1982); *City of Mobile v. Bolden*, 446 U.S. 55 (1980); *Village of Arlington Heights v. Metropolitan Housing Development Corp.*, 429 U.S. 252 (1977).

58. *Village of Arlington Heights v. Metropolitan Housing Development Corp.*, 429 U.S. 252, 266 (1977).

59. *Rogers v. Lodge*, 458 U.S. 613, 618 (1982). "Relevant facts" include the magnitude of the disparity, foreseeability of the consequences of the government's actions, legislative history, patterns of conduct, and the government's knowledge of the disparate impact (*Dowdell v. City of Apopka*, 698 F.2d 1181, 1186 [11th Cir. 1983]). See also *Zimmer v. McKeithan*, 485 F.2d 1297, 1305–1307 (5th Cir. 1973), aff'd per curiam on other grounds sub nom. *East Carroll Parish School Board v. Marshall*, 424 U.S. 636 (1976).

60. *Personnel Administrator v. Feeney*, 442 U.S. 256 (1979).

61. Id. at 279.

62. *Rogers v. Lodge*, 458 U.S. 613, 643, 645 (1982).

63. Id. at 647.

64. For further discussion of the intent test in a legislative context, see John Ely, "Legislative and Administrative Motivation in Constitutional Law," *Yale Law Journal* 79 (1970): 1205–1340; "Legislative Motivation," Symposium, *San Diego Law Review* 15 (1978): 925–1183.

65. Zimmer, Sullivan, and Richards, *Cases and Materials on Employment Discrimination*, p. xxxiv.

66. For a discussion of the distinction between voluntary and involuntary racial preferences, see Roy L. Brooks, "Affirmative Action in Law Teaching," *Columbia Human Rights Law Review* 14 (1982): 25–27. On the importance of voluntary use of racial preferences, see, e.g., *Johnson v. Transportation Agency, Santa Clara County, California*, 480 U.S. 616, 616n.8 (1987) (cases cited); *United Steelworkers of America v. Weber*, 443 U.S. 193, 204 (1979). On the use of the benign quotas in housing, see, e.g., Bell, *Race, Racism, and American Law*, pp. 535–541.

67. See Bruce Ackerman, "Integration for Subsidized Housing and the Question of Racial Occupancy Controls," *Stanford Law Review* 26 (1974): 251–253; Grover Hankins, "Starrett City and Other Race-Conscious Methods of Achieving Integration," in Schwemm, *The Fair Housing Act After Twenty Years*, pp. 109–110.

68. Newman's testimony is quoted from *United States v. Starrett City Associates*, 660 F. Supp. 668, 673–674 (E.D.N.Y. 1987), aff'd, 840 F.2d 1096 (2d Cir. 1988), cert. denied, 109 S. Ct. 376 (1988).

69. Anthony Downs, *Opening Up the Suburbs* (New Haven, Conn.: Yale University Press, 1973), p. 99. For discussion of additional social science data, see Bell, *Race, Racism, and American Law*, pp. 531–532, 535–537. See also *Issues in Housing Discrimination: A Consultation/Hearing of the United States Commission on Civil Rights, Washington, D.C., November 12–13, 1985* (Washington, D.C.: U.S. Civil Rights Commission, 1986), vol. 1, *Papers Presented*, pp. 145–199 (papers presented by Roger Starr, Rodney A. Smolla, and Oscar Newman).

70. For decisions in which courts have upheld the use of racial occupancy controls, see e.g., *Schmidt v. Boston Housing Authority*, 505 F. Supp. 988 (D.C. Mass. 1981); *Otero v. New York City Housing Authority*, 484 F.2d 1122 (2d Cir. 1973). For decisions in which use of such controls was not upheld, see, e.g., *Williamsburg Fair Housing Commission v. N.Y.C. Housing Authority*, 493 F. Supp. 1225 (S.D.N.Y. 1980). See also Rodney Smolla, "Integration Maintenance: The Unconstitutionality of Benign Programs That Discourage Black Entry to Prevent White Flight," *Duke Law Journal* 1981 (1981): 891–939.

71. *United States v. Starrett City Associates*, 660 F. Supp. 668 (E.D.N.Y. 1987), aff'd, 840 F.2d 1096 (2d Cir. 1988), cert. denied, 109 S. Ct. 376 (1988). *Starrett City* was decided on statutory grounds, namely, the Fair Housing Act (id. at 677). The district court distinguished it from *Otero* on the grounds that *Otero* was decided on a constitutional standard (id. at 677–678). This distinction is somewhat odd, because the Constitution is generally more restrictive in the use of racial classifications than Congress is (see, e.g., *Johnson v. Transportation Agency, Santa Clara County, California*, 480 U.S. 616, 627–628n.6 [1987]). *Starrett City* is the major case in the Reagan administration's long assault on racial occupancy quotas; see Robert G. Schwemm, "Introduction," in Schwemm, *The Fair Housing Act After Twenty Years*, p. 12.

72. Fair Housing Act of 1968 (Title VIII), Pub. L. No. 90–284, 82 Stat. 81 (1968) (codified as amended at 42 U.S.C. §§ 3601–3619 [1982 and Supp. 1987]).

73. See, e.g., John O. Calmore, "Proving Housing Discrimination: Intent vs. Effect and the Continuing Search for the Proper Touchstone," in *Issues in Housing Discrimination*, vol. 1, *Papers Presented*, pp. 77–92.

74. 42 U.S.C. §§ 3604–3606.

75. Id. at §§ 3604, 3605, 3601.

76. Roger Spencer, "Enforcement of Federal Fair Housing Law," *Urban Lawyer* 9 (1977): 514. The policy behind the 1949 Housing Act is stated in 42 U.S.C. § 1441 (1970).

77. These exemptions are codified in 42 U.S.C. §§ 3603(b)(1), 3603(b)(2).

78. *Reitman v. Mulkey*, 387 U.S. 369 (1967).

79. 42 U.S.C. § 3612(c). The next section of this chapter discusses damages in greater detail.

80. Id. at §§ 3610, 3612.

81. See "Racism Next Door" p. 40; Celis, "Justice, HUD Oppose Housing Segregation."

82. See Brooks, "Use of the Civil Rights Acts of 1866 and 1871," pp. 258, 261–262 (sources cited therein).

83. 42 U.S.C. § 1982.

84. *Jones v. Alfred H. Mayer*, 392 U.S. 409, 412–413 (1968); emphasis in original. See also "Civil Rights—Racial Discrimination and Property Rights: The Scope of 42 U.S.C. § 1982," Note, *Wayne Law Review* 29 (1982): 203–239.

85. *Jones v. Alfred H. Mayer*, 392 U.S. 409, 441–442 (1968). Although Justice White believes that the intent test applies to section 1982 actions (*City of Memphis v. Green*, 451 U.S. 101, 129 [1981]), the Court itself has not so ruled. The Court has, however, ruled that Section 1982's sister provision, Section 1981 (42 U.S.C. § 1981 [1982]), requires proof of intent to discriminate (*General Building Contractors Association v. Pennsylvania*, 458 U.S. 375 [1982]). See "Dead-End Street: Discrimination, the Thirteenth Amendment, and Section 1982, *City of Memphis v. Green*," Comment, *Chicago-Kent Law Review* 58 (1982): 873–905.

86. See, e.g., *Marable v. Walker*, 704 F.2d 1219 (11th Cir. 1983) (trial court limited damages to $1,000). But see also *Philips v. Hunter Trails Community Association*, 685 F.2d 184, 191 (7th Cir. 1982) ($100,000 in punitive damages awarded under Section 1982).

87. See James A. Kushner, *Fair Housing: Discrimination in Real Estate, Community Development, and Revitalization*, with annual supplements (Colorado Springs: Shepards/McGraw-Hill, 1983), p. 478; Bell, *Race, Racism, and American Law*, 516–520. See also *Philips v. Hunter Trails Community Association*, 685 F.2d 184, 190 (7th Cir. 1982).

88. Office of the Attorney General of California, John K. Van de Kamp, news release, July 10, 1986, Sacramento, California, p. 1.

89. Bell, *Race, Racism, and American Law*, pp. 516–518.

90. In particular, civil rights litigation in which the trial court retains subject-matter jurisdiction, such as school desegregation cases, seems never-ending; see, e.g., Chayes, "Role of the Judge."

91. See, e.g., *Dayton Board of Education v. Brinkman*, 433 U.S. 406 (1977); *Austin Independent School District v. United States*, 429 U.S. 990 (1976) (remanded for reconsideration in light of *Washington v. Davis*, 426 U.S. 229 [1976] and *Village of Arlington Heights v. Metropolitan Housing Development Corp.*, 429 U.S. 252 [1977]).

92. *Swann v. Charlotte-Mecklenburg Board of Education*, 402 U.S. 1 (1971). See also *Missouri v. Jenkins*, 1105. Cf. 1651 (1990).

93. *Davis v. Board of School Commissioners*, 402 U.S. 33, 37 (1971); emphasis added.

94. See, e.g., Douglas Longshore and Jeffrey Prager, "The Impact of School Desegregation: A Situational Analysis," *Annual Review of Sociology* 11 (1985): 75–91.

95. *Milliken v. Bradley [Milliken I]*, 418 U.S. 717, 743–744 (1974).

96. See, e.g., *Kelly v. Metropolitan County Board of Education of Nashville and Davidson County, Tenn.*, 687 F.2d 814 (6th Cir. 1982), cert. denied, 459 U.S. 1183 (1983); *Clark v. Board of Education of Little Rock School District*, 705 F.2d 265 (5th Cir. 1983).

97. *Milliken v. Bradley [Milliken II]*, 433 U.S. 267, 281 (1977).

98. See, e.g., the cases cited in note 96, above (Chapter 3).

99. The prototype desegregation plan for predominantly African American schools has come to be known as the "Atlanta Compromise." Implemented in 1973 in Atlanta, Georgia, the compromise gave African Americans the right to obtain control of the predominantly African American Atlanta school district and to select an African American educator as superintendent. They were also given financial backing to implement an ambitious educational enrichment program that gave special emphasis to mathematics and reading by a most unusual feature: the school board was given power to set its own tax rate without having to resort to a public referendum to raise money. The assessed valuation on Atlanta's commercial and residential property nearly doubled, from $2.7 billion in 1973 to $5 billion in 1986. The only major problem with the compromise, from my point of view, was the lack of cultural diversity. Atlanta's demographics meant that there were simply not enough whites in the school district to make racial balancing meaningful, and the Supreme Court's restrictions on interdistrict remedies (*Milliken v. Bradley*, 418 U.S. 717 [1974]) made cultural diversity in Atlanta public schools not even a remote possibility. For more on the Atlanta

Compromise, see Dudley Clendinen, "Urban Education That Really Works," *New York Times*, April 13, 1986, sec. 12 (Educational Life, special section).

100. For a full discussion of the problems of standardized testing, see Howard F. Taylor, *The I.Q. Game: A Methodological Inquiry into the Heredity-Environment Controversy* (New Brunswick, N.J.: Rutgers University Press, 1980).

101. Duffey is quoted in Fiske, "Enrollment of Minorities." See also Brent Staples, "The Dwindling Black Presence on Campus," *New York Times Magazine*, April 27, 1986, p. 52; Watkins, "Losing Ground"; Simpson, "Black College Students"; "Dramatic Drops for Minorities"; "Wrong Message from Academe." There has also been a general increase in racial tension throughout America; see Leavy, "What's Behind the Resurgence of Racism?"; Freedman, "Racial Tension in New York"; David Hatchett, "The State of Race Relations," *Crisis*, November 1989, pp. 14–19. Europe has also experienced an increase in racial problems ("Rising Racism on the Continent," *Time*, February 6, 1984, pp. 40–45).

102. Simpson, "Black College Students."

103. These incidents are reported, respectively, in id.; Staples, "Dwindling Black Presence on Campus," p. 52; and Watkins, "Losing Ground."

104. Simpson, "Black College Students."

105. See, e.g., Staples, "Dwindling Black Presence on Campus," p. 46; Elizabeth Kolbert, "Minority Faculty: Bleak Future," *New York Times*, August 18, 1985, sec. 12 (Education, special section); "Minorities Studies Show More Students But Fewer Teachers," *San Diego Union*, February 9, 1986; Thomas Johnson, "Ivy League Blacks Find Life in Microcosm on the Campus," *New York Times*, May 20, 1979, sec. 1 (main).

The shortage of African American faculty tends to feed on itself. "If a black child never encounters a black professional, that suggests a lot to him about his own potential" (*San Diego Union*, February 9, 1986, interview with H. Dean Propst, chancellor of the University of Georgia).

106. Hastings and Hastings, *Index*, p. 467.

107. See Watkins, "Losing Ground"; Wayne King, "Bakke Case Still Affects Davis Medical School," *New York Times*, December 6, 1981, sec. 1 (main).

108. William Raspberry, "Aid That Isn't Charity," *Washington Post*, April 13, 1987.

109. Cook is quoted in id. See also Vander Zanden, *The Social Experience*, p. 476.

110. Staples, "Dwindling Black Presence on Campus," pp. 51–52.

111. *Regents of the University of California v. Bakke*, 438 U.S. 265 (1978).

112. Id. at 320, 414. Pertinent sections of the Civil Rights Act are found at 42 U.S.C. § 2000d–2000d-4 (1982).

113. *Regents of the University of California v. Bakke*, 438 U.S. 265, 314–316, 370–378 (1978).

114. Id. at 358–362, 327.

115. Id. at 387, 294–295.

116. See, e.g., *City of Richmond v. J. A. Croson Co.*, 109 S. Ct. 706 (1989); *Wygant v. Jackson Board of Education*, 476 U.S. 267 (1986).

117. King, "Bakke Case."

118. Id.

119. "Affirmative action, in its most fundamental form, simply instructs the employer to look beyond traditional qualifications and to look at the 'whole person.' This means that the employer should be conscious of the applicant's race or gender as well as such neutral qualities as motivation, how far the person has traveled to get to where he or she is today, and whether the person satisfies a legitimate institutional interest (e.g., educational diversity or maximization of the institution's total utility) or social responsibility (e.g., maximization of antidiscrimination values or acting as responsible neighbors in the community). Given the legacy of slavery and legalized segregation, this is the only manner in which most minorities can realistically compete with whites on an equal footing today" (Brooks, "Civil Rights Scholarship," p. 403 [citations omitted]).

120. *Local 28, Sheet Metal Workers v. EEOC*, 478 U.S. 421, 450 (1986).

Chapter 4

1. See U.S. Bureau of the Census, *Current Population Reports: Money Income and Poverty Status, 1988*, p. 127; Rose, *American Profile*, p. 7.

2. Rose, *American Profile*, p. 21.

3. Ken Auletta, *The Underclass* (New York: Random House, 1982).

4. "The Vanishing Black Family: Crisis in Black America," CBS Reports, January 25, 1986, television documentary.

5. The conference proceedings are reported in "Joint Center for Political Studies Conference Report: Defining the Underclass," *Focus*, June 1987, pp. 8–12. The consensus definition is cited in id., p. 11.

6. See id., p. 9; Wilson, *The Truly Disadvantaged*, p. 10.

7. Rose, *American Profile*, p. 35.

8. See "Joint Center for Political Studies Conference Report"; Wilson, *The Truly Disadvantaged*, p. 60; Vander Zanden, *The Social Experience*, p. 239; Isabel V. Sawhill, "Poverty and the Underclass," in *Challenge to Leadership: Economic and Social Issues for the Next Decade*, ed. Isabel V. Sawhill (Washington, D.C.: Urban Institute Press, 1988), p. 227.

9. Wilson, *The Truly Disadvantaged*, p. 60.

10. See Vander Zanden, *The Social Experience*, p. 239; Sawhill, "Poverty and the Underclass," pp. 227–230; David Whitman and Jeannye Thorton, "A Nation Apart," *U.S. News and World Report*, March 17, 1987, pp. 18–21.

11. A 1987 congressional study conducted by the Joint Economic Committee contends that a "low-wage explosion," which began in 1979, is keeping more than thirty million Americans below the poverty line. "Between 1979 and 1985—the most recent year for which government data are available—44 percent of the net new jobs created paid poverty-level wages" (Barry Bluestone and Bennett Harrison, "A Low-Wage Explosion: The Grim Truth About the Job 'Miracle,' " *New York Times*, February 1, 1987, sec. 8 [Business]).

12. See, e.g., Thurow, *Zero-Sum Society*, pp. 184–187; Joel Kotken, "The Reluctant Entrepreneurs: Are American Blacks Still Stuck on the Bottom Rung of the Economic Ladder Because So Few Start Businesses on Their Own?" *Inc.*, September 1986, pp. 81–86; Anthony Ramirez, "America's Super Minority," *Fortune*, November 24, 1986, pp. 148–149; "Asian Americans: Are They Making the Grade?" *U.S. News and World Report*, April 2, 1984, pp. 41–43; "Racial Tensions Mount Between Blacks, Koreans," *Jet*, July 1, 1985, p. 5. Other minority groups often experience less racial discrimination and segregation than African Americans do, which helps to explain their relative progress. Farley and Allen, for example, report that even the most recently emigrated minority groups experience less housing discrimination and segregation than African Americans (*Color Line*, p. 148). These authors also claim that foreign-born blacks, such as West Indians, are only marginally better off than those born in the United States and are far worse off than whites (id., pp. 362–405).

13. See Edward C. Banfield, *The Unheavenly City Revisited* (Boston: Little, Brown, 1974); Oscar Lewis, *The Children of Sanchez* (New York: Random House, 1961).

14. See Wilson, *The Truly Disadvantaged*.

15. See William Ryan, *Blaming the Victim*, rev. ed. (New York: Vintage Books, 1976).

16. See, e.g., Luix Overbea, "Youths Hold Key to Black Family Survival," *Christian Science Monitor*, April 1, 1987; "Growing Up Poor," Transcript no. 403, "Frontline" television series, February 2, 1986 (Boston: WGBH Educational Foundation, 1986); Carlyle C. Douglas, "Future of Young Black Men Looks Bleak, Panelists Say," *New York Times*, May 19, 1985, sec. 1 (main); "Children Having Children," *Time*, December 9, 1985, pp. 78–90; "A Threat to the Future," *Time*, May 14, 1984, p. 20. At the release of the Urban League's annual report *The State of Black America 1986*, National Urban League president John Jacob remarked that the plight of young African American men is one of the most pressing problems facing America today (*San Diego Union/Tribune*, February 2, 1986). The role of teenagers in the breakdown of the African American family was highlighted in "The Vanishing Black Family," the controversial television report; for an excellent discussion of the program, see William Raspberry, "America's Black Family Crisis," *San Diego Union*, January 24, 1986.

17. See, e.g., "Children Having Children," p. 81.

18. The remark of the Atlanta teenager is quoted in "Main Street," *TV Guide*, June 14–20, 1986, p. A-69; the Newark teenager appeared in the televised report "The Vanishing Black Family" in January 1986.

19. "Growing Up Poor," p. 17.

20. Andrew Stein, "Children of Poverty: Crisis in New York," *New York Times Magazine*, June 8, 1986, p. 68.

21. Id.

22. "Growing Up Poor," p. 5.

23. Stein, "Children of Poverty," p. 68.

24. "Growing Up Poor," p. 6.

25. Studies have shown that food prices in poverty-stricken areas are above average; see, e.g., Rose, *American Profile*, pp. 7–8.

26. "Growing Up Poor," p. 6.

27. James P. Comer and Alvin Poussaint, *Black Child Care: How to Bring Up a Black Child in America—A Guide to Emotional and Psychological Development* (New York: Simon and Schuster, 1975), pp. 22–23, 19–21.

28. See, e.g., Thomas Morgan, "The World Ahead: Black Parents Prepare Their Children for Pride and Prejudice," *New York Times Magazine*, October 27, 1985, pp. 32–35.

29. Claude Brown, *Manchild in the Promised Land* (New York: Signet, 1965).

30. Claude Brown, "Manchild in Harlem" *New York Times Magazine*, September 16, 1984, pp. 38–40. See also Douglas, "Future of

Young Black Men"; "When Brother Kills Brother," *Time*, September 16, 1985, pp. 32–36.

31. "Welcome, America, to the Baby Bust," *Time*, February 23, 1987, p. 28.

32. Id., p. 29. See also "Growing Up Poor."

33. John Edgar Wildeman, *Brothers and Keepers* (New York: Penguin, 1984), pp. 57–58, 64.

34. See Williams, *Eyes on the Prize*; Higginbotham, *In the Matter of Color*; Winthrop D. Jordan, *White Over Black: American Attitudes Toward the Negro, 1550–1812* (Chapel Hill: University of North Carolina Press, 1968); Julius Lester, *To Be A Slave* (New York: Dell, 1968); Herbert Aptheker, *Nat Turner's Slave Rebellion* (New York: Grove Press, 1966); Kenneth Stampp, *The Era of Reconstruction, 1865–1877* (New York: Vintage Books, 1965); Kenneth Stampp, *The Peculiar Institution: Slavery in the Antebellum South* (New York: Vintage Books, 1956).

35. See National Advisory Commission on Civil Disorders (Kerner Commission), *Report of the National Advisory Commission on Civil Disorders: Summary of Report* (New York: Bantam Books, 1968; New York: A. Philip Randolph Institute, 1970), pp. 9–16, 5. See also "The Cycle of Despair," *Life*, educational reprint, March 8, 1968. For an account of how local governments, through the unequal distribution of municipal services, helped to create the impoverished conditions under which many African Americans now live, see Haar and Fessler, *Wrong Side of the Tracks*.

36. Statistics on the unemployment rate are found in U.S. Bureau of the Census, *Current Population Reports: The Social and Economic Status of the Black Population in the United States—An Historical View, 1970–1978*, Special Studies Series P-23, Publication no. 80 (Washington, D.C.: U.S. Government Printing Office, 1979), pp. 69, 70. See also Farley and Allen, *Color Line*, p. 214, figure 8.1. On the poverty rate, see U.S. Bureau of the Census, *Current Population Reports: The Social and Economic Status of the Black Population, 1970–1978*, pp. 29, 49, 50. On income levels, see Smith and Welch, *Closing the Gap*, p. 104. See also U.S. Bureau of the Census, *Statistical Abstract of the United States, 1971*, 92d ed. (Washington, D.C.: U.S. Government Printing Office, 1972), p. 316; U.S. Bureau of the Census, *Historical Statistics of the United States: Colonial Times to 1970*, pt. 1, G (Washington, D.C.: U.S. Government Printing Office, 1975), pp. 189–256.

37. U.S. Bureau of the Census, *Current Population Reports: The Social and Economic Status of the Black Population, 1970–1978*, p. 74.

38. Smith and Welch, *Closing the Gap*, pp. 6, 23–26.

39. Statistics on housing are taken from U.S. Bureau of the Census, *Current Population Reports: The Social and Economic Status of the Black Population, 1970–1978*, pp. 137, 139, 141. Statistics on education are taken from id., p. 93.

40. Carl Rowan, "The Blacks Among Us," *Reader's Digest*, June 1985, p. 72.

41. "Strivers and Defeatists," *New York Times*, November 2, 1986, sec. 4 (Week in Review).

42. Rowan, "The Blacks Among Us," pp. 74–75.

43. National Advisory Commission, *Report*, pp. 15–16.

44. See, e.g., "When Brother Kills Brother."

45. James Baldwin, *The Evidence of Things Not Seen*, (New York: Holt, Rinehart and Winston, 1985), p. 19.

46. Fiss, "Theory of Fair Employment Laws," pp. 237–240. For a more detailed discussion of racial sensibility, see Brooks, "Life After Tenure." For a discussion of other deleterious psychosocial consequences of racism, see Oscar A. Barbarin et al., eds., *Institutional Racism and Community Competence*, DHHS Publication no. (ADM) 81–907 (Washington, D.C.: U.S. Department of Health and Human Services, 1981); Alexander Thomas and Samuel Sillen, *Racism and Psychiatry* (New York: Brunner/Mazel, 1972); Joel Kovel, *White Racism: A Psychohistory* (New York: Vintage Books, 1970).

47. These statistics are reported in Sheldon H. Danziger, Robert H. Haveman, and Robert D. Plotnick, "Antipoverty Policy: Effects on the Poor and the Nonpoor," in *Fighting Poverty: What Works and What Doesn't*, ed. Sheldon H. Danziger and Daniel H. Weinberg (Cambridge, Mass.: Harvard University Press, 1986), pp. 50–77; and Kornblum and Julian, *Social Problems*, pp. 232–234.

48. National Opinion Research Center, *General Social Surveys, 1972–1983*, p. 117; Converse et al., *American Social Attitudes*, pp. 61, 91. See also Chapter 3 for further discussion.

49. See, e.g., Greg J. Duncan, *Years of Poverty, Years of Plenty* (Ann Arbor: Institute for Social Research, University of Michigan, 1984); Mary Jo Bane, "Household Composition and Poverty," in Danziger and Weinberg, *Fighting Poverty*, pp. 209–231.

50. Wilson, *The Truly Disadvantaged*, pp. 7, 30, 49, 56, 60–61, 143–144, 160.

51. See "Strivers and Defeatists."

52. Comer and Poussaint, *Black Child Care*, pp. 19–21.

53. Wilson, *The Truly Disadvantaged*, p. 60. A recent article (Donald S. Massey and Mitchell L. Eggers, "The Ecology of Inequality: Minorities and the Concentration of Poverty, 1970–1980," *American Jour-*

nal of Sociology 95 (March 1990): 1153–1188) confirms the view that African American interclass spatial separation has increased since the 1960s, but questions the importance of this trend in explaining the emergence of "concentrated urban poverty." Among the article's empirical findings that challenge this relationship are the following: the "highest levels of interclass segregation are observed in black communities notable for their lack of concentrated black poverty (e.g., Anaheim, San Jose), while metropolitan areas with very high concentrations of black poverty (e.g., New York, Philadelphia, and Detroit) have low to moderate levels of segregation by income" (id., p. 1171). As important as these findings are, they do not, however, measure the degree of interclass social and cultural interaction or otherwise disprove the theory advanced in this book that increased interclass separation helps to explain the emergence of the underclass subculture, especially dysfunction and self-destruction (see p. 121). Moreover, the article defines the African American underclass solely in terms of urban poverty, failing to differentiate among the working poor, the welfare poor, and other subgroups within the poverty class as discussed earlier in this chapter. The article simply demonstrates that upper-income migration from African American ghettoes fails to account for concentrated African American poverty; it says little about the relationship between that exodus and the African American underclass subculture.

54. James Comer, "Black Americans' Problems Are the Orphan of History," *Los Angeles Times*, February 14, 1986, pt. 2, sec. J.

55. See, for example, the discussion in Chapter 3 concerning insufficient resources in predominantly African American public schools.

56. Allan Bloom, *The Closing of the American Mind* (New York: Simon and Schuster, 1987), p. 91. Bloom expressly criticizes African American college students who have "veered off toward black separation" by demanding "segregated tables in dining halls" and "separation in housing and in areas of study" (meaning African American studies programs).

Chapter 5

1. For discussion of various institution support programs, see, e.g., Dirk Johnson, "Companies Create 'Model School' for Urban Poor," *New York Times*, October 20, 1988, sec. B.

2. Id.

3. My views on Delancey Street are taken from several sources, including the following: a conversation in January 1990 with Mary Lynn Samios, currently an attorney in San Jose, California; Samios's research presented in her paper "Delancey Street: A Preliminary Report" (type-

script, July 25, 1985); Ann Japenga, "She's a Partner in Criminology," *Los Angeles Times*, April 5, 1984, pt. 5; Diana Sperrazza, "Special New Mexico Community Gives Losers 2nd Chance: Delancey Street Program," *Albuquerque Journal*, March 21, 1982; and a conversation in 1985 with the former president of the Delancey Street Foundation, Mimi Silbert, who holds a Ph.D. in criminology and psychology and who was teaching at the University of California at Berkeley in the 1970s when John Maher asked her to help run Delancey Street. Other useful sources include Grover Sales, *John Maher of Delancey Street: A Guideline to Peaceful Revolution in America* (New York: Norton, 1975); "The Delancey Street Gang," *Newsweek*, September 23, 1974, p. 81; and "Getting Straight on Delancey Street: San Francisco Therapeutic Community," *Time*, March 19, 1973, p. 82.

4. Gilbert Ware, *William Hastie: Grace Under Pressure* (New York: Oxford University Press, 1984), p. 16.

5. See Brooks, "Affirmative Action Issue."

6. "Images (1987), Farewells," *Time*, December 28, 1987, p. 59.

7. See the Introduction, above, for discussion of Booker T. Washington's theory of race relations. "Uncle Tom" is the name used for African Americans who try to ingratiate themselves with whites rather than demanding respect and equal rights. It is taken from Harriet Beecher Stowe's nineteenth-century novel *Uncle Tom's Cabin*, in which a slave by that name suffers submissively through beating after beating by Simon Legree, his master. Tom shows no anger toward the master, who finally beats him to death.

8. See, e.g., Schaefer, *Sociology*, pp. 63–83, 86, 182, 202, 609.

9. Some African American scholars claim that African American children have a distinct learning style as well as a distinct language style. This learning style may be a cultural liability, because it is deemed to be incompatible with the cognitive approach reflected in standardized tests and classroom instruction. The extremely controversial idea of an African American cognitive style requires more research. For a more detailed discussion of the theory, see Janice E. Hale-Benson, *Black Children: Their Roots, Culture, and Learning Styles* (Baltimore: Johns Hopkins University Press, 1986). See also New York State Department of Education, *Increasing High School Completion Rates* (Albany: New York State Department of Education, 1987), pp. 15–16.

10. See, e.g., Committee on Policy for Racial Justice, *Visions of a Better Way: A Black Appraisal of Public Schooling*, prepared by Sara Lawrence Lightfoot (Washington, D.C.: Joint Center for Political Studies Press, 1989).

Chapter 6

1. Murray, *Losing Ground*, pp. 227–228.

2. See this chapter's later discussion of the strict scrutiny test and *Bakke* for further elaboration of the concepts of racial inclusion and "unnecessarily trammeling the interests" of white Americans.

3. As mentioned in Chapter 2, this discussion focuses only on disparate-treatment discrimination. Middle-class African Americans also find disparate-impact litigation to be a problem, however.

4. See, e.g., Cleary, "Presuming and Pleading," pp. 11–12.

5. For a discussion of the frequency of perjured testimony in civil litigation, see Geoffrey Hazard, "Ethics in the Practice of Law," in *Pleading and Procedure*, 4th ed., edited by David Louisell and Geoffrey Hazard (Mineola, N.Y.: Foundation Press, 1979), pp. 1165, 1167.

6. *McDonnell Douglas Corp. v. Green*, 411 U.S. 792, 801 (1973). Also see the discussion in Chapter 2, above.

7. See 42 U.S.C. § 2000e-5.

8. *Price Waterhouse v. Hopkins*, 109 S. Ct. 1775, 1796 (1989).

9. Shipp, "Litigiousness of Academe," p. 63.

10. California Government Code §§ 12900–12996 (West 1980 and Supp. 1985). For extensive discussion of the Fair Employment and Housing Act, see Marjorie Gelb and Joanne Frankfurt, "California's Fair Employment and Housing Act: A Viable State Remedy for Employment Discrimination," *Hastings Law Review* 34 (1983): 1055–1105.

11. Fair Housing Amendments Act of 1988, P.L. 100–430, 102 Stat. 1619, September 13, 1988, amending 42 U.S.C. §§ 3601–3617 (1982).

12. For a good discussion of other strategies for dealing with the problem of intra-class racial disparity in primary education, see Hochschild, *New American Dilemma*.

13. As a former director of a special academic and admissions program for prospective minority law students, I placed great weight on a student's motivation and college grade point average, as did my predecessors. In a conversation with me, Trina Grillo, who is a professor of law and director of the academic support program at the University of San Francisco Law School, agreed with this approach and further stated that standardized admissions test scores were less predictive for African Americans than for any other group at her school. Narissa Skillmen, who is the well-respected pioneer of academic support programs in law schools in California and who now owns a private consulting firm in New York and Oakland, strongly recommends that less attention be given to standardized admissions tests and that more attention be given

to grade point average and motivation when evaluating African American applicants.

14. *Wygant v. Jackson Board of Education,* 106 S. Ct. 1842, 1861 (1986) (quoting *Regents of the University of California v. Bakke,* 438 U.S. 265, 359 [1978]).

15. Id. at 1867. See generally *United States v. Paradise,* 107 S. Ct. 1053, 1064 (1987).

16. *Local 28, Sheet Metal Workers v. EEOC,* 106 S. Ct. 3019, 3036–3037 (1986) (cases cited therein). See generally *United Steelworkers of America v. Weber,* 443 U.S. 193, 202–203, 208 (1979); *Johnson v. Transportation Agency, Santa Clara County, California,* 107 S. Ct. 1442, 1450–1451 (1987).

17. See e.g., *Johnson v. Transportation Agency, Santa Clara County, California,* 107 S. Ct. 1442, 1451 (1987) (citing *United Steelworkers of America v. Weber,* 443 U.S. 193, 208 [1979]).

18. For fuller treatment of this argument and of the morality issue, see, e.g., Kupperman, "Relations Between the Sexes."

19. The government may no longer be the sole provider of remedial education. Citing an oral report given by the American Society for Training and Development recently, the *Wall Street Journal* lists the following statistics: "22% of [large employers] . . . offer basic training in reading, 41% in writing, and 31% in arithmetic" ("Labor Letter," *Wall Street Journal,* February 20, 1990).

20. "Labor Letter," *Wall Street Journal,* December 3, 1987.

21. See Roy L. Brooks and Sharon A. Cheever, "The Federal Loan Guarantee Program: A Unified Approach," *Journal of Corporate Law* 10 (1984): 204–205.

Bibliography

Ackerman, Bruce. "Integration for Subsidized Housing and the Question of Racial Occupancy Controls." *Stanford Law Review* 26 (1974): 245–309.

"Affirmative Word from Washington." *New York Times*, December 13, 1981, sec. 4 (Week in Review).

Allport, Gordon W. *The Nature of Prejudice.* Unabridged ed. Reading, Mass.: Addison-Wesley, 1979.

Annual Report of the Director of the United States Courts, 1987. Washington, D.C.: U.S. Government Printing Office, 1987.

Aptheker, Herbert. *Nat Turner's Slave Rebellion.* New York: Grove Press, 1966.

Asante, Molefi Kete. *The Afrocentric Idea.* Philadelphia: Temple University Press, 1987.

Ashmore, Harry S. *Hearts and Minds: The Anatomy of Racism from Roosevelt to Reagan.* New York: McGraw-Hill, 1982.

"Asian Americans: Are They Making the Grade?" *U.S. News and World Report*, April 2, 1984, pp. 41–43.

Auletta, Ken. *The Underclass.* New York: Random House, 1982.

Austin, Regina. "Resistance Tactics for Tokens." *Harvard Blackletter Journal* 3 (1986): 52–53.

Baldwin, James. *The Evidence of Things Not Seen.* New York: Holt, Rinehart and Winston, 1985.

Bane, Mary Jo. "Household Composition and Poverty." In *Fighting Poverty: What Works and What Doesn't,* edited by Sheldon H. Danziger and Daniel H. Weinberg, pp. 209–231. Cambridge, Mass.: Harvard University Press, 1986.

Banfield, Edward C. *The Unheavenly City Revisited.* Boston: Little, Brown, 1974.

Barbarin, Oscar A., Paul R. Good, O. Martin Phan, and Judith A. Sis-
kind, eds. *Institutional Racism and Community Competence*. DHHS
Publication no. (ADM) 81–907. Washington, D.C.: U.S. Department
of Health and Human Services, 1981.

Bartholet, Elizabeth. "Application of Title VII to Jobs in High Places."
Harvard Law Review 95 (1982): 947–1027.

Becnel, Barbara. "Minority Lawyers: Some Firms Fear Client Objections." *Los Angeles Daily Journal*, May 11, 1987.

Bell, Derrick A., Jr. *And We Are Not Saved: The Elusive Quest for Racial Justice*. New York: Basic Books, 1987.

———. "The Price and Pain of Racial Perspective." *Stanford Law
School Journal*, April 1986, p. 5.

———. *Race, Racism, and American Law*. 2d ed. Boston: Little,
Brown, 1980.

———. "Serving Two Masters: Integration Ideals and Client Interest
in School Desegregation Litigation." *Yale Law Journal* 85 (1976):
470–516.

———, ed. *Shades of Brown: New Perspectives on School Desegregation*. New York: Teachers College Press, 1980.

Bentham, Jeremy. *An Introduction to the Principles of Morals and Legislation*. New York: Hafner, 1948.

Bergmann, Barbara. "An Affirmative Look at Hiring Quotas." *New York
Times*, January 10, 1982, sec. 3 (Business).

"Beyond the Prima Facie Case in Employment Descrimination: Statistical Proof and Rebuttal." Note. *Harvard Law Review* 89 (1975): 387–
422.

"Black Leaders Gather at the Fifth National Policy Institute to Discuss Critical Policy Issues." Conference Report. *Focus*, May 1988,
pp. 7–11.

"Blacks and the Wall Street Purge." *Newsweek*, February 1, 1988, p. 38.

"Black vs. White in Howard Beach." *Time*, January 5, 1987, p. 48.

Blau, Peter M., and Otis Dudley Duncan. *The American Occupational
Structure*. New York: Free Press, 1978.

Bloom, Allan. *The Closing of the American Mind*. New York: Simon and
Schuster, 1987.

Bluestone, Barry, and Bennett Harrison. "A Low-Wage Explosion: The
Grim Truth About the Job 'Miracle.' " *New York Times*, February 1,
1987, sec. 8 (Business).

Bompey, Stuart H., and Barry N. Saltman. "The Role of Statistics in
Employment Discrimination Litigation—A University Perspective."
Journal of College and University Law 9 (1982): 263–278.

Book Note. *American Law Review* 14 (1880): 233–236.

Brimmer, Andrew F. "Income and Wealth." *Ebony* (special issue), August 1987, pp. 42–48.

Brodin, Mark. "The Standard of Causation in the Mixed-Motive Title VII Action: A Social Policy Perspective." *Columbia Law Review* 82 (1982): 292–326.

Brooks, Roy L. "Affirmative Action in Law Teaching." *Columbia Human Rights Law Review* 14 (1982): 15–48.

————. "The Affirmative Action Issue: Law, Policy, and Morality." *University of Connecticut Law Review* 22 (1990): 323–372.

————. "Anti-Minority Mindset in the Law School Personnel Process: Toward an Understanding of Racial Mindsets." *Law and Inequality: A Journal of Theory and Practice* 5 (1987): 1–31.

————. "Beyond Civil Rights Restoration Legislation: Restructuring Title VII." *Saint Louis University Law Journal* 34 (1990): 551–566.

————. "Civil Rights Scholarship: A Proposed Agenda for the Twenty-First Century." *University of San Francisco Law Review* 20 (1986): 397–417.

————. "Life After Tenure: Can Minority Law Professors Avoid the Clyde Ferguson Syndrome?" *University of San Francisco Law Review* 20 (1986): 419–427.

————. "Twentieth Century Black Thought: Ideology and Methodology." *Phi Kappa Phi Journal* 53 (1973): 46–57.

————. "Use of the Civil Rights Acts of 1866 and 1871 to Redress Employment Discrimination." *Cornell Law Review* 62 (1977): 258–288.

Brooks, Roy L., and Sharon A. Cheever. "The Federal Loan Guarantee Program: A Unified Approach." *Journal of Corporate Law* 10 (1984): 185–232.

Brown, Claude. "Manchild in Harlem." *New York Times Magazine*, September 16, 1984, pp. 36–44.

————. *Manchild in the Promised Land.* New York: Signet, 1965.

Bumiller, Kristin. *The Civil Rights Society: The Social Construction of Victims.* Baltimore: Johns Hopkins University Press, 1988.

Burke, Edward. "3,700 Partners, 12 Are Black." *National Law Journal*, July 2, 1979, p. 1.

Calmore, John O. "National Housing Policies and Black America: Trends, Issues, and Implications." In *The State of Black America 1986*, edited by Janet Dewart, pp. 115–149. New York: National Urban League, 1986.

————. "Proving Housing Discrimination: Intent vs. Effect and the Continuing Search for the Proper Touchstone." In *Issues in Housing Discrimination: A Consultation/Hearing of the United States Commission on Civil Rights, Washington, D.C., November 12–13, 1985,* vol. 1, *Papers Presented,* pp. 77–92. Washington, D.C.: U.S. Civil Rights Commission, 1986.

Cardozo, Benjamin N. *The Growth of the Law.* New Haven, Conn.: Yale University Press, 1924.

———. *The Nature of the Judicial Process.* New Haven, Conn.: Yale University Press, 1921.

———. *The Paradoxes of Legal Science.* New York: Columbia University Press, 1928.

Carter, Robert L. "A Reassessment of *Brown v. Board.*" In *Shades of Brown: New Perspectives on School Desegregation,* edited by Derrick A. Bell, Jr., pp. 20–28. New York: Teachers College Press, 1980.

———. "The Warren Court and Desegregation." *Michigan Law Review* 67 (1968): 237–248.

Celis, William, III. "Justice, HUD Oppose Housing Segregation, But Enforcement Lags." *Wall Street Journal,* October 28, 1985.

Chayes, Abraham. "The Role of the Judge in Public Law Litigation." *Harvard Law Review* 89 (1976): 1281–1316.

"Children Having Children." *Time,* December 9, 1985, pp. 78–90.

Chused, Richard. "The Hiring and Retention of Minorities and Women on American Law School Faculties." *University of Pennsylvania Law Review* 137 (1988): 537–569.

"Civil Rights—Racial Discrimination and Property Rights: The Scope of 42 U.S.C. § 1982." Note. *Wayne Law Review* 29 (1982): 203–239.

Cleary, Edward W. "Presuming and Pleading: An Essay on Juristic Immaturity." *Stanford Law Review* 12 (1959): 5–28.

Clendinen, Dudley. "Urban Education That Really Works." *New York Times,* April 13, 1986, sec. 12 (Educational Life, special section).

"Come Back When You're White." *San Diego Reader,* July 26, 1984.

Comer, James P. "Black Americans' Problems Are the Orphan of History." *Los Angeles Times,* February 14, 1986, pt. 2, sec. J.

Comer, James P., and Alvin Poussaint. *Black Child Care: How to Bring Up a Black Child in America—A Guide to Emotional and Psychological Development.* New York: Simon and Schuster, 1975.

Committee on Policy for Racial Justice. *Visions of a Better Way: A Black Appraisal of Public Schooling,* prepared by Sara Lawrence Lightfoot. Washington, D.C.: Joint Center for Political Studies, 1989.

Converse, Philip E., Jean D. Dotson, Wendy J. Hoag, and William H. McGee III. *American Social Attitudes Data Sourcebook: 1947–1978.* Cambridge, Mass.: Harvard University Press, 1980.

Cruse, Harold. *Plural But Equal: Blacks and Minorities in America's Plural Society.* New York: William Morrow, 1987.

"The Cycle of Despair." *Life*, educational reprint, March 8, 1968.

Danziger, Sheldon H., Robert H. Haveman, and Robert D. Plotnick. "Antipoverty Policy: Effects on the Poor and the Nonpoor." In *Fighting Poverty: What Works and What Doesn't*, edited by Sheldon H. Danziger and Daniel H. Weinberg, pp. 50–77. Cambridge, Mass.: Harvard University Press, 1986.

Danziger, Sheldon H., and Daniel H. Weinberg, eds. *Fighting Poverty: What Works and What Doesn't*. Cambridge, Mass.: Harvard University Press, 1986.

Davidson, Joe. "Private Schools for Black Pupils Are Flourishing." *Wall Street Journal*, April 15, 1987.

"Dead-End Street: Discrimination, the Thirteenth Amendment, and Section 1982, *City of Memphis v. Green*." Comment. *Chicago-Kent Law Review* 58 (1982): 873–905.

"The Delancey Street Gang." *Newsweek*, September 23, 1974, p. 81.

Department of Housing and Urban Development. *Fair Housing Enforcement Demonstration*. Washington, D.C.: U.S. Department of Housing and Urban Development, Office of Development and Research, 1983.

"Developments in the Law—Equal Protection." Note. *Harvard Law Review* 82 (1969): 1065–1192.

Diamond, Mark. "A Trace Element in the Law." *American Bar Association Journal*, May 15, 1987, pp. 46–49.

Dickens, Floyd, and Jacqueline Dickens. *The Black Manager: Making It in the Corporate World*. Saranac Lake, N.Y.: American Management Association, 1987.

Dingle, Derek. "Will Black Managers Survive Corporate Downsizing?" *Black Enterprise*, March 1987, pp. 49–55.

Dorn, Edwin. "Truman and the Desegregation of the Military." *Focus*, May 1988, pp. 3–4, 12.

"Double Jeopardy in the Newsroom." *Time*, November 29, 1982, p. 90.

Douglas, Carlyle C. "Future of Young Black Men Looks Bleak, Panelists Say." *New York Times*, May 19, 1985, sec. 1 (main).

Dowd, Gregory Evans. "Declarations of Dependence: War and Inequality in Revolutionary New Jersey, 1776–1815." *New Jersey History* 103 (1985): 47–67.

Downs, Anthony. *Opening Up the Suburbs*. New Haven, Conn.: Yale University Press, 1973.

"Dramatic Drops for Minorities: Black and Hispanic Enrollments Are Down at All College Levels." *Time*, November 11, 1985, p. 84.

DuBois, W. E. B. *The Autobiography of W. E. B. DuBois*. New York: International Publishers, New World Paperbacks, 1970.

Ducat, Craig C., and Harold W. Chase. *Constitutional Interpretation.* 3d ed. St. Paul, Minn.: West Publishing, 1983.

Duncan, Greg J. *Years of Poverty, Years of Plenty.* Ann Arbor: Institute for Social Research, University of Michigan, 1984.

Edwards, Harry T., and Barry L. Zaretsky. "Preferential Remedies for Employment Discrimination." *Michigan Law Review* 74 (1976): 1–47.

Edwards, Richard. *Contested Terrain: The Transformation of the Workplace in the Twentieth Century.* New York: Basic Books, 1979.

"Eight Whites Shot by Black Man After Harassment." *Los Angeles Times* (San Diego ed.), June 12, 1986, pt. 1.

Ellison, Ralph. *Invisible Man.* New York: Random House, 1952.

Ely, John. "Legislative and Administrative Motivation in Constitutional Law." *Yale Law Journal* 79 (1970): 1205–1340.

Equal Employment Opportunity Commission (EEOC). *Eighteenth Annual Report—1983.* Washington, D.C.: EEOC, 1984.

———. *Twenty-Third Annual Report—1988.* Washington, D.C.: EEOC, 1989.

Executive Director, Association of American Law Schools. Memorandum to Deans of Member Schools. Memorandum no. 86–57, September 5, 1986.

Farley, Reynolds. "The Residential Segregation of Blacks from Whites: Trends, Courses, and Consequences." In *Issues in Housing Discrimination: A Consultation/Hearing of the United States Commission on Civil Rights, Washington, D.C., November 12–13, 1985, vol. 1, Papers Presented,* pp. 14–19. Washington, D.C.: U.S. Civil Rights Commission, 1986.

Farley, Reynolds, and Walter R. Allen. *The Color Line and the Quality of Life in America.* New York: Russell Sage Foundation, 1987.

"Fear of Blacks, Fear of Crime." *New York Times,* December 28, 1986, sec. 4 (Week in Review).

Fernandez, John P. *Racism and Sexism in Corporate Life: Changing Values in American Business.* Lexington, Mass.: Lexington Books, 1981.

Fiske, Edward. "Enrollment of Minorities in Colleges Stagnating." *New York Times,* April 19, 1987, sec. 1 (main).

Fiss, Owen. "A Theory of Fair Employment Laws." *University of Chicago Law Review* 38 (1971): 235–341.

Foner, Eric. *Reconstruction: America's Unfinished Revolution, 1863–1877.* New York: Harper and Row, 1988.

Frank, Jerome. *Law and the Modern Mind.* New York: Tudor, 1930.

Franklin, John Hope. *From Slavery to Freedom: A History of Negro Americans.* 3d ed. New York: Vintage Books, 1969.

Frazier, Thomas R., ed. *Afro-American History: Primary Sources*. New York: Harcourt Brace and World, 1970.

Freedman, Samuel. "Racial Tension in New York Is on Increase Despite Gains." *New York Times*, March 29, 1987, sec. 1 (main).

Gates, Henry, Jr. *The Signifying Monkey: A Theory of Afro-American Literary Criticism*. New York: Oxford University Press, 1988.

Gayle, Addison, Jr., ed. *The Black Aesthetic*. Garden City, N.Y.: Doubleday, 1972.

Gelb, Marjorie, and Joanne Frankfurt. "California's Fair Employment and Housing Act: A Viable State Remedy for Employment Discrimination." *Hastings Law Review* 34 (1983): 1055–1105.

"Getting Straight on Delancey Street: San Francisco Therapeutic Community." *Time*, March 19, 1973, p. 82.

Goldfarb, Sally. "Education Without Representation." *Student Lawyer*, May 1981, pp. 11–13.

"Grapevine." *TV Guide* (San Diego ed.), April 18–24, 1987, p. A–2.

Green, Lorenzo G. *The Negro in Colonial New England, 1620–1776*. New York: Columbia University Press, 1942.

Griffin, Noah. "Broadcasting." *Crisis*, June/July 1989, pp. 28–32, 66.

"Growing Up Poor." Transcript no. 403, "Frontline" television series, February 2, 1986. Boston: WGBH Educational Foundation, 1986.

Gunther, Gerald. *Constitutional Law*. 11th ed. Mineola, N.Y.: Foundation Press, 1985.

Haar, Charles M., and Daniel W. Fessler. *The Wrong Side of the Tracks*. New York: Simon and Schuster, 1986.

Hacker, Andrew. "American Apartheid." *New York Review of Books*, December 3, 1987, pp. 26–33.

Hale-Benson, Janice E. *Black Children: Their Roots, Culture, and Learning Styles*. Baltimore: Johns Hopkins University Press, 1986.

Hankins, Grover, "Starrett City and Other Race-Conscious Methods of Achieving Integration." In *The Fair Housing Act After Twenty Years: A Conference at Yale Law School, March 1988*, edited by Robert G. Schwemm, pp. 109–110. New Haven, Conn.: Yale Law School, 1989.

Hastings, Elizabeth Hann, and Philip K. Hastings, eds. *Index to International Public Opinion, 1987–1988*. New York: Greenwood Press, 1989.

Hatchett, David. "Blacks and the Mass Media." *Crisis*, June/July 1989, pp. 18–26, 68.

——— . "The State of Race Relations." *Crisis*, November 1989, pp. 14–19.

Hawley, Willis. "Equity and Quality in Education: Characteristics of Effective Desegregated Schools." In *Effective School Desegregation:*

Equity, Quality, and Feasibility, edited by Willis Hawley, pp. 297–307. Beverly Hills, Calif.: Sage, 1981.

Hays, Scott. "Capturing the Black Experience." *TV Guide,* November 29, 1986, pp. 10–14.

Hazard, Geoffrey. "Ethics in the Practice of Law." In *Pleading and Procedure,* edited by David Louisell and Geoffrey Hazard, pp. 1165–1169. 4th ed. Mineola, N.Y.: Foundation Press, 1979.

Higginbotham, A. Leon, Jr. *In the Matter of Color: Race and the American Legal Process—The Colonial Period.* New York: Oxford University Press, 1978.

Hill, Robert B. "The Black Middle Class Defined." *Ebony* (special issue), August 1987, pp. 30–32.

Hirschman, Charles. "America's Melting Pot Reconsidered." *Annual Review of Sociology* 9 (1983): 397–423.

Hochschild, Jennifer L. *The New American Dilemma: Liberal Democracy and School Desegregation.* New Haven, Conn.: Yale University Press, 1984.

————. *Thirty Years After Brown.* Washington, D.C.: Joint Center for Political Studies, 1985.

Holmes, Oliver Wendell, Jr. *The Common Law.* Edited by Mark Howe. Cambridge, Mass.: Harvard University Press, Belknap Press, 1963.

————. "The Path of the Law." *Harvard Law Review* 10 (1987): 457–478.

Hope, Richard O. *Racial Strife in the U.S. Military: Toward the Elimination of Discrimination.* New York: Praeger, 1979.

Horowitz, Joy. "Hollywood's Dirty Little Secret." *American Visions,* August 1989, pp. 16–21.

Howard-Filler, Saralee R. "Two Different Battles." *Michigan History* 71 (January/February 1987): 30–33.

Humphrey, Melvin. *Black Experience Versus Black Expectations.* Research Report no. 53. Washington, D.C.: Equal Employment Opportunity Commission, 1977.

Hwang, Sean-Shong, Steven H. Murdock, Banoo Parpia, and Rita R. Hamm. "The Effects of Race and Socioeconomic Status on Residential Segregation in Texas, 1970–1980." *Social Forces* 63 (March 1985): 732–747.

Hymowitz, Carol. "Many Blacks Jump Off the Corporate Ladder to Be Entrepreneurs." *Wall Street Journal,* August 2, 1984.

"Images (1987), Farewells." *Time,* December 28, 1987, pp. 58–59.

Issues in Housing Discrimination: A Consultation/Hearing of the United States Commission on Civil Rights, Washington, D.C., November 12–13, 1985. Vol. 1, *Papers Presented.* Washington, D.C.: U.S. Civil Rights Commission, 1986.

Japenga, Ann. "She's a Partner in Criminology." *Los Angeles Times,* April 5, 1984, pt. 5.

Jaynes, Gerald D., and Robin M. Williams, Jr., eds. *A Common Destiny: Blacks and American Society.* Washington, D.C.: National Academy Press, 1989.

Johnson, Dirk. "Companies Create 'Model School' for Urban Poor." *New York Times,* October 20, 1988, sec. B.

Johnson, Thomas. "Ivy League Blacks Find Life in Microcosm on the Campus." *New York Times,* May 20, 1979, sec. 1 (main).

"Joint Center for Political Studies Conference Report: Defining the Underclass." *Focus,* June 1987, pp. 8–12.

Jordan, Winthrop D. *White Over Black: American Attitudes Toward the Negro, 1550–1812.* Chapel Hill: University of North Carolina Press, 1968.

"Jury Finds Bias by Daily News." *New York Times,* April 19, 1987, sec. 4 (Week in Review).

Kamerman, Sheila, and Alfred Kahn. "Europe's Innovative Family Policies." *Transatlantic Perspectives,* March 1980, pp. 9–12.

Kennedy, Randall. "Racial Critiques of Legal Academa." *Harvard Law Review* 101 (1989): 1745–1819.

King, Martin Luther, Jr. *Stride Toward Freedom: The Montgomery Story.* Perennial Library ed. New York: Harper and Row, 1964.

King, Wayne. "Bakke Case Still Affects Davis Medical School." *New York Times,* December 6, 1981, sec. 1 (main).

Kluger, Richard. *Simple Justice.* New York: Alfred A. Knopf, 1976.

Kolbert, Elizabeth. "Minority Faculty: Bleak Future." *New York Times,* August 18, 1985, sec. 12 (Education, special section).

Kornblum, William, and Joseph Julian. *Social Problems.* 6th ed. Englewood Cliffs, N.J.: Prentice-Hall, 1989.

Kotken, Joel. "The Reluctant Entrepreneurs: Are American Blacks Still Stuck on the Bottom Rung of the Economic Ladder Because So Few Start Businesses on Their Own?" *Inc.,* September 1986, pp. 81–86.

Kovel, Joel. *White Racism: A Psychohistory.* New York: Vintage Books, 1970.

Kuhn, Thomas S. *The Structure of Scientific Revolutions.* 2d ed. Chicago: University of Chicago Press, 1970.

Kulik, Chen-Lin, and James Kulik. "Effects of Ability Grouping on Secondary School Students: A Meta-Analysis of Evaluation Findings." *American Educational Research Journal* 19 (Fall 1982): 415–428.

Kupperman, Joel. "Relations Between the Sexes: Timely vs. Timeliness Principles." *San Diego Law Review* 25 (1988): 1027–1041.

Kushner, James A. *Fair Housing: Discrimination in Real Estate, Community Development, and Revitalization.* With annual supplements. Colorado Springs: Shepards/McGraw-Hill, 1983.

"Labor Letter." *Wall Street Journal,* December 3, 1987.

"Labor Letter." *Wall Street Journal,* February 20, 1990.

Landry, Bart. *The New Black Middle Class.* Berkeley and Los Angeles: University of California Press, 1987.

——— . "The New Black Middle Class," pts. 1 and 2. *Focus,* September 1987, pp. 5–7; October 1987, pp. 6–7.

Langdell, Christopher C. *A Selection of Cases on the Law of Contracts.* Boston: Little, Brown, 1871.

Lawrence, Charles. "The Id, the Ego, and Equal Protection: Reckoning with Unconscious Racism." *Stanford Law Review* 39 (1987): 317–388.

Leavy, Walter. "What's Behind the Resurgence of Racism in America?" *Ebony,* April 1987, pp. 132–139.

"Legislative Motivation." Symposium. *San Diego Law Review* 15 (1978): 925–1183.

Lester, Julius. *To Be a Slave.* New York: Dell, 1968.

Levi, Edward. "The Business of the Courts: A Summary and a Sense of Perspective." *Federal Rules of Decision* 70 (1976): 212–223.

Levine, Richard L. "The Plight of Black Reporters: Why 'Unconscious Racism' Persists." *TV Guide,* July 25, 1981, pp. 22–28.

Lewis, Leon. "About Men: In On the Game." *New York Times Magazine,* February 3, 1985, p. 70.

Lewis, Oscar. *The Children of Sanchez.* New York: Random House, 1961.

Llewellyn, Karl N. *Jurisprudence: Realism in Theory and Practice.* Chicago: University of Chicago Press, 1962.

Logan, John R., and Mark Schneider. "Racial Segregation and Racial Change in American Suburbs, 1970–1980." *American Journal of Sociology* 89 (January 1984): 874–888.

Longshore, Douglas, and Jeffrey Prager. "The Impact of School Desegregation: A Situational Analysis." *Annual Review of Sociology* 11 (1985): 75–91.

Louisell, David, and Geoffrey Hazard, eds. *Pleading and Procedure.* 4th ed. Mineola, N.Y.: Foundation Press, 1979.

Loury, Glenn. "The Better Path to Black Progress: Beyond Civil Rights." *New Republic,* October 7, 1985, pp. 22–25.

McGuire, Philip. "Desegregation of the Armed Forces: Black Leadership, Protest, and World War II." *Journal of Negro History* 63 (Spring 1983): 147–158.

Macionis, John J. *Sociology.* Englewood Cliffs, N.J.: Prentice-Hall, 1987.

McManis, Sam. "Campanis Fired in Wake of Racial Remarks." *Los Angeles Times* (San Diego ed.), April 9, 1987, pt. 3.

"Main Street." *TV Guide,* June 14–20, 1986, p. A-69.

Marcotte, Paul. "The Changing of the Guard." *American Bar Association Journal,* May 15, 1987, pp. 56–62.

Massey, Donald S., and Nancy A. Denton. "Hypersegregation in U.S. Metropolitan Areas: Black and Hispanic Segregation along Five Dimensions." *Demography* 26 (August 1989): 373–391.

Massey, Donald S., and Mitchell L. Eggers. "The Ecology of Inequality: Minorities and the Concentration of Poverty, 1970–1980." *American Journal of Sociology* 95 (March 1990): 1153–1188.

Meier, August, and Elliott Rudwick. *Black History and the Historical Profession, 1915–1980.* Urbana: University of Illinois Press, 1986.

Meier, August, Elliott Rudwick, and Francis Broderick, eds. *Black Protest Thought in the Twentieth Century.* 2d ed. Indianapolis: Bobbs-Merrill, 1971.

Mendez, Miguel. "Presumptions of Discriminatory Motive in Title VII Disparate Treatment Cases." *Stanford Law Review* 32 (1980): 1129–1162.

"Minorities Studies Show More Students But Fewer Teachers." *San Diego Union,* February 9, 1986.

Morgan, Thomas. "The World Ahead: Black Parents Prepare Their Children for Pride and Prejudice." *New York Times Magazine,* October 27, 1985, pp. 32–35.

Morrow, Lance. "The Powers of Racial Examples." *Time,* April 16, 1984, p. 84.

Moskos, Charles C. "Blacks in the Army: Success Story." *Current,* September 1986, pp. 10–17.

Moynihan, Daniel P. *Family and Nation.* San Diego: Harcourt Brace Jovanovich, 1986.

Murray, Charles. *Losing Ground: American Social Policy, 1950–1980.* New York: Basic Books, 1984.

Myrdal, Gunnar. *An American Dilemma: The Negro Problem and Modern Democracy.* New York: Harper and Brothers, 1944; New York: Pantheon, 1964.

Naipaul, Vidiadhar S. *The Enigma of Arrival.* New York: Alfred A. Knopf, 1987.

National Advisory Commission on Civil Disorders (Kerner Commission). *Report of the National Advisory Commission on Civil Disorders: Summary of Report.* New York: Bantam Books, 1968; New York: A. Philip Randolph Institute, 1970.

National Opinion Research Center. *General Social Surveys, 1972–1983: Cumulative Codebook*. Chicago: National Opinion Research Center, 1983.

————. *General Surveys*. Chicago: National Opinion Research Center, 1983.

New York State Department of Education. *Increasing High School Completion Rates*. Albany: New York State Department of Education, 1987.

"The 1985 Minority Law Teachers' Conference." Symposium Report. *University of San Francisco Law Review* 20 (1986): 383–576.

Office of the Attorney General of California, John K. Van de Kamp. News release, July 10, 1986. Sacramento, Calif.

O'Hare, William P., Jane-yu Li, Roy Chatterjee, and Margaret Shukur. *Blacks on the Move: A Decade of Demographic Change*. Washington, D.C.: Joint Center for Political Studies, 1982.

Orfield, Gary. *Public School Desegregation in the United States, 1968–1980*. Washington, D.C.: Joint Center for Political Studies, 1983.

Overbea, Luix. "Youths Hold Key to Black Family Survival." *Christian Science Monitor*, April 1, 1987.

Pear, Robert. "Study Says Affirmative Rule Expands Hiring of Minorities." *New York Times*, June 19, 1983, sec. 1 (main).

Pholman, H. L. *Justice Oliver Wendell Holmes and Utilitarian Jurisprudence*. Cambridge, Mass.: Harvard University Press, 1984.

Polyviou, Polyvios G. *The Equal Protection of the Laws*. London: Duckworth, 1980.

Postema, Gerald J. *Bentham and the Common Law Tradition*. Oxford: Clarendon Press, 1986.

"Racial Tensions Mount Between Blacks, Koreans." *Jet*, July 1, 1985, p. 5.

"The Racism Next Door." *Time*, June 30, 1986, pp. 40–41.

Ramirez, Anthony. "America's Super Minority." *Fortune*, November 24, 1986, pp. 148–149.

Raspberry, William. "Aid That Isn't Charity." *Washington Post*, April 13, 1987.

————. "America's Black Family Crisis." *San Diego Union*, January 24, 1986.

Reibstein, Larry. "Many Hurdles, Old and New, Keep Black Managers Out of Top Jobs." *Wall Street Journal*, July 10, 1986.

Reynolds, Christopher. "Incidents of Racism Increase." *San Diego Union*, December 31, 1983.

"Rising Racism on the Continent." *Time*, February, 6, 1984, pp. 40–45.

Rivlin, Gary. "Climbing the Legal Ladder: Some Kinds of Discrimination Die Hard." *American Bar Association Update*, Fall 1981, pp. 28–49.

Rose, Stephen. *The American Profile Poster.* New York: Pantheon, 1986.

Rowan, Carl. "The Blacks Among Us." *Reader's Digest*, June 1985, pp. 72–75.

Rudwick, Elliott. *W. E. B. DuBois: Propagandist of the Negro Protest.* New York: Atheneum, 1969.

Ryan, William. *Blaming the Victim.* Rev. ed. New York: Vintage Books, 1976.

Sales, Grover. *John Maher of Delancey Street: A Guideline to Peaceful Revolution in America.* New York: Norton, 1975.

Samios, Mary Lynn. "Delancy Street: A Preliminary Report." Typescript, July 25, 1985.

Sawhill, Isabel V. "Poverty and the Underclass." In *Challenge to Leadership: Economic and Social Issues for the Next Decade*, edited by Isabel V. Sawhill, pp. 215–252. Washington, D.C.: Urban Institute Press, 1988.

Sawhill, Isabel V., ed. *Challenge to Leadership: Economic and Social Issues for the Next Decade.* Washington, D.C.: Urban Institute Press, 1988.

Schaefer, Daniel L. "Freedom Was as Close as the River: The Blacks of Northeast Florida and the Civil War." *Escribano* 23 (1986): 91–116.

Schaefer, Richard T. *Sociology.* 3d ed. New York: McGraw-Hill, 1989.

Schatzki, George. "United Steelworkers of America v. Weber: An Exercise in Understandable Indecision." *Washington Law Review* 56 (1980): 51–73.

Schlei, Barbara, and Paul Grossman. *Employment Discrimination Law.* 2d ed. Washington, D.C.: Bureau of National Affairs, 1983.

Schultz, Stanley K. *The Culture Factory: Boston Public Schools, 1789–1860.* New York: Oxford University Press, 1973.

Schwemm, Robert G. "Introduction." In *The Fair Housing Act After Twenty Years: A Conference at Yale Law School, March 1988*, edited by Robert G. Schwemm, pp. 11–13. New Haven, Conn.: Yale Law School, 1989.

Schwemm, Robert G., ed. *The Fair Housing Act After Twenty Years: A Conference at Yale Law School, March 1988.* New Haven, Conn.: Yale Law School, 1989.

Shipp, E. R. "The Litigiousness of Academe." *New York Times*, November 8, 1987, sec. 12.

Shoben, Elaine W. "Differential Pass-Fail Rates in Employment Testing: Statistical Proof Under Title VII." *Harvard Law Review* 91 (1978): 793–813.

"Shop Here, But Don't Stop Here." *Time*, March 10, 1986, p. 46.

Simpson, Janice. "Black College Students Are Viewed as Victims of a Subtle Racism." *Wall Street Journal*, April 3, 1987.

Smith, James P., and Finis R. Welch. *Closing the Gap: Forty Years of Economic Progress for Blacks*. Santa Monica, Calif.: Rand, 1986.

Smith, Lincoln B. "Juri-Statistical Methods in Legal Research." Typescript, December 1989.

Smith, Ralph. "The Invisible Lawyer." *Barrister*, Fall 1981, pp. 42–49.

Smolla, Rodney. "Integration Maintenance: The Unconstitutionality of Benign Programs That Discourage Black Entry to Prevent White Flight." *Duke Law Journal* 1981 (1981): 891–939.

"Social Issues: The Roots of Poverty." *Time*, January 5, 1987, p. 49.

Sorenson, Annemette, Karl E. Taeuber, and Leslie Hollingsworth, Jr. "Indexes of Racial Residential Segregation for 109 Cities in the United States, 1940 to 1970." *Sociological Focus* 8 (April 1975): 125–142.

Sowell, Thomas. *Civil Rights: Rhetoric or Reality?* New York: William Morrow, 1984.

————. *The Economics and Politics of Race: An International Perspective*. New York: William Morrow, 1983.

"Special Issues—Progress Report on the Black Executive: The Top Spots Are Still Elusive." *Business Week*, February 20, 1984, pp. 104–105.

Spencer, Roger. "Enforcement of Federal Fair Housing Law." *Urban Lawyer* 9 (1977): 514–558.

Spencer, Samuel, Jr. *Booker T. Washington and the Negro's Place in American Life*. Boston: Little, Brown, 1955.

Sperrazza, Diana. "Special New Mexico Community Gives Losers 2nd Chance: Delancey Street Program." *Albuquerque Journal*, March 21, 1982.

Stampp, Kenneth. *The Era of Reconstruction, 1865–1877*. New York: Vintage Books, 1965.

————. *The Peculiar Institution: Slavery in the Antebellum South*. New York: Vintage Books, 1956.

Staples, Brent. "The Dwindling Black Presence on Campus." *New York Times Magazine*, April 27, 1986, pp. 46–47, 51–52.

The State of Black America 1986. Edited by Janet Dewart. New York: National Urban League, 1986.

Stein, Andrew. "Children of Poverty: Crisis in New York." *New York Times Magazine*, June 8, 1986, pp. 38–39, 68.

Stevens, William K. "Philadelphia Neighborhood Is Starting to Simmer Down." *New York Times*, December 1, 1985, sec. 1 (main).

"Strivers and Defeatists." *New York Times*, November 2, 1986, sec. 4 (Week in Review).

"Subtle Racism Said to Prevail in East County Area." *East County To-day* (San Diego), November 30, 1983.

Taeuber, Karl E. "Causes of Residential Segregation." In *The Fair Housing Act After Twenty Years: A Conference at Yale Law School, March 1988*, edited by Robert G. Schwemm, pp. 33–39. New Haven, Conn.: Yale Law School, 1989.

Taylor, Howard F. *The I.Q. Game: A Methodological Inquiry into the Heredity-Environment Controversy.* New Brunswick, N.J.: Rutgers University Press, 1980.

Thomas, Alexander, and Samuel Sillen. *Racism and Psychiatry.* New York: Brunner/Mazel, 1972.

Thorton, Mary. "Affirmative Action Found to Diversify Work Force." *Washington Post,* June 20, 1983, sec. 1.

"A Threat to the Future." *Time,* May 14, 1984, p. 20.

Thurow, Lester. *The Zero-Sum Society: Distribution and the Possibilities for Economic Change.* New York: Basic Books, 1980.

Unger, Roberto. "The Critical Legal Studies Movement." *Harvard Law Review* 96 (1983): 561–675.

Updegrave, Walter L. "Personal Finance: Race and Money." *Money,* December 1989, pp. 152–172.

U.S. Bureau of the Census. *Census of Population and Housing: 1980.* Public Use Microdata Samples. Washington, D.C.: U.S. Government Printing Office, 1981.

———. *Current Population Reports: Money Income of Households, Families, and Persons in the United States: 1987.* Series P–60, no. 162. Washington, D.C.: U.S. Government Printing Office, 1989.

———. *Current Population Reports: Money Income and Poverty Status in the United States: 1988.* Series P–60, no. 166. Advance data from the March 1989 Current Population Survey. Washington, D.C.: U.S. Government Printing Office, 1989.

———. *Current Population Reports: The Social and Economic Status of the Black Population in the United States—An Historical View, 1970–1978.* Special Studies Series P–23, Publication no. 80. Washington, D.C.: U.S. Government Printing Office, 1979.

———. *Historical Statistics of the United States: Colonial Times to 1970.* Pt. 1, G. Washington, D.C.: U.S. Government Printing Office, 1975.

———. *Sixteenth Census of the United States: 1940, Population.* Vol. 3, pt. 1. Washington, D.C.: U.S. Government Printing Office, 1940.

———. *Statistical Abstract of the United States, 1971.* 92d ed. Washington, D.C.: U.S. Government Printing Office, 1972.

———. *Statistical Abstract of the United States, 1985.* 106th ed. Washington, D.C.: U.S. Government Printing Office, 1986.

———— . *Statistical Abstract of the United States, 1986*. 107th ed. Washington, D.C.: U.S. Government Printing Office, 1987.

Vaas, Francis J. "Title VII: Legislative History." *Boston College Industrial and Commercial Law Journal* 7 (1966): 431–458.

Vander Zanden, James W. *The Social Experience*. New York: Random House, 1988.

"The Vanishing Black Family: Crisis in Black America." CBS Reports, January 25, 1986. Television documentary.

Ware, Gilbert. *William Hastie: Grace Under Pressure*. New York: Oxford University Press, 1984.

Washington, Erwin. "Racism and the Movie Industry." *Crisis*, June/July 1989, pp. 34–40, 66.

Watkins, Linda M. "Losing Ground: Minorities' Enrollment in College Retreats After Its Surge in 70's." *Wall Street Journal*, May 29, 1985.

Watson, Glegg, and George Davis. *Black Life in Corporate America: Swimming in the Mainstream*. Garden City, N.Y.: Anchor/Doubleday, 1982.

Weinrib, Ernest J. "Legal Formalism: On the Immanent Rationality of Law." *Yale Law Journal* 97 (1988): 949–1016.

Weisenhaus, Doreen. "White Males Dominate Firms: Still a Long Way to Go for Women and Minorities." *National Law Journal*, February, 8, 1988, p. 1.

"Welcome, America, to the Baby Bust." *Time*, February 23, 1987, pp. 28–29.

Westlaw: Introductory Guide to Legal Research. St. Paul, Minn.: West Publishing, 1988.

West's Federal Practice Digest Edition, 1975 to Date. St. Paul, Minn.: West Publishing, 1984.

"When Brother Kills Brother." *Time*, September 16, 1985, pp. 32–36.

White, Arthur O. "The Black Leadership Class and Education in Antebellum Boston." *Journal of Negro Education* 42 (1973): 505–515.

Whitman, David, and Jeannye Thorton. "A Nation Apart." *U.S. News and World Report*, March 17, 1987, pp. 18–21.

Wildeman, John Edgar. *Brothers and Keepers*. New York: Penguin, 1984.

Wilkins, Roger. *A Man's Life: An Autobiography*. New York: Simon and Schuster, 1982.

Williams, Juan. *Eyes on the Prize: America's Civil Rights Years, 1954–1965*. New York: Viking, 1987.

Williams, Linda. "Stress of Adapting to White Society Cited as Major Cause of Hypertension in Blacks." *Wall Street Journal*, May 28, 1986.

Williams, T. Harry, Richard N. Current, and Frank Freidel. *A History of the United States to 1877*. 3d ed. New York: Alfred A. Knopf, 1969.

Wilson, Reginald, and Deborah J. Carter. *Eighth Annual Status Report on Minorities in Higher Education*. Washington, D.C.: American Council on Education, 1989.

Wilson, William Julius. *The Truly Disadvantaged: The Inner City, the Underclass, and Public Policy*. Chicago: University of Chicago Press, 1987.

Woodson, Carter G. *The Education of the Negro Prior to 1861*. Washington, D.C.: Associated Publishers, 1919.

Woodward, C. Vann. *The Strange Career of Jim Crow*. 2d rev. ed. New York: Oxford University Press, 1966.

Wright, Skelly. "Professor Bickel, the Scholarly Tradition, and the Supreme Court." *Harvard Law Review* 84 (1971): 769–805.

"Wrong Message from Academe." *Time*, April 6, 1987, p. 57.

Zimmer, Michael J., Charles A. Sullivan, and Richard Richards. *Cases and Materials on Employment Discrimination*. 2d ed. Boston: Little, Brown, 1988.

Table of Cases

Statutes

U.S. Constitution

Amend. V
Amend. XIV

29 U.S.C.

§§ 151–169 (National Labor Relations Act)

42 U.S.C.

§ 1441 (Housing Act of 1949)
§ 1971 (Voting Rights Act of 1965)
§§ 1971–2000h-6 (Civil Rights Act of 1964, all titles)
§ 1981
§ 1982
§ 2000d–2000d-4
§ 2000e–2000e-17 (Civil Rights Act of 1964, Title VII)
§§ 3601–3619 (Fair Housing Act of 1968, Title VIII)
§§ 3601–3617 (Fair Housing Amendments Act of 1988)

West's California Government Code

§§ 12900–12996

Code of Federal Regulations

3 C.F.R. 957 (1941) (from Exec. Order No. 8802)
3 C.F.R. 720 (1948) (from Exec. Order No. 9980)
3 C.F.R. 722 (1948) (from Exec. Order No. 9981)

Index

Compositor: BookMasters, Inc.
Text: 11/13 Caledonia
Display: Caledonia
Printer: Thomas-Shore, Inc.
Binder: Thomas-Shore, Inc.